Shoshee Chunder Dutt

The Young Zemindár; His Erratic Wanderings and Eventual Return

Shoshee Chunder Dutt

The Young Zemindár; His Erratic Wanderings and Eventual Return

ISBN/EAN: 9783337187224

Printed in Europe, USA, Canada, Australia, Japan

Cover: Foto ©ninafisch / pixelio.de

More available books at **www.hansebooks.com**

THE YOUNG ZEMINDÁR;

HIS ERRATIC WANDERINGS AND EVENTUAL
RETURN:

Being a Record of Life, Manners, and Events in Bengal of from Forty to Fifty Years ago.

BY

SHOSHEE CHUNDER DUTT.

> Where'er I roam, whatever realms to see,
> My heart, untravell'd, fondly turns to thee,
> Still to my mother turns.
>   Goldsmith's *Traveller* (slightly altered).

LONDON:
LOVELL REEVE AND CO.,
5, HENRIETTA STREET, COVENT GARDEN.
1885.

[*All rights reserved.*]

CONTENTS.

CHAPTER	PAGE
I. THE RÁIS OF BONÁ GHÁT	7
II. THE DEWÁN'S MELÁ	13
III. THE FIRST EXERCISE OF AUTHORITY	20
IV. THE REFERENCE TO THE DEITY	27
V. THE SABÁIT'S STORY	34
VI. THE LECTURE AT HOME	40
VII. THE FERÁZEE RISING	48
VIII. A MYSTERIOUS BURGLARY	55
IX. IN THE TRAP AT LAST	61
X. ASSERTION OF CIVIL AUTHORITY, AND ITS RESULTS	69
XI. THE FIRE PUT OUT, AND THE RUN FOR A SHAVE	74
XII. THE REVELATION	81
XIII. THE LOVES OF THE RIVERS	87
XIV. A MYSTERIOUS LETTER	95
XV. HOOKED AGAIN	103
XVI. THE FOREST RISING	110
XVII. REBELLION IN THE KOLEHÁN, AND HOW IT WAS EXTINGUISHED	118
XVIII. A MOTHER'S DISTRESS	124

CONTENTS.

CHAPTER	PAGE
XIX. Inundation, Famine, Pestilence, and Death	131
XX. The Zohur Stone	138
XXI. The Emissary again, and a Step-Mother's Story	145
XXII. Jagganáth ke Jai	154
XXIII. The Mine ready once more	161
XXIV. The Chilká Lake, and the Story of the Serpent's Rock	170
XXV. The New Rebellion	178
XXVI. The Bediyá Domes	187
XXVII. Adaysto	195
XXVIII. Home, as Monohur found it	203
XXIX. The Paramhangsa	211
XXX. The Shástric Scheme	219
XXXI. The New Arrival	227
XXXII. The Jal Rájáh of Burdwán	234
XXXIII. Byjanáth, or Deoguru	242
XXXIV. At Gayá	250
XXXV. Sákya, and some Stories about him	258
XXXVI. At Benáres	267
XXXVII. Stories about the Dakshya Jagya, and the Pisách Mochan	277
XXXVIII. The Nawáb's Rule	285
XXXIX. The Rámáyana, and a Missing Chapter of History recovered	294
XL. The Dhatoora Poisoner	303
XLI. The Mahábhárut heard and sifted	309
XLII. Miracles over the Dead	319

CONTENTS.

CHAPTER	PAGE
XLIII. THE MAID OF ROHILKUND	326
XLIV. HIMÁLAYAN STORIES, AND A NEW ROUTE TO CHINA	341
XLV. A TRUE DESCRIPTION OF CHINA, WITH A *So* AND *Do* WIFE STORY IN THE BARGAIN	349
XLVI. AT PÁTNÁ, AND ABOUT THE MOHURRUM	357
XLVII. A MOHURRUM QUARREL	364
XLVIII. AT ECHÁPORE	371
XLIX. THE AGGRIEVED VYSNUBI	379
L. THE NIGHT CONFERENCE, AND RECONCILIATION OF ACCOUNTS	385
LI. A CHANGE OF MASTERS	393
LII. ESTABLISHED AT ECHÁPORE	398
LIII. AT BONÁ GHÁT, AND ABOUT AN INDIGO DISPUTE	405
LIV. THE ENGLISH *VERSUS* THE MAHOMEDANS	413
LV. THE HOGS	421
LVI. THE DEVIL NOT SO BLACK AS HE IS PAINTED	427
LVII. THE QUESTION MOOTED	433
LVIII. THE KNOT TIED HARD	442
LIX. THE RETURN TO BONÁ GHÁT	449

THE YOUNG ZEMINDÁR.

CHAPTER I.

THE RÁIS OF BONÁ GHÁT.

There is a place named Boná Ghát, on the banks of the Bhetná Nuddee, in Pergunnáh Datteáh, of 24-Pergunnáhs, in the province of Bengal, which is well situated, and surrounded on all sides by a fairly cultivated and flourishing country. It is now a small and almost insignificant village, but in times past was the headquarters of a family of Ráis, or Zemindárs, who had the reputation of great wealth and power, several of the members being further described as being good and humane landlords, who did much service in their day to the poor. The story about them says that they possessed a fort and a palace in the village, which were occupied by the family for nearly a century, and the remains of the first were yet traceable on the ground during the earlier years of the English power, though scarcely attesting at that time to the might or affluence which the building had originally symbolised. The palace, or residence, of the Ráis seems to have been rebuilt some forty years ago, and is yet standing; but its present condition is very ruinous, owing to the family having since got poor, and being now represented by some minor children only, whose guardians, in the usual native fashion, have enriched themselves at the expense of their wards. The more remarkable peculiarities of the village to this day are: a large mango-grove, commencing from a short distance to the west of the Zemindár's house, and extending over nearly fifty acres of land, several tanks of clean and wholesome water, and the neighbourhood of the Nuddee referred to, all which advantages together render the spot too well-fitted for the purposes of a fair for that circumstance to have been overlooked. Markets are accordingly held at the place on two days of the week, besides which a *melá* is celebrated there annually during the Bárooni festival in March, which goes by the name of the *Dewán's Melá*, on the following account.

The Zemindárs of Boná Ghát were Bráhmans, descended from Bhatta Náráyana of the Sándilya family, the chief of the five pure Bráhmans who came to Bengal from Kanouj, and from whom the Rájáhs of Nuddeá also claim their descent. The founder of the family was one Bistoo Hari Sándyal, who came to Boná Ghát with the intent of leading the life of an anchorite there. But his son, Srimanta, who was of a more pugnacious character, having followed him thither, succeeded in a short time to secure all the wealth of the pergunnáh by various means, after which he got his usurpations confirmed by the Nawáb of Moorshedábád, who was glad to accept the presents that were offered to him, accompanied as they were by a promise of an increased *kházáná*, or revenue, for the imperial treasury.

The fifth in succession to Srimanta was Hullodhur Sándyal, who rendered great services to the Nawáb, in

THE RÁIS OF BONÁ GHÁT. 9

connection with the Mahrattá incursions, and, having amassed an immense fortune during those disturbances, was enabled to augment his ancestral estate still further by buying up and adding thereto the estates of several defaulting Zemindárs. The title of Rái was now conferred on him by the Nawáb for his services to the State, and this was assumed by the family in place of the sept name of "Sándyal," which had intermediately become plebeian; and the palace and fortress at Boná Ghát were both erected by Hullodhur, with the express permission of the Nawáb.

We need not follow the family-history of the Ráis further. Rughoonáth Rái was the Zemindár of Boná Ghát when the battle of Plássey was fought and lost, and, as all the adherents of the Nawáb were obliged to fly, Rughoonáth with his family proceeded in the direction of Dhumraii, in the hope of cutting his way through the Soonderbuns to Jagganáth. Whether he did reach Jagganáth or not was never known, for no tidings of his arrival there were ever received at Boná Ghát. The wife of the pilgrim was overtaken with the pains of labour on the banks of the Kool-Kooli Nulláh, on the borders of the Soonderbuns, upon which she was deserted by her husband and left to her fate, and, being shortly after delivered of a boy, lay with her child in a dense jungle helpless and alone.

Both the mother and child would have been inevitably destroyed by wild beasts but for having been accidentally discovered by a kind-hearted *goáláh*, or herdsman, named Nobin, who had come to the spot in search of his cows, just when the lady had recovered her senses and was looking uncomfortably about herself. She was prevailed upon by him to take refuge with her son in his house in the absence of any better place to go to; and in the course of a few years Kooláye Goáláh, the reputed son of Nobin, became a strapping cowherd, respected and feared by other cowherd boys of the same age.

Within these ten or twelve years the British *Ráj* had been fully established all over Bengal, and the wife of Rughoonáth, not having heard from her husband, thought it high time now to go back to Datteáh in the interests of her son.

"What do you want to go to Datteáh for?" asked Nobin, when the matter was broached to him. "Have you any friends in that quarter?"

"Yes, we had relations and friends there," said the lady, "but do not know whether they are living or dead. My son is shooting up into youth, and I want to introduce him to my uncle, who was a well-to-do *chásá* of Boná Ghát."

The lady still kept the secret of her former life she hardly knew wherefore. She was afraid that things had gone wrong both at Datteáh and with the fugitive Zemindár. Why should poor Kooláye Chánd then know anything whatever in respect to his real position in life, merely to get discontented with his present lot?

"It is well to go and know the worst of it now, if only to be relieved of the suspense that has been weighing so heavily on us," thought the lady to herself. "We shall be able to shape our future course better after the mystery that envelopes us has been cleared up." And she went forward accordingly with a resolute heart, accompanied by Nobin and her son.

They reached Boná Ghát with various feelings, the Zemindár's lady in expectation and silence, but quite unable to arrange her thoughts; Nobin watching her face thoughtfully, but without being able to read her heart; Kooláye Chánd, with the usual hilarity of his years, enjoying himself as boys only can whenever there is anything new to look at or hunt for.

"Well, we have arrived at Boná Ghát at last," said Nobin, "and fortunately before nightfall. The *gurh* and the palace of the Ráis are before us. In what direction do we go now to find out the relative you seek?"

"I really do not know," said the Zemindár's lady, with a sigh, looking steadfastly at her family-residence, which was gradually becoming undistinguishable in the gloom. "Can we not make inquiries of him at the big house before us?"

They groped their way up accordingly to the Zemindár's house, and noiselessly pushed open the outer gate; but the building was tenantless, and it was considered unsafe to enter it at that hour.

"Since we don't exactly know where this friend of yours lives it would be best, I think," said Nobin, "to take up our quarters for the night at the village inn, if there be any such place here;" and, this being agreed to, they went back to the public road, and pursued it till they came to a *moodi's* shop, which represented a lodging-house for strangers. The proprietor was accommodating, and gave them a couple of small rooms to rest in, and, as they were tired with their day's journey, they were very anxious to go to sleep. One of the rooms was therefore quickly taken up by the lady and her son, and the other by Nobin, who got a lamp from the *moodi* and placed it at a door which joined the two apartments.

"Ha! whom have we here?" exclaimed the *moodi*, who had followed Nobin, and was looking attentively at the lady's face. "O, my honoured mistress, are you come home at last, and in such plight as this?"

"Are you quite sure that you know me?" asked the lady in excessive fright. "Who do you take me for that you address me as your mistress?"

"Who do I take you for? Who can I take you for, but your own good self, and the owner of all these estates? Every feature, every line of your kind face is imprinted in our recollections. You have become older and thinner now than before, but you are our own dear mother still, and can never, never be forgotten by us."

There was no denying the honour further; the poor have very retentive memories, and the virtues of the Zemindár's lady had made her servants her friends. The *moodi* had been one of her household lackeys, and this the lady recollected just as much as he remembered the mistress he had served.

The story of the lady and her son was listened to with intense interest by the whole village of Boná Ghát on the following morning, and Kooláye Chánd had no difficulty in assuming possession of his ancestral estates and importance. Nobin offered to return to his obscurity and a herdsman's life; but this neither Kooláye Chánd nor his mother would permit. They made him the Zemindár's *Dewán*, and after his death the *melá* we have spoken of was established to commemorate his worth.

CHAPTER II.

THE DEWÁN'S *MELÁ*.

WE must here at the very commencement take a leap over sixty years and more, to introduce the reader to the eventful period of 1831, when the young Zemindár of the day, Monohur Rái, the great-grandson of Kooláye Chánd Rái, had just attained his majority, or the age of eighteen, and was bent on solemnising the event along with the Dewán's *Melá*, which had fallen in at the same time, with the greatest *éclat*. He was a fine specimen of a high-bred Bengali youth, of slim but wiry build, with an expressive and handsome face scarcely disfigured by a pair of small and deep-set eyes, and having many good qualities of the heart, mixed unfortunately with an intense, or immoderate, love for frolics and adventures.

"I am determined to make the present *melá* an immense success," said he, "so that it may never cease to be remembered, and you must not scold me for that, mother mine!"

"Be it so," replied the mother, a lady thirty-five or thirty-six years old, of rather delicate features, but having a peculiar air of amiability and truthfulness about her, blended with a slight tinge of sadness for her widowed state. "But take care, my son, that you do not mark it with any discredit to your house and family-name."

"O, mother, have I not become a big man now, and don't I know how to uphold the family honours? You will soon hear from all sides how well the people will speak of me; and won't you be proud, Má, of having such a youth for your son?"

"Heaven bless and prosper you in everything, Monohur!" returned the lady, with a sad, sweet smile. "But I am sure it would please me better to see you applying to your work as diligently as your ancestors did, than that you should be going about gathering praises from the mob at a *melá*. Empty praises from the mass must not turn your young head, my son. You run so frequently after frolics and adventures that you really do alarm me at times."

"Ah, mother dear! just look down on the mango-grove yonder and see what a multitude of men have assembled there to celebrate my majority-day. Can you possibly disapprove of my furthering their enjoyment to the best of my power, when they have met so eagerly solely for the purpose of welcoming me as their lord and master? We shall have business, pleasure, frolic, and adventures all in concert there, and, surely, they can be united together in a *melá*. Can they not?"

"Yes, to a certain extent they can," answered the lady; "but the present is no fit occasion for frolic and pleasure, and all business cannot be associated with them, as you seem to think, Monohur. Some very important matters have suddenly and unexpectedly thrust themselves forward into notice which demand our immediate attention, and it is very unfortunate indeed that the *melá* comes up just at this particular time."

"O, mother! we cannot defer the *melá*, you know, for it has certain days. and those only, fixed for it. But your other business, of whatever importance, can surely lie over for the time—for only three short days, dear mother —after which I shall be as wholly attentive to it as you yourself may direct."

Saying this he bounced out of the house almost without waiting for his parent to reply, to superintend the *melá* preparations on which his whole heart was set, and which, sooth to say, were not very indifferently regarded by the lady herself, for all the brave words she had spoken to her son.

It was a grand *melá*, and an immense multitude, variously reckoned at from ten to fifteen thousand persons, were congregated within the mango-grove to celebrate it. There were all kinds of men among them, from the *chásá* and the cowherd, who had taken short leave of their fields, to the Hindu *Mohunt*, and the Mahomedan *Fakir* who had emerged from their retreats to take part in the festivity; and even the village girls and matrons had ceased working for the time at their *dhenki* and with the *koolá*,[1] though such immunity from labour falls rarely to their lot.

The Zemindár had offered to provide accommodation and convenience for all who came, and had spared no expense in doing justice to what he had undertaken. From an early hour all was stir and animation on the part of his people throughout the grove, and while several places were got ready with seats and canopies for the convenience of the more respectable visitors when they got tired of walking over the grounds, booths were erected in different directions for distributing sweetmeats and fruits among those who might seek for them, and

---

[1] *I.e.* at threshing corn.

others for the grant of largesses of money among the Bráhmans and the poor. One centrical spot, provided with a daïs and a rich canopy over it, was especially reserved for the Zemindár; and the birds of the grove gave a charm to the tree-tops around it, preferring its neighbourhood to all others for reasons best known to themselves, and adding therefrom their melodious voices to soften, as it were, the general clamour arising from every side.

There was business and pleasure certainly united at the *melá*, as the boy-Zemindár had unthinkingly asserted, the first being represented by the products of the country brought to it for sale, and the second by the amusements which were generally indulged in. Here were displayed paddy and grains of diverse sorts; there *ghee*, oil, sugar, molasses, fruits and vegetables, curds and sweetmeats; and, further on again, clothes, mats, pottery, straw and bamboo ware, brass ornaments, and metal utensils of all kinds—everything, in fact, which was in use in, or could be useful to, village life. But even the sellers of the articles were not engrossed in clearing their bargains, for the games and amusements of the *melá* were shared in by them almost as eagerly as by the rest. The boys of tender age were playing *jore-ke-bejore* (odd or even) with great earnestness; bigger lads were intent on the games of *bágbandi* and *mongul-páthán*; yet bigger ones were either for *nouko-chooree* or *hádoo-gádoo*, the latter known elsewhere as the *kabádi*. The men were similarly playing *páshá*, cards, or *satranchi*, particularly those who had brought goods to the fair for sale; while thorough idlers were amusing themselves with the *beená* and the *shitár*, the *behálá*, *tublá*, and *mirdung*, not a few finding relief even in the discordant music of the *dholuk*, the *kánsi*, and the *shánáye*. And the enjoyment was unrestrained and noisy, as such enjoyments always are.

The Zemindár, attired in holiday clothes, and with a walking-stick in his hand, strolled over the whole ground, inspecting almost every arrangement with care, while the eyes of all were drawn on him kindly and respectfully as they made room for him in whichever direction he went. He was smiles and attention to everybody, and listened patiently to every suggestion that was made for either augmenting or prolonging the amusement; and the people were charmed by his manners and condescension, and praised him with hearty untiring cheers.

The rejoicings were continued for three whole days, and were resolving into revelry, when the Zemindár's *Surburákár*, or manager, came forward to suggest that it was time now to put an end to the fair. He was an old servant of the family, who had more of his will at present than he ever had when his late master was alive, for Monohur's mother had the most implicit confidence in his management.

"We had better break up now," said he to Monohur, in a suggesting tone. "We have had the usual three days' amusement already, and business of great importance has been accumulating which has to be attended to."

"What business, Nilkant? Why should any business interfere with the natural frolics of the day? You look as if you had something of great moment to unfold. What is it about?"

"Very bad news has come to us from Pergunnáhs Ánoorpoor and Balleáh, where our neighbours, the Mahomedans, are, it is said, becoming restive, and we have not always been on the best terms with them."

"You look more gloomy over the news than I have

c

seen you do on greater fears. Are you afraid of the Mahomedans much?"

"No, not afraid of them exactly; but the information received relates to matters of serious importance, and requires very careful sifting, and—and—I would not care to speak further about them in the open air."

The Zemindár looked dissatisfied, the more so perhaps that his servant was so reticent; but, still heedless of the warning given to him, he separated himself from his would-be Mentor, and pierced further into the midst of the mango-tope, in the direction of the daïs erected for his reception. Here he was closely followed and accosted by a religious mendicant, who had so put on his headgear as almost entirely to conceal his features. He had the outward appearance of a Mahomedan Fakir, but might well have been mistaken for a Hindu Mohunt, or a beggar of any race.

"What was that old servant of yours speaking to you about, sir?" asked he of the Zemindár.

"I really don't know; I hardly understood what he said. He spoke of some Mahomedan doings at Ánoorpoor and Balleáh, which I don't care to know of to-day."

"You need not listen to what he says. The *melá* is over; let it break up. If you will give me a private hearing I shall tell you something that should be of advantage to you."

"Who art thou, father, and what business can you have with me? I can hardly understand why my affairs should interest you, you being a Mahomedan, apparently, and I a Hindu."

"Ah, I am an anchorite, and was dead to this world for twenty years. If I have come back to it since it is because my Master requires my services further. But I cannot indicate the direction in which I can serve you unless you give me a private hearing."

"Really, all this is perfectly unintelligible to me," said the perplexed youth, speaking rather displeasedly to himself, but loud enough to be heard by those immediately around him. "There is my manager hints to me of important disclosures which must be confidentially made. Here turns up a Mahomedan Fakir and demands a private ear. I have, surely, no time for either at present; but when the fair is over I shall be at the service of both."

So saying he bowed his head courteously towards the Fakir, and passed on through the tope as unconcernedly as before. He was a young man, barely escaped from boyhood, and could hardly be expected to prefer business to pleasure so soon, especially to such pleasure as now monopolised his mind.

"I must get him quickly married," said his mother to herself, after listening to the grumblings of the Surburákár. "He is too wild to be kept loose, and must be speedily mated."

Ah, mother dear ! your colt is too unruly to bear the harness yet. He must sow his wild oats before he will allow of being controlled.

CHAPTER III.

THE FIRST EXERCISE OF AUTHORITY.

THERE was a *Muktab*, or Mahomedan school, in the outskirts of Boná Ghát for imparting instruction to Mahomedan youths in Arabic, and this became a scene of great confusion one morning a short time after the breaking up of the *melá*, from a dispute having occurred in it between two students named Abdool Gohur and Syed Jooman, respectively. They were both of them good scholars, and often had arguments with each other on learned questions. But on the present occasion from arguments they came to altercation, and from altercation to abuse, which was followed by a scuffle; and, when the combatants were parted, it was discovered that Abdool Gohur had received a wound on the side from a knife which was lying on the ground.

"How fearful these Mahomedans are!" exclaimed the Zemindár's mother, when the matter was reported to her. "I trust the wounded youth has not since succumbed under his wound?"

"No, madam, not up to this time at least," said the Surburákár. "But the fellow who used the knife was not the less a ruffian for the narrow escape of his victim, and has to be brought to account for what he has done."

"Ah, that of course," said the lady; "but what was

the subject under discussion between them which led to the stabbing? Have we any information on that point?"

"None," said the Surburákár. "One of the contending parties is said to be a Ferázee, and the other not, and they were probably quarrelling about those very tenets of which we have heard so much lately from Pergunnáh Balleáh. What we have to do now is simply to send the Zemindár to the spot, for, as he is a resident Zemindár, the Government will expect him to institute a personal inquiry into the matter, after which he has to make over one or both the combatants to the district authorities."

"Then must Monohur perform his duty in the way you point out," said the mother; "but I shall await his return from the place with some anxiety."

"Why? What for, mother?" exclaimed Monohur. "What is there to be anxious for?"

"Nothing, certainly," answered the lady; "but I always feel uncomfortable when we have anything to do with our Mahomedan ryots. Go and perform your duty by all means, my son; but don't forget to return to me as soon as the work is over."

This was the first occasion on which the young Zemindár had been called upon to exercise his authority formally, and he went out with a brave assumption of the honours of his post. He had a small following with him, and was very respectfully received at the Muktab, having won golden opinions already even from the Mahomedans by his behaviour at the *melá*.

"He looks very much like his father," observed a gray-bearded Moslem as he came forward to make his obeisance to him, "and has the same broad forehead, and the same bright eyes."

"I trust he has the same large heart also," remarked another, "for our deceased lord had a generous and feeling heart."

"There can be no doubt of that," said a third, "for his heart is in his face, and that is very kindly and fair."

The manner in which the Zemindár commenced his inquiries also gave satisfaction. He asked questions pleasantly, listened attentively to what was said in reply, and cross-examined the speakers with much acumen and intelligence.

"You have received a knife-wound, Abdool Gohur. Let me see the wound."

"Here it is, sir," said the student, tucking up his *koortá*. "It is very slight, and scarcely worth being examined by yourself."

"You don't think it was accidental; do you?"

"I don't know, sir. It may have been so; and probably was."

"You did not anticipate or expect it from Jooman? You were never on bad terms with him before?"

"Certainly not, sir."

"Has the knife been identified?"

"Yes, sir," said one of the bystanders. "Syed Jooman has acknowledged it as belonging to him."

"Nor does he deny having inflicted the wound," put in another of the bystanders, who was no other than our old friend the Fakir who had accosted the Zemindár at the *melá*. "But this is a matter which the students might well be left to settle between themselves. There is little necessity for the Zemindár to trouble himself about it."

"No, no, that won't do," said the Surburákár, who formed one of the party that had accompanied Monohur·

to the Muktab. "The case is a criminal one, and the Zemindár must perform his duty and make over the offender to the police."

"To the police!" exclaimed the Fakir, with affected surprise. "And whereabouts then is this police? See, Zemindár *Mohásoy*, that thin, ragged chuprássi standing in the background there, whom any one of your peons might eat up when hungry, represents the police to which your Surburákár says you ought to make over the student. Is not the proposal silly on the face of it? Will you submit to do that?"

"Why not?" again interposed the Surburákár. "This is a very serious business. Two students in a private seminary quarrel with each other, and one uses a knife against the other. We don't know but that the wounded youth may yet die from the effects of the wound, though he seems to think so lightly of it at present; and what would the Government say to the Zemindár if he did not secure and make over the homicide into custody while having it in his power to do so?"

The Fakir did not even condescend to look at the Surburákár while he spoke so volubly, but, addressing the Zemindár, said,—

"You, sir, are the *de facto* Rájáh, or king, of these parts, and why should you make over any case from your jurisdiction to what your manager calls the 'Government,' which has no position anywhere, and cannot enforce its authority of itself? This is a mere school-squabble. The wound, you have seen, is only slightly deeper than a petty scratch. Even the youth who has been wounded does not wish for the punishment of his offending comrade. Why should you not inflict some nominal punishment, if any, and terminate the case?"

"Don't think of that," urged again the Zemindár's Surburákár. "We must not dream of ignoring the authority of the Government, from which that of the Zemindár is derived; and don't you mind the suggestions of such a beggarly counsellor as yonder fellow, who, under his tattered clothing, seems to hide some deep design of his own."

The Surburákár looked hard at the Fakir's face as he spoke; but the latter only smiled contemptuously in reply, without vouchsafing a single word to him in return. He only winked at the Zemindár, and then, suddenly coming up to him, said—

"I have been waiting to have a word with you. Do give me a private hearing when this case is over."

The case was disposed of very leniently by the Zemindár. This was his first exercise of authority, and he was too young yet to wish to act with severity. His decision was, in fact, just what the Fakir had suggested it should be.

"There is no malice proved against Syed Jooman, though he used the knife," said the Zemindár. "He simply acted without forethought, and as even his adversary does not wish for his punishment, and as the wound does not threaten to assume a serious character, it is hardly necessary to send up the case to the magistrate;" and the chowkeydár, who had received his hush-money from the friends of Syed Jooman, grinned approval of the Zemindár's decision.

The Surburákár was red-hot with wrath, and walked off from the place at once to the Zemindár's mother, but he was not accompanied by the Zemindár. Monohur Rái had promised a private conference with the Fakir, and, having sent away his followers in different directions, proceeded with him alone into the mango-grove, which was almost contiguous to the Muktab.

"How far do you want me to go with you?" asked Monohur of the man.

"O, a few paces only," was the reply; "to such a spot as will not expose us to the risk of being overheard."

The Fakir was an elderly man with a stooping head and a sunken chest, and the Zemindár had no harm to apprehend from him personally.

"I cannot guess what he can have to say to me," communed Monohur with himself, "but it does not look as if he had any sinister intent against me, and it is certain that he isn't an unsafe person for one of my make and age to go with;" and so the two went together into the gloomiest part of the tope.

What they talked of has not been reported to us, but Monohur did not return from the conference at once to his expecting mother. A good understanding was established between the Zemindár and the Fakir, but there was still a point of difference between them; and this point was referred for settlement, not to the Zemindár's mother or to his Surburákár, but to the most powerful Hindu divinity of the place, speaking through the lips of his *Sabáit*, or priest. This deity was named Nággesur Mahádeva, whose shrine was much resorted to at the time, not only by the Hindus, but frequently also by the Mahomedans living within several miles around Boná Ghát. At one time the idol had large funds allotted for its maintenance, the law under the Hindu Rájáhs having conferred on the Sabáit the power of levying a tax of one *trisulá* pyce on each bullock that entered Pergunnáh Datteáh, and one *pootáh* of grass out of each bundle exported therefrom. But these exactions having been subsequently abolished by the British Government, a small money-compensation in lieu of them had to be paid to the shrine by the Zemindár. It is said that the amount of this stipend having on one occasion been further reduced by Monohur's grandfather, Godádhur, the god assumed the appearance of a *daitya* of ferocious form and took his seat at the top of the temple, which caused a total cessation of rain in the village in the sultriest part of the year, the tanks becoming simultaneously filled with blood, or water of that colour. The whole village, with the Zemindár at their head, turned out thereupon to pacify the deity; his allowance was fully restored, and the arrears of it paid down before him; and, his old temple having become ruinous, a new temple was raised for him on the banks of the Bhetná, upon which he was mollified. This new temple is the one that still stands, and has always been kept in good repair; and the deity has been so feared ever since that no business of any importance is undertaken in this part of the country to the present day without previously consulting him.

"Why consult your mother on matters which it is not possible for her to understand?" said the Fakir to the Zemindár. "We, as Mahomedans, have consulted our own most sacred shrines, and you as a Hindu are welcome to do likewise. Have you no faith in Nággesur Mahádeva, or do you apprehend his misdirecting you?"

"I have the fullest confidence in the god of my fathers," answered Monohur, devoutly, "and I accept your suggestion to refer the point of difference between us for his decision."

CHAPTER IV.

THE REFERENCE TO THE DEITY.

THE temple at Boná Ghát stands on the very brink of the Bhetná, on an elevated platform paved with Chunár stones. It possesses no striking features of grandeur or beauty, but is not an uninteresting building of its kind either—namely, of the four-cornered and vaulted temple kind, surmounted by a spire at the top, edifices of which description are to be seen almost everywhere throughout India. The approach to the platform from three sides is by three distinct roads, while from the fourth the ascent from the river is by a staircase of granite which goes far below the water's edge. The river flows by in a dark and muddy channel, and is overlooked by a clump of tall palm-trees growing almost immediately on its banks.

The morning was bright. The sun had arisen about an hour, and the gardens on three sides of the platform, refreshed by the dews of the night, were breathing out a luxuriant fragrance. But the hearts assembled before the shrine scarcely appreciated the charm of the scenery around them. They had come there with excited hopes and ambitions, excited griefs and fears, and their eyes scarcely ever strayed from the stone image of the god within the temple, which was fixed and inert, and the form of the Sabáit, a thin, middle-aged man, who seemed deeply absorbed in prayer.

The devotions of the priest being at last concluded, he

came forward to the temple gate to go through the accustomed routine of listening to and answering the inquiries of the crowd collected before him, and the first who accosted him was a woman who had been forced to come there by her neighbours. An orphan child of the village had fallen down from a *Chálta* tree into a pool of water infested by alligators, and had not afterwards been seen. The woman had brought the news into the village. Her version was that she had seen the boy climb up the tree, had prevented him from doing so, but was not attended to, had witnessed his fall into the deepest part of the pool, and also his being seized upon and carried down by an alligator.

"That cannot be a true tale, surely," said one of the villagers to her; "for there seems to be no reason for the boy to have got upon the tree at all. Children never climb Chálta trees of their own will, since the fruit cannot be eaten raw. Did you not tell the boy to get up and fetch some Cháltás for you?"

"No; why should I have sent up a poor orphan on such an errand? Don't I know that the pool has a bad name, and the tree also?"

"Will you swear before Nággesur Mahádeva that the story, as you have told it, is wholly true?"

"Yes," said the woman, boldly; and she was marched up at once to the temple to take the oath.

The Sabáit heard the reference with a smile; then, taking down a garland of flowers from the top of the Lingam, he placed it into the woman's hand.

"Mind, you are now speaking to the god himself, with his sacred garland in your hand. Tell him the story as you wish it to be believed."

The woman attempted to speak, but could not. She

coughed two or three times, and spat out blood with her spittle.

"There, behold," said the Sabáit, "a convicted liar!" and that very moment the boy that was believed to have been carried off by an alligator ran out of the temple to the wonder of the villagers and their relief, for he was well loved by them.

"Well, what is your version of the story, boy?"

"Why, that woman there sent me up the Chálta tree to get Cháltás for her. I fell from the tree into the pool beneath, and struggled hard to gain the shore. I do not know how I succeeded; the woman did not help me, for I saw that she had run off."

The next applicant before the shrine was a young woman of fifteen or sixteen, who was believed to be possessed of the devil, and had been brought there by her friends that she might be cured by the deity.

"Describe her ailment as it broke out," said the Sabáit to her friends.

"O, sir! she complained first of pains all over her body, and afterwards spoke and behaved strangely, gnashed her teeth, and twirled and twisted her limbs in an indescribable manner. Two kobirájes were called in, but could not say what was the matter with her. A rojáh saw her after them, and declared that she was possessed of the devil. He beat her violently with shoes on the head, breast, and back to exorcise the evil-spirit. We remonstrated, but he said that there was no other treatment. His usage, however, did her no good, and, as we would not permit its repetition, we have brought her hither, feeling certain that Nággesur Mahádeva is quite able to effect the expulsion of the devil from her, if it pleases him to do so."

"You are right in thinking so," said the Sabáit. "Nággesur Mahádeva can of course do what no rojáh will ever accomplish. Take charge of this *billipatra*[1] from his feet. Immerse it in a jar of water and give the patient a mouthful of the water to drink every morning and evening. If you do this regularly for a week the evil-spirit will be only too glad to get out of her."

The third case was that of a woman who had lost her child and could not find him. The child had a few silver trinkets on his person worth about two or three rupees. The mother had sought for him all over the village and beyond it, but without success. She was exhausted and crying bitterly on the road-side, when her neighbours suggested that she should go to the temple to inquire.

"Don't you know," said they, "that Nággesur Mahádeva can direct you aright in the search if it pleases him?"

"But how can I go to him? I have spent all I had in the search already, and have not a pyce now to buy offerings with to place before his shrine."

"It does not matter. If you are really so poor as that he will undoubtedly answer your heart's wishes without expecting any offering from you."

"And here I am, sir, with my rent heart before the god."

"You have done right, daughter, to come here in your distress. Your child has been kidnapped by the *Bájikars*, or gipsies, who passed this way two days ago. It is a small party of some sixteen or seventeen persons; all of them thieves and kidnappers. They have crossed the Hindangá Gáng already, and are now selling animal oils

---

[1] Leaf of the wood-apple tree, held sacred in the worship of Mahádeva.

at Pulláshpole. Ask your friends to be alert. If you can overtake the party before they reach Chándpore you will recover your child, but not the trinkets he wore."

After having given these and other similar answers with celerity, the Sabáit advanced towards a young man who was standing apart from the rest, though he had come to consult the deity even as they had done.

"You wish to take counsel of the deity, young man, but still hesitate to prefer your request. You need not be afraid. You are known to me, and the god of your fathers will always be a help to you in your difficulties."

"I have, indeed, something very serious to consult him about, father, but I find it difficult to break the matter even to you."

"Ah, I understand. The subject is very weighty, surely, and one may well hesitate to confide it to others. But I know all about the matter already, and, besides that, what you have to tell me concerns not you alone, but the public weal also, of which we are the best protectors. Don't fear then to speak of it as becomes a man of your position in life, for what you say you say to Nággesur Mahádeva, not to me. Describe your difficulty and you shall know the mind of the god about it at once."

"What I want to know of Nággesur Mahádeva is this only—Should I remain at home to get wived, as my mother wishes? or go out to fight the battles of my country, if my services are asked for?"

"If your country requires your services, young man, your first duty is to her and to your fellowmen. You will have plenty of time hereafter to cultivate the domestic virtues."

"Think again, sir, and give me the exact dictum of the deity in its integrity. I am an only son, and have a widowed mother at home. I am, moreover, the sole heir of a long line of eminent ancestors. The duties I owe to my mother and my family-name must be as important as any other."

"They are so, and it pleases the deity much to find that you are not forgetful of them. But they are not urgent, and there is no particular reason to fear that they would suffer by a short delay."

"How so, sir? I am eighteen years old already, and the practice in my family has always been for boys to get married before their sixteenth year, and for girls before their tenth."

"You have already departed from the rule then, young man, and may well give an additional year or two to your country before you get bound by your domestic duties and sit down to beget and rear children."

"But, my mother? Would it not be unnatural to thwart her wishes when she has set her heart on marrying me without delay?"

"Do you know whom your mother wants you to marry? She wants the Zemindár of Boná Ghát to wed the heiress of Paithulli. The match is an unequal one for you in every respect, and very undesirable. Nággesur Mahádeva is the best friend of your house, and wishes you to seek and secure a better wife."

"Would it be right and becoming in me, sir, to set aside my mother's choice?"

"Right, to be sure," answered the Sabáit, deliberately. "A good wife is a great gain, young man, and it is most proper that the Zemindár of Boná Ghát should be well-married. But you must dare and deserve before you can get such a wife; and the deity may not help you to find one if you do not deserve and dare. Sit down and listen to a story of old days, and you may gather wisdom from it to invigorate your heart and hands."

It will be convenient to tell the story in a separate chapter.

CHAPTER V.

THE SABÁIT'S STORY.

"A HOLY Bráhman had one son and three daughters, all of whom were handsome and well-accomplished. When the father died he told his son not to give away his sisters to ordinary men, nor for himself to take an ordinary wife. The orphans lived quietly together for a year, and the girls, being very lovely, had many suitors. These, however, were ordinary persons, and were therefore summarily rejected.

"After the expiration of the first year there was a tremendous thunder-storm, accompanied by heavy rain, and, while the lightnings flashed across the sky, a bright, beaming youth entered the Bráhman's house.

"'Who art thou?' asked the young Bráhman of the intruder, in surprise.

"'O, I am the Spirit of the Storm,' said he, 'and have come to take away your eldest sister with me as my wife.'

"'Take her off then, and God bless you both!' returned the Bráhman youth; and the Spirit of the Storm married the young girl, and took her away with him into the air.

"Next year there was a violent earthquake, and the earth was split and broken asunder in several places, and a brave, fair youth entered the Bráhman's house.

"'Who art thou?' demanded the master of it again, as before, of the being who now confronted him.

"'O, I am the Spirit of the Earthquake, and have come to woo your second sister to be my wife.'

"'Take her away then, and God bless you both!' said the young Bráhman, and the Spirit of the Earthquake married her, and took her down underneath the earth.

"In the third year there was a tremendous inundation, and crocodiles and alligators from the sea covered the land, while a brave, bright youth entered the Bráhman's water-covered house.

"'Who art thou?' demanded the young Bráhman of him, as on previous occasions.

"'O, I am the Spirit of the Waters, and would fain have your third sister for my wife.'

"'Take her then, and God bless you both!' and the Spirit of the Waters married her, and carried her off to the regions under the waters.

"'Well, I have married away all my sisters fairly, even according to my father's injunction,' said the Bráhman youth to himself. 'Where am I to find an extraordinary wife now to keep house for me?'

"He was overheard from a neighbouring tree by a beautiful bird with many-coloured wings, which chirped out in reply that it had seen a most extraordinary girl in the depth of the forest. 'She is the daughter of a Dánava, and is very much beloved by her father, and very carefully guarded. She is lovelier than all your sisters, and the words drop from her mouth like pearls of wisdom.'

"'How, O bird, is she to be wooed and won?'

"'O, her father goes out every night seeking whom

to devour, and if you can see her then and induce her to elope with you she may be yours.'

"Brave was the Bráhman youth, and very fond of excitement and adventure, and he entered the forest in the night alone, and traced the Dánava's daughter to her home.

"'Will you come away, bright eyes, with me? Your life here must be very lonely, and we could be so happy with each other elsewhere.'

"'Willingly,' said the girl, 'for I have got weary of my seclusion, and uneasy also, as not knowing for what purpose I am here so rigidly detained. But I fear it will be very difficult for us to escape hence; the risk, I assure you, is very great.'

"'Well, I must take it notwithstanding,' said the youth in reply; 'such a prize as you are is well worth a lot of troubles and fears.'

"They tried hard to get out of the forest before the Dánava's return, but were unable to do so, being overtaken almost at its borders.

"'Ha, girl! hast thou got a lover and wouldst escape from me? Get home, fool, and I shall soon come to you after I have punished your seducer suitably;' and he bound the Bráhman youth and suspended him from the highest tree in the forest that the owls and other nightbirds might come and peck at him. But the Spirit of the Storm, seeing the distress of his brother-in-law, came promptly to his aid, and, raising a furious gale, levelled the tree with the ground, wafting the youth at the same time safe to his home.

"'I must try again to secure that precious wife,' said the youth to himself after passing a wretched and sleepless night. 'Never was such a beautiful dream seen in life before, and I must not give up the prize without further attempts;' and he entered the forest again with a bold heart at night, and appeared before the Dánava's house.

"The girl uttered a cry of pleasure on seeing him safe and sound, and fastened her arms around his neck, and hung from it as a bridal garland.

"'Ah, why hast thou come hither again, my lover? Hast thou not felt already how fearful my father is?'

"'I would not be worthy of thee, sweet maid, if I did not dare thus much for you. Let us fly again, dearest, and it may be that this time we shall be able to escape him.'

"'I am quite as willing to go as ever,' replied the maiden, 'but am not so hopeful of success as you are; and if we fail again you are sure to be more fearfully punished than before.'

"'So be it,' said the youth; and they fled once more, but were again unable to clear the forest prior to the Dánava's return.

"'Ha! hast thou ventured to repeat thy bold game so soon, young man, notwithstanding the punishment I inflicted on thee last night? This time then, I shall bury thee underground and deprive thee of daylight for ever.'

"But the Spirit of the Earthquake was alive to the danger of his brother-in-law, and splitting up the ground in his rage he liberated him and conveyed him safe to his home.

"'A third time must I try to get that girl as my wife. I have given away my heart to her already, and, if this suspense be not promptly ended, it will be all over with me soon;' and he entered the forest again at night to carry out his intent.

"The girl was delighted as before to receive him, though remonstrating that he should have come risking a fresh capture; and they eloped once more, but to be apprehended again before the forest was quite cleared.

"'Now, by the souls of the undying gods,' swore the Dánava, addressing the young Bráhman, 'this time I shall surely fling thee into the sea that thou may'st never turn up again;' and he threw him out of the forest with such force that he sped through the air like a falling star, and fell into the ocean at a distance of more than a hundred miles.

"But the Spirit of the Waters had observed the peril of his brother-in-law, and, rescuing him from the waves, carried him safely to his house.

"Sore, sore grieved was the Bráhman youth at these repeated failures in securing the wife of his choice.

"'O, friendly bird, you told me where the peerless bride was to be found; can you not tell me how she is to be secured?'

"'Thou art a Bráhman's son, O, youth, and dost thou ask advice on such a subject from a little miserable thing like me? Take a jar of Gungá water with you and some Tulsi leaves, and, when you run away with your bride-elect, scatter the water and the leaves behind you, and no Dánava will dare to cross them to approach you.'

"Armed as advised, the Bráhman youth entered the forest for the fourth time, and mighty glad was the Dánava's daughter to see him alive and well, yet terribly afeared that he should have come after her once more.

"'O, my dearest lover, why have you ventured hither again for me? This time my father will surely kill you.'

"'So be it, my love; I would rather die at his hands than live without you. But come away quickly with me.

This time our plan is well laid, and your father will not be able to overtake us.'

"They fled as before, and the Bráhman youth scattered Gungá water and Tulsi leaves on their wake, and the Dánava, though he could see them from a distance, was unable to approach them. He uttered a fearful cry, like the howl of a wild beast deprived of its young; raved and tore his hair in rage; and his daughter was greatly terrified at the outburst of his wrath. But she was carried through the forest by her lover with great celerity, and they lost no time in getting married the moment they were out of it; and the Dánava's daughter became a good, dutiful, and pious Bráhmani."

"This is a rather long tale, sir," said Monohur, somewhat pettishly; "and I could have heard just as good a one at home from my old grandaunt, were I disposed to listen to her patiently. But I don't see what connection the story has with my case, or what lesson I am expected to learn from it."

"This only: you must venture as much, or more even, for your bride than the youth I have spoken of did for his; and, if your choice be of the right sort, you shall have the Spirits of the Storm, Earthquake, and Waters to assist you, and, over and above them, the Spirit of Purity and Peace. They are all, I assure you, at work at this moment; and it is well for thee, my son, to take part in their labours, to which your mind has been already directed."

CHAPTER VI.

THE LECTURE AT HOME.

A FEW hours later in the day Monohur had to meet his mother, who had been anxiously awaiting his return. He would have avoided seeing her if he could have managed it, but it was simply impossible to do so. She had been watching closely for him, and sprang towards him with a scream as she saw him coming into the house.

"Where have you been all this time, Monohur? And why did you not return home at once after disposing of the school-quarrel case, as I had asked you?"

"O, mother, I had business out of the village to attend to; and I also went to consult Nággesur Mahádeva on matters that deeply affect my interest and welfare."

"What may those matters be, my son? and why was I not told of them before you went? Your interests are mine, Monohur; you are nothing apart from me, nor I from you."

"I know that well, mother dear, for I know that you are the best and kindest mother that ever breathed. But I do not wish that you should be mixed up with the matters I was referring to. I am a big boy now, and may have especial secrets of my own, you know."

"Do you really think so, Monohur? Are you already tired of my control?" asked the mother, looking up almost reproachfully at his face. "You are young, boy, and therefore apt to be led astray if not carefully watched over. You can have no secrets from me at this age but such as are sure to lead you into difficulties."

But there was no disposition on the part of the son to trust his personal affairs to his mother's keeping.

"A woman can have no correct knowledge of men and public matters," thought he to himself. "She has hitherto been led entirely by the Surburákár, to whose tutoring I shall not submit."

His spoken reply, however, was both kinder and more respectful, though still very vague.

"O, mother, you shall know all in time. Just let me have a short while to understand my own heart aright; and I shall then be able to reproduce it before you with better effect."

"Which is as much as to say, Monohur, that you will not trust me with your secret at present. Ah, boy, I did not expect this want of confidence in me from you. I only hope you understand your position aright."

"What do you mean, mother? I certainly do understand my position, I think; but I cannot say that I understand your words in the least."

"Why, I was told by the Surburákár that in that school-squabble case you have discharged the delinquent who made use of the knife, instead of sending him up to the district magistrate, as the Government orders require. Is not that mistaking your position as a Zemindár greatly? Don't you know that you are bound to make over such offenders to the Government authorities?"

"How bound? My impression always was that the Zemindárs are the *de facto* Rájáhs or rulers within their respective estates, and that the power to discharge or punish offenders rests with them alone."

"No, certainly not. That may have been the case in the past, but is not so now. We hold our lands from the Government, and are in every respect subordinate to it. There is Nilkant coming, who will explain all this to you more clearly. I only wish you would learn your duties and responsibilities properly before attempting to cut off your leading-strings."

"The leading-strings, mother, I will not endure. I might have borne your control well enough, but I see that you can do nothing without Nilkant, and I will not put myself under his guidance if I can help it. I am willing, however, to learn whatever you or he may have to communicate to me."

He then turned to the Surburákár who had come up, and said rather proudly—

"Well, Nilkant, I find that you have reported unfavourably of me to my mother with reference to that quarrel-case in the Muktab. Will you explain to me why my proceedings in that matter have received your disapproval?"

"I have brought these papers with me, and if you will read them attentively you will find that in such matters Zemindárs have no such discretion as you were pleased to exercise. First read this paper, which is a copy of the original *Kuboolyat*, or engagement, which was executed by Kooláye Chánd Rái, your ancestor of revered memory, when the zemindáry was conferred on him by the British *Ráj*."

Monohur took the paper that was handed to him, and began to read it very carefully. It ran as follows:—

"I, Kooláye Chánd Rái, Zemindár of Boná Ghát, do execute this Kuboolyat on my part out of my free will and consent. Having been appointed to hold the office of Zemindár in Boná Ghát, I agree to collect the rents according to the rates sanctioned by the Government. I shall pay the annual revenue due to the Government in the instalments specified in the annexed schedule, without excuse or delay. I shall keep the ryots prosperous and contented, and exert myself to improve the lands, so that they may bring forth more crops than they yield at present. I shall not allow cultivated lands to fall waste, nor inferior crops to be grown on superior lands. I shall not be prodigal in my own expenses, nor allow my ryots to be so. I shall never grant *jygheres*, or lands in free gift, without obtaining the permission of the Government. I shall at all times keep a careful watch over the boundaries of my zemindáry. I shall not allow guns, or swords, or other offensive weapons to be manufactured, sold, or used on my estate without the sanction of the Government. I shall prevent, to the best of my power, the commission of murders, robberies, disturbances, thefts, and other offences within my zemindáry; and, when they are committed, I shall make over all offenders to the Government authorities for trial and punishment, with such stolen property as may be recovered, etc., etc."

Monohur read the document twice over before he returned it to the Surburákár.

"If I had been Kooláye Chánd Rái," said he, "I would certainly not have submitted to such terms as are here stated."

"Then you would not have received the *Sunnud* which was granted to your honoured ancestor in return for his Kuboolyat," answered Nilkant, in a quiet, impassive tone, handing another paper to him for perusal.

The wording of the Sunnud was as follows:—

"Be it known to all Kánoongoes, Pradháns, Mátabars, and Ryots of Boná Ghát, in Pergunnáh Datteáh, in the district of 24-Pergunnáhs, that, whereas Rái Kooláye Chánd Sándyal is in possession of the zemindáry aforesaid, and has signed an engagement to discharge his duties honestly and faithfully to the Government, the said zemindáry is hereby granted and assigned to him, subject to the terms of the Kuboolyat executed by him. You are all accordingly ordered to honour him as your lawful Zemindár, and never to wander from his rightful commands. You are never to conceal any matters from his knowledge, and are to pay rent to him punctually, according to the laws promulgated by the Government and the rules and customs which have hitherto obtained. The Zemindár, on his part, is required to keep his ryots contented, protect them with a watchful eye, prevent the commission of crimes within his estate, and deliver over all offenders to the Government authorities for trial and punishment."

"Were such the terms under which the predecessors of Kooláye Chánd Kortá held their office under the Mahomedans?"

"No; the Mahomedans left more power in the hands of their manager-substitutes than the British Government has done; but they also exercised greater atrocities over them, if all that is said of them be true."

"I don't believe all that is said against them," cried Monohur, in a fretful tone. "It is the English only who traduce them, and their reason for doing so is obvious. I say again that had I been Kooláye Chánd Rái I would not have accepted the zemindáry under such documents as these; nor do I understand how the terms enunciated in them are binding on me."

"How foolishly you speak, indeed," observed his mother, expostulatingly. "The English Government is a paternal one, and all that we have we owe to it. The terms of the engagements referred to are binding on us by those of the Perpetual Settlement. Don't you know what that is?"

"But the land, mother, the land is the free gift of the gods! The English did not bring it out with them in their ships; did they? The country belongs to its inhabitants, who were placed in it by the gods. The English understand this well enough in their own country. Why have the Hindu and Mahomedan laws then been interfered with and overturned? Why have not all the privileges we enjoyed before under the Mahomedans been continued to us? O, mother! if all Zemindárs were of my mind they would throw up their zemindáries rather than hold them under such conditions as have been shown to me."

The young man uttered these words with sparkling eyes and in an animated and resolute voice, which brought to his mother's face an expression of deep distress and anxiety.

"I fear this comes of your having listened to the whisperings of a Mahomedan Fakir who has been frequently seen in your company," gasped out the poor woman at last. "O, Monohur, do not speak in that vehement way, nor use such dangerous words again, if you would not break my heart! The Mahomedans are arrant knaves themselves, and would fain make knaves of the Hindus also, if they can. The English have conquered the country; what good then can come of your reviling them? Every word that you say may be true in the abstract; but still ought not such words to be uttered. We are happy as we are, O, my son! Don't aspire to be wiser and greater, or you will only bring down ruin on yourself and yours, for the Government, though paternal, is eagle-eyed and iron-armed."

"She is right," said Nilkant. "If you continue to think as you have expressed yourself you will only be putting the rope round your own neck."

Monohur let the subject drop. The issues raised in his mind by the documents shown to him were too weighty and important for a passionate discussion.

"I have already liberated the school-boys, mother, and there is nothing more to be done in that matter now. If the authorities take offence at what I have done I must submit to such punishment as they may choose to inflict on me. I have no objection to your and Nilkant's disposing of all such cases for me in future."

The mother would have remonstrated further with him, but could not, and Monohur took advantage of her silence to rush out of the house to the wood that skirted it on the north and east, to commune with himself in silence and alone.

The house was bounded on both those sides by bamboo-clumps, which gird nearly all Bengali houses in the Mofussil almost in every direction. The English reader asks—"Wherefore?" The question has never been answered correctly, though the answer is a very simple one. The country for centuries was a very unquiet one, as there were nothing but raids and invasions in every part of it throughout the Mahomedan era; and these bamboo-clumps often saved the inhabitants from great and various calamities in those days. All persons who had houses worth saving belted them round with dense bamboo-thickets to render them unapproachable except by one or two narrow

THE LECTURE AT HOME. 47

winding passages, or, as in the case of the Zemindár's house, from one side only; and within these thickets whole communities found refuge when, elsewhere, the land was being plundered and harried. O, Monohur, if you had read them aright those bamboo-clusters alone ought to have taught you a lesson sufficient to balance your mind! But an entire set of new ideas had been foisted into his mind, and was playing the deuce with his brain.

"The whole country is now ripe for a revolt," muttered the Zemindár to himself. "Why should I not take advantage of the circumstance to better my position if I can?"

CHAPTER VII.

THE FERÁZEE RISING.

WHILE the events recorded in the preceding chapters were occurring in one portion of the district, a Mahomedan conspiracy was being matured in another—namely, in the pergunnáhs of Ánoorpoor, Bálindáh, and Balleáh, all of which were almost adjacent to Datteáh. The village of Chándpore, in Bálindáh was the original home of a cowherd youth, named Teetoo Meer, who was generally known as a good-for-nothing fellow, much complained of by the farmers for the manner in which he treated their cows. This man acquired afterwards a reputation for sanctity by the performance of a pilgrimage to Meccá, where he is said to have met with a distinguished Wáhábee leader, named Syed Ahámud, who exhorted him to undertake the reformation of the Mahomedan religion in his part of India. In furtherance of this project Teetoo, on returning from his pilgrimage, repaired to the fair at Hurwá, which is celebrated in commemoration of Gorá Chánd, a Mahomedan *Pir*, and took the opportunity to promulgate the Ferázee doctrines, or a slight modification of Wáhábism, requiring at the same time that all good Mahomedans should wear a long beard. His language was far from being conciliatory; no attempt at persuasion or instruction was ever made by him; he preferred, even from the outset, to see what could be done

THE FERAZEE RISING. 49

by abuses and threats. But there was no want of success on that account. He managed in a short time to secure a large following, and, being joined by another *budmásh* named Miskeen Sháh, began to arm his followers with clubs and other weapons, which soon converted them into a dangerous gang.

"How are we to put down this new movement?" asked Rámdhone Ghuttack, the Zemindár of Sáduckpore, of some of his brother Zemindárs. "The innovations introduced by Teetoo are unsettling our estates, and may eventually lead to mischief and confusion."

"What if we levy a tax on beards?" suggestingly answered Kristo Prosád Rái, the Zemindár of Poorú. "If the distinguishing mark of the sect be removed would not that act as a determent and prevent more of our ryots from joining it?"

"It may or may not," responded a third Zemindár; "but the idea is a very good one, and should be carried out at once."

An order was accordingly issued simultaneously by all the Hindu Zemindárs of Ánoorpoor, Bálindáh, Balleáh, and Surfarázpore authorising the levy of a tax of one rupee and four annas annually on each beard, whether cultivated by a Mahomedan or a Hindu. The Mahomedans protested against this as an unjust exaction, and, on their objection not being heeded, they complained of it to Teetoo.

"Ah!" exclaimed Teetoo, "don't I understand what the Kaffirs mean? It was I that directed the cultivation of the beard, and surely their order is levelled against me personally, more than against others. Have the fools then forgotten their old cowherd boy so soon, and shall I not hasten to remind them that I live?"

E

The threat was significant, and the opportunity to give effect to it was not difficult to find. The Hindu festival of Rámnavami had fallen on the same day with the Akhiree Cháhár Sambá of the Mahomedans, and, while Kristo Prosád was celebrating the former at Poorá with great *éclat*, Teetoo collected a large party of his followers at Ekdil Sháh's Durgáh, which stood in the immediate neighbourhood of the Zemindár's house.

"Is it right," said Teetoo to his men, "that the Hindus should be deafening us with their cries while we are here at prayer? Should we not attack their deity and pound it into dust?"

"Dare we?" asked Miskeen Sháh. "The Dárogá is personally present at the Zemindár's house."

"Then we shall break the Dárogá's head along with that of the Zemindár if either ventures to interfere with us. Could we not do that much in defence of our faith?"

And Teetoo's valour was much applauded by his adherents.

The Zemindár's house was immediately after attacked by an infuriated mob armed with swords and bludgeons, and, as the Hindus resisted, there was a great fight to begin with. The Dárogá attempted, but in vain, to put down the affray, and the Zemindár's men, being as tens against hundreds, were eventually beaten, and obliged to fly. Flushed with their success the Mahomedans now slaughtered a cow in the house to desecrate it, and defiled the chapel especially, by sprinkling the blood of the animal on its floor and walls.

"I have heard," said Miskeen Sháh, "that the women of the Zemindár's house are very pretty. Must we not see them?"

THE FERÁZEE RISING.

"No, no," said the Dárogá, "that would fix an indelible disgrace on the family. You have done mischief enough already, and should retire."

But Teetoo would listen to no remonstrance, and, the Zemindár's inner house being broken into, the females were pulled about and insulted, much household property being at the same time destroyed and looted. After that the assailants went off, but not till they had set fire to some piles of hay which sent forth dense clouds of smoke and flame, the final result of the act being that a good part of the village was consumed; and, in the confusion that occurred, a sweet girl of ten or eleven, the only child of a respectable household, was lost or carried off.

"What will you do with the girl, Miskeen Sháh?" asked Teetoo. "Will you make her your wife?"

"My wife! No. I have a good many of them already, and don't wish to be more heavily encumbered. But I shall certainly make a Mahomedan of her, and then marry her to Gházee Myán."

The idea was so good that it was warmly applauded by the bulk of the Sháh's hearers, for it was a religious sacrifice to which he had referred. The Mahomedans of the lower classes, who have lost their previous children, make a vow that if they have a child that will survive, he or she, or a substitute for him or her, would be devoted to the service of Gházee Myán, or the Bamboo. When the child is a boy they make him a Fakir; when a girl she is married to the Bamboo, and then assigned to the village Fakir, but cannot be married by anyone.

"Our Fakir is much too old, I think," said Teetoo, "to appreciate such a precious sacrifice."

"O, never mind that. The Fakir has his rights and is

working for the cause zealously, and the first capture of our sword and spear may well go to him."

"Nonsense!" exclaimed the Dárogá. "Who ever heard of such a nice little girl as that being so sacrificed! I beseech you again, friends, to liberate her."

"You have not chosen your friends wisely, Dárogá Sáheb," said Teetoo in reply, in a grim, sarcastic vein. "Don't you see the light there? What is to prevent us from roasting you over that fire?"

The Dárogá was an old man, but bearing on his features the traces of an energy that age had not altogether obliterated. The threat of Teetoo did not seem to affect him much; but he looked anxiously about him lest any act of his should complicate matters yet further, and, preferring to bide his time, he left the place.

Then followed a series of other outrages perpetrated indiscriminately on all who had chanced to give offence either to Teetoo or to any of his followers.

"We have plenty of work to perform," said Teetoo; "let us lose no time in getting through it;" and they lost no time in harrying, burning, and slaying, such being the work they had selected for themselves.

The first attack after the Poorá outrage was on a native Christian named Smith, who was severely beaten and tortured.

"We have one remedy only for all distempers," said Miskeen Sháh, "and must not hesitate to apply it alike on Christians, Mahomedans, and Hindus;" and it was applied with remorseless cruelty in every instance.

The next following attacks were mostly on Mahomedans—namely, on those who had come within the range of Teetoo's hatred by abandoning their beards; and even.

the mosques they usually prayed in were burnt to the ground.

"What are these fellows but Káffirs?" said Gholám Másoom, whom Teetoo had appointed Commander-in-Chief of his army. "If they fear the orders of their Zemindárs more than the orders we issue to them, whom have they to blame but themselves for the consequences?"

The greatest sufferers everywhere were, however, the Hindus, on whom no atrocities were left unused. Not only was the celebration of their religion rigorously prohibited, but oxen and fowls were killed in large numbers in their villages, and the temples desecrated by their blood. The raw hides of the oxen were at the same time scoffingly hung up in the houses of the inhabitants, and the female members of their families were invariably maltreated when unable to fly. And the area of the outrages was gradually widened so as to embrace not only several divisions of 24-Pergunnáhs, but also of Nuddeá and Furreedpore.

As a rule the Hindus succumbed under the violence inflicted on them; but at some places a show of opposition was occasionally made, notably at Ráikoti, by a Zemindár named Hurdeb Rái, who was eventually defeated. All resistance of this kind was, in fact, invariably beaten down in the end; and Teetoo was easily persuaded to believe that his power had become invincible.

"Should we not now turn our arms against the English Government," said he, "and drive out the Ferángees from the country? That would best enable us to further the re-establishment of the Prophet's faith in it on a basis of purity, and what have we to fear in the undertaking?"

And, taking a house at Nárkelberiáh, a village in Ballcáh, he built a mud fort there, which became his headquarters; while the emblem of royal dignity, the imperial music, was also assumed by him by the *Nákará* being beat morning and evening from the gateway of his palace, which soon assumed a fearful significance in peaceful ears, as it always preceded the raids made every now and then from the fort on the villages by which it was surrounded.

CHAPTER VIII.

A MYSTERIOUS BURGLARY.

On the same night that Hurdeb Rái was attacked by Teetoo Meer, at Ráikoti, there was a burglary in the Zemindár's house at Boná Ghát, which caused much confusion and excitement in the village next morning, and kept it in ferment for some days.

"Who could have believed this possible?" exclaimed the Surburákár. "A burglary in the Zemindár's house! Where could the burglars have come from?"

"That is just what I want to know, Nilkant," said the Zemindár's mother, "for they have taken away everything valuable we had in the house—almost all the family jewellery and all the hard cash saved during the last ten years."

She wiped her eyes with the end of her garment as she concluded, for the last ten years referred to meant the interval that had elapsed since her husband's death, which was sharply recalled to her memory. But she got over her weakness quickly, and continued—

"Where is Monohur now? The boy has attention for everything but what concerns him most. I wish he would return from his morning exercise soon, and inquire into this matter personally. Did he go out on horseback to-day, do you know?"

"I really don't know, lady," said Nilkant. "I don't

think I have seen him at all this morning. I must have been otherwise engaged when he went out."

"I do wish you or somebody else had seen him when he went; I want very particularly to know where he has gone to, and what is delaying him there."

But no one could give her the information she sought, and she left the room in vexation, muttering dissatisfaction at everything, and with everybody; and there was good cause indeed for her discontent. The burglary committed was a most daring one. The private *kházá-nághur* of the Zemindár, in which all the family-jewels and the *kházáná* were kept, had been opened and entered, but how it was not understood, as neither the door nor its lock showed any marks of violence. Inside the room was a large chest, the key of which was kept by Nilkant. This had been broken open, and the smaller boxes which were in it, and contained jewellery and gold, had all disappeared. The keys of these boxes were, some of them, in the possession of Monohur, and others in the possession of his mother; and it was only natural that the latter should be getting very impatient that no clue to the robbery could be discovered. Nilkant also was in much distress, for he had always been a faithful servant of the family; and the loss to the Zemindár, if the property carried off were not recovered, would, he knew, be very great.

"It is useless waiting for the Zemindár's return," said he to himself. "He is a wild boy, and there is no knowing when he may come back; and, after all, it is not likely that he will be able to help the inquiry much. I must assume, therefore, the Zemindár's functions myself for the time, even though his mother, in her discontent, has not asked me to do so."

Nilkant was an efficient servant, and could be backed

against any detective in an inquiry like the one now forced on him. He set on foot a diligent search, sending out people in all directions with very precise instructions for their guidance; but no trace of the thieves could yet be found. They only discovered the boxes in a field at a mile's distance from the house, all broken open and their contents gone, with the exception of some documents, bills of exchange, and half-notes, which the burglars had thrown away as useless.

This was very disheartening news for the Zemindár's mother, and, getting more and more displeased every hour, she did not hesitate to utter unflattering words of all her servants.

"It is twelve o'clock now," said she, "and Monohur has not yet come back. Have you sent anyone to look out for him?"

"No; it would be useless to do so, for we don't know whither he has gone. He is so fond of taking long rides now and of staying away whole days from home that it would not be easy to trace out his retreat."

"Do try, though, Nilkant. I am very anxious that he should know at once what has happened here, even though he should prove to be of no greater assistance to me in this matter than you are. Was anyone with him last evening, do you know?"

The question threw a flood of new light into the Surburákár's mind. The Fakir had been with the Zemindár till a late hour of the night. With what object? Had he any hand in the burglary? Worse still, was it possible that he had so far duped Monohur as to make him a thief of his own goods?

The Surburákár looked sadly perplexed, and could only stammer out an imperfect reply.

"Yes, I believe I saw the Fakir with him till a late hour in the night."

"What for?"

"I—I really don't know; I am perfectly puzzled what to think of, or what to say."

"Why, speak out your mind boldly, Nilkant. Tell me each thought as it comes up, I beseech you. Do you think the Fakir may have had a hand in the robbery?"

"I would not be surprised at all, lady, if it should turn out to be so; and I am afraid—"

Nilkant could not get on.

"Of what more? Speak out truly and bluntly, as has always been your wont. I like a direct man and a direct way of speaking, Nilkant."

"Why, what can you expect but treachery from these Mahomedan knaves, though I am not altogether sure that the Fakir is a Mahomedan? And the Zemindár being so wilful and silly, what so likely but that he should have been trepanned?"

The Zemindár's mother started as if she were shot through, and then looked pale as death.

"Impossible!" said she. "I cannot believe that of Monohur, Nilkant;" but even while she said so she was already half convinced that the view which had occurred to the Surburákár was likely to be true.

"What are we to do now, then?" asked she after a long pause, with a deep drawn breath, looking out reproachfully at the open sky, which was as bright and gay as ever, as if it had never had a bit of grief to disturb its cheerfulness. "What is your advice now?"

The Surburákár had not made up his mind yet for anything, and looked almost as disconsolate as his mistress; but the question recalled him to his duty, and he presently answered—

"We must look sharply out now both for Monohur and the Fakir, and await disclosures as they turn up."

"But were there none others with the Zemindár but the Fakir?"

"Yes, of course there were; I mean his servants were waiting in the anteroom as usual. I think I saw Kesto Mánná, Seeboo Sing, Láll Chuprássi, Hurry Cowár, and Pear Gáyn in attendance."

"Don't you suspect any of them of having acted as an accomplice to the Fakir?"

"I don't know whom to suspect and whom not. But I have had the houses of all our servants overhauled, and nothing has been found in them. The men just named are besides all of them present here at this moment, with the exception of Pear Gáyn."

The lady returned to her inmost apartments in a state of mind that cannot be described, while the Surburákár passed on to his work, musing over his plans.

When an Indian is following a trail he is never discouraged by any difficulties in his way, but goes on continuously till he comes to the end of it. This was exactly what Nilkant was doing; but the case bore a very ugly appearance yet, notwithstanding all his endeavours to unravel it, and he felt at times that he was perhaps not on the right scent after all. He had not only had the houses of the servants, but of several other persons in the village who were suspected by him, very carefully searched; but all to no purpose. Pear Gáyn's disappearance not having been accounted for, he had brought away his wife and children from his house, and had kept them under careful though kind surveillance. He had also had all the *Kurmokárs'*, or goldsmiths', shops explored, as these people in all villages are generally in league with thieves and burglars, and melt down stolen property for them almost before hue and cry about the loss can be raised.

"What more can I do?" said he to himself almost in despair. "I am afraid it is the good-for-nothing boy himself that has voluntarily put his head into the noose."

At this moment some fresh clamouring was heard nearly all over the house, and everything in it was once again in commotion as before.

"Why, what is the matter this time? What does this new tumult mean?" asked the Surburákár in a loud voice.

"O, sir, Pear Gáyn was captured by our people near Mádhubkáttee, but has been rescued."

"Rescued? By whom?"

"By a large body of Ferázees, headed by the Fakir, who was seen here so often with the Zemindár."

"Ah! Then my worst fears have been realised. Alas, poor mother! How shall I dare to tell you such tidings of your son?"

CHAPTER IX.

IN THE TRAP AT LAST.

ONE of the most important rivers passing through the district of 24-Pergunnáhs is the Schámutti, or Jabooná, which runs in a very tortuous course, but is deep throughout its entire length, and navigable for boats of the largest size. It is the largest and most important of all the streams lying between Boná Ghát and Nárkelberiáh, and here on the left bank of it some eight or ten persons were seen four days after the burglary at Boná Ghát, with a jaded palfrey at their side, awaiting the return of the ferry-boat to cross over.

"You are carrying me to new scenes and new faces, Fakir. What bribe will you give me to forget the old faces I leave behind?" asked the youngest of the party of his friend and guide.

"O, you leave them for a short time only, my son, till you have made an undying name for yourself, and acquired an independent position in the world," was the Fakir's reply.

"That is, indeed, the hope and inducement that has brought me out," rejoined the young man; "and I only wish I could have come over with my mother's consent and blessing. So good a mother she is, and yet I have both deceived and disobeyed her!"

"You must not think of that now, young man,"

remarked the Fakir. "The die is cast; you have thrown your lot with ours, and must go through the ordeal you have accepted, till time rights both your condition and ours."

"True, indeed," said the young man. "But I am a stranger here, and this is the first time that I have come out among men who do not know me in the least. No one, in fact, of all the warriors I come to knows anything of me but yourself, and I cannot help feeling somewhat uncomfortable, as not knowing what reception I may meet with among the rest."

"Have I not assured you already of a warm and cordial welcome by all? Have you any good reason to doubt my truth?"

"None whatever, my friend. My only fear is that you may not have sufficient influence with your party to make me very acceptable to them. The Ferázees are said to be fanatics, and they have been fighting from the commencement with all the Hindu Zemindárs in their neighbourhood."

"Yes, that was, indeed, the first phase of our development, but that phase has since gone by. The Ferázee doctrines were originally enunciated at Dowlutpore, in the Furreedpore district, whence I come. Their objects are twofold; first, to purify Mahomedanism, and next, to liberate the country from foreign thraldom. It was Teetoo and his party who commenced to fight with the Hindus, but he has now been overruled in council by us. The country belongs to the Hindus and the Mahomedans, and the two religionists could not act in opposition without weakening each other. We have a common object now to attain—namely the expulsion of the Ferángees from Bengal, and are as assiduously seeking for the aid of the Hindus at this moment as we had opposed them before."

"Have you got any other Hindus yet besides me and my party to join you?"

"Yes, we count them by hundreds already, and in a short time expect to count them by thousands."

"And then I shall be only one of the thousands who will have come forward to help you!"

"One man must be *one* under all circumstances, my son, for it is morally impossible that he should be more. But Kharga Báhádoor shall be an unit as prominent as Miskeen Sháh, or Gholám Másoom, or may be as Teetoo Meer himself, for you have the means of commanding your position."

Kharga Báhádoor was gratified at being so spoken of and assured, and jumped into the boat with alacrity as it touched the beach. The river was quickly crossed, and a couple of hours later they approached Nárkelberiáh, which they found well stockaded and watched with zealous care.

"Who are the people whom the Fakir is bringing in?" asked Miskeen Sháh of Teetoo, looking at them with suspicious eyes. "They are most of them Kaffirs apparently. Have we not more of them already than is safe to keep about us?"

"O, this is that rich Zemindár who is in a hurry to become an independent prince. He has lots of money to throw away, and we want the sinews of war sadly," said Teetoo.

"There, Gholám Másoom, there is another sub-commander for you to drill and educate. He is a Zemindár and must have a separate command; must he not?"

"No, not a separate command, surely," said Teetoo;

"but we must find him a post of honour, if only for the wealth he brings with him."

"Is there no other price for his adherence to us?" asked Miskeen Sháh. "I can hardly believe that he has come out with his money-bags simply from an expectation of independence."

"Simply for that, and for nothing else," replied Teetoo, "though the Fakir has got another springe ready for him, I hear."

"What may that be?"

"A wife! The child you captured at Poorá, who was to have been married to the Bamboo, and made over to the Fakir, the Fakir wishes to be married to this youth."

"That is hardly fair, chief. The child is my prize. I was willing enough to devote her to the service of Gházee Myán for the benefit of our cause; but why should I give her up to a Kaffir?"

"I don't ask you to give her up at all. Only allow him to play with her, and remain entangled in our snare for the time. When we have got from him what we want it will not be difficult to throw him overboard."

While this colloquy was passing on one side the Fakir was introducing his friends to Kharga Báhádoor on the other—that is, as well as he could do so from the distance that yet separated them.

"Do you see who are coming forward to welcome you, my son? That warrior there with a long face, brown complexion, and hollow eyes, who wears the coarse cloth of a *Hájee*, that is Teetoo Meer, the life and soul of our enterprise."

"And the chief on his right, who towers above him by a whole head, and is talking less with Teetoo than with the people around him?"

"O, that is Gholám Másoom, the commander of our forces. He is always distinguishable alike by his superior stature and the enormous club he carries with him. Don't you see him brandishing the club every now and then as he talks?"

"I do. The cudgel, I suppose, is understood as the insignia of his office?"

"Just so; and it does good service in keeping the mob in order, for they do not care much for any one who cannot impress them with fear."

"And the man on Teetoo's left? I mean him with pale cheeks, aquiline nose, and thin lips; who is he?"

"O, that is Miskeen Sháh, a man terrible in counsel, and scarcely less terrible in arms."

"But he seems to have a singularly unpleasant expression in his face though. Has he not?"

"Well, we need not remark that. They say that his private life is that of a demon. But he is a very useful ally to us at this juncture; and that is all we care for now."

Further talk was stopped by the two parties coming up to and facing each other; and the welcome Teetoo gave to his new recruits was so frank, courteous, and cordial, that Kharga Báhádoor was immensely flattered and obliged.

"Meer Sáheb, you really overpower me by your kindness and courtesy," said he to him thankfully. "Heaven be my witness that I have brought my whole heart to your cause."

"It is the best of all causes, brother," said Teetoo, "and I congratulate you on your having joined it. Let Hindu and Mahomedan exert side by side in it, and show who can do most for securing the freedom of his country."

F

"I shall certainly do my best to justify your selection of me to share with you the honours of this enterprise," returned Kharga Báhádoor; " but I fear I make an indifferent figure in the scene since I come to you almost alone."

"O, that does not signify in the least," said Miskeen Sháh. "We have men, but not the money wherewith to pay for their exertions, and since you bring money to make up for what you are wanting in, you contribute equally with us to the good cause to be sure."

They were now drifting into complete confidence seemingly on both sides, and on the part of the recruits in perfect sincerity also; and, absorbed by the bustle and animation around him, Kharga Báhádoor forgot for the moment the mother and home he had left behind. The forces under Teetoo were not less than four thousand strong, but consisting mainly of shepherds, wood-cutters, and bargemen, with a sprinkling of smugglers and cut-throats to give strength and stamina to the combination. Gholám Másoom, who had seen service as a soldier, had tried hard to introduce something like martial order among these, but apparently not with much success; though in the eyes of Kharga Báhádoor they seemed to form as good an army as he had any conception of. The stir and tumult which pervaded them were mistaken by him for enthusiasm; and he already felt certain that the cause of liberty and nationality would be easily won.

The attention of the new warrior was at this moment drawn away in another direction by the Fakir. Not to leave things half-done the latter had brought forward some of the other Hindu chiefs to see him, and with them the little girl captured by the Mahomedans at Poorá. A creature more elf-like had never crossed the vision of

Kharga Báhádoor, and he gazed at her with intense delight.

"Whose is that little child there, so slim and straight, and fresh in her tender grace; and what is her business here?"

The questions were addressed to the Fakir, but he had already left the place.

"O, that is my daughter," said one of the Hindus present, "and my name is Thákoor Bhunj;" and he laughed much, and by winking significantly encouraged the young man to speak to and make friends with the child. But the child hid her face in her tiny hands, partly from bashfulness and partly from fear, and would not respond to the advances of familiarity made to her, which made Kharga Báhádoor ask her in an undertone if he had in any way annoyed her.

"O, I am not offended," said she; "but I don't know you, and cannot think of cultivating any close acquaintance with one I do not know."

"Why not? Your father wishes us to become good friends. Has he not said so?"

"My father? No, no; that man is not my father. I have lost all hopes of meeting with my parents, and do not know what will become of me here."

"Indeed! Do tell me your story then, and I shall try my best to serve you, and to be as a brother to you."

"My story? What story? They have forced me away from my parents, and I only live with that man here because he is a Hindu and of my caste. I have lost all hopes of happiness in this life, and that is the beginning and end of my story."

"Have you no friends at this place, then?"

"None."

"Will you allow me to be a friend to you, little one? I will give my heart's blood to help you."

"Will you take me back to my parents?" asked the child, with an almost irradiant face.

"Yes, after our most important business here is over."

"What is that? and how long will it take?"

"It is—fighting with the oppressors of our country. I think it will come on very soon, though I do not know when it may terminate."

"In that case you cannot serve me, for I wish to go back to my parents now;" and she put up her little hands to her face again, and was at once in tears.

All the aspirations of Kharga Báhádoor were for war, but the turns of the human mind are so uncertain that he almost felt as if he could desert the cause he had embraced just to escape from that place with that grieved and gentle child.

But the Fakir was at his side again by this time.

"This is the wife I have selected for you, my son, and a much better selection it is than what your mother would have made. You do not get her, however, till you have made a name worthy of her by liberating your country. The Spirits of the Storm, Earthquake, and Waters are at work now to secure that end, and you must work with them heartily to win the precious prize that has been reserved for you."

"O, father, am I not here for that work alone?"

CHAPTER X.

ASSERTION OF CIVIL AUTHORITY, AND ITS RESULTS.

THE acts of violence perpetrated by the Ferázees culminated towards the close of 1831, when, provided with money and arms by the wealthier recruits who had latterly joined them, they pillaged all the districts of Furreedpore, Nuddeá, and 24-Pergunnáhs, robbing all Hindus and Mahomedans without distinction who were found inimical to their pretensions.

"How mischievous the fellows are, surely!" exclaimed the Magistrate of Baraset, "and how foolishly too they are acting! Their conduct is quite incomprehensible to me, for they are making enemies on all sides of them by their devilries."

"What do you think of doing, sir, under the circumstances?" inquired the Station Moonsiff.

"O, I must go out amongst them to see if I cannot put down the disturbance by my presence at the spot."

"But your following is too small, sir," observed the Sheristádár. "You will make no impression on them with your policemen and sepoys."

"Ah! but I don't want to fight them at all. I only wish to put a stop to further mischief if I can, and I am sure that if they see me before them they will quietly come back to their allegiance."

The Moonsiff and the Sheristádár did not regard the

matter so hopefully, but they could not well contradict the Magistrate, who, as the head officer of the district, had a right to consider himself to be the best-informed man in it; and he went out against the insurgents the very next morning with about a hundred policemen and twenty-five sepoys.

"The English are coming out to meet us," exclaimed the Fakir, speaking to Teetoo.

"How do you know?" asked the chief.

"My scouts have seen them," rejoined the Fakir. "They are only about four miles distant from this place now."

"Impossible!" said Teetoo, "for I would have known of it long before if they were so near, unless my watchmen are all dead or drunk."

"You will soon find, Meer Sáheb, that my news is true," replied the Fakir; and it was fully verified within two hours after.

"They have come out indeed," said Gholám Másoom, "but only with some chuprássis and a handful of sepoys. We can ground them very fine with our clubs in half an hour if we care to do so."

And he marshalled forth the Ferázees in a body, all armed with clubs, swords, and spears, and ready for a fight.

"Ah! who are you coming to fight with?" exclaimed the Magistrate, as soon as he saw them advancing towards him. "Don't you see that I am the Magistrate of the district, and have repaired hither to restore order amongst you? Will you lay down your arms and return to your homes and occupations at once?"

"Wherefore should we?" asked Miskeen Sháh in reply. "Who are the English that the children of Alláh and

Mahádeva should call them lords and masters in their own native land? Who has made you a Magistrate over us? What right have you to dictate any terms whatever to us?"

"Ha, Miskeen Sháh! I know you for a double-dyed traitor," replied the Magistrate, "and you shall receive hereafter the punishment due to your many crimes. My immediate business is not with you, but with these misguided people whom you and their other chiefs, to serve their own personal interests, have led into danger. I call upon these to lay down their arms and return to loyalty and their homes, so that their folly may not be remembered against them."

"Indeed!" exclaimed the Fakir, thrusting himself forward as the spokesman of the mob. "Have you, indeed, come hither to preach loyalty to us? But loyalty to whom? Does not loyalty to you and your race mean disloyalty to country, nationality, and faith? We have searched the records of our fathers, but have nowhere met with any rule or injunction that says that the Mahomedans and the Hindus are to be as slaves unto the Christians. We despise your suggestion, therefore, O, Magistrate, and will not listen to it."

"I am not come hither," said the Magistrate, "to discuss politics with you. I am here in the name of the law, to warn you that, if you do not break up your combination at once and return to your homes quietly, you will leave me no alternative but to proceed against you as traitors and disturbers of the public peace, and to punish you very severely for the crime."

"You crow much too loud, Magistrate Sáheb," said Teetoo derisively, "considering the small following at your back. Had you not better take time by the forelock and decamp? My people are looking with very unfriendly eyes at you as the representative of a power steeped in falsehood and guile, that entered our country begging to be allowed to traffic with us, but has ever since taken every opportunity to insult and oppress us. If you wish to save your life you have barely time to fly."

"The fellows mean mischief, sir," said the chief native officer with the Magistrate. "We have very few fighting men with us, and Teetoo's suggestion is perhaps the best for us to adopt."

There were some Europeans, however, with the Magistrate—three or four only—who were unwilling to admit this, and, being strong and well-made men, they were naturally averse to fly.

"Suppose we wait till we get a mauling," said one of these. "Would it be too late then to think of acting in accordance with Teetoo's advice?"

"So far as I see," said another, "there is no occasion for us to get funky yet. The fellows are blustering, but I don't believe they will care to come to the scratch."

But a shout was now raised by Gholám Másoom of which the meaning was not to be misunderstood; and his followers, answering in the same voice, rushed in a body against the Magistrate and his party, pelting brickbats at them, which made the policemen to fly.

It is useless to attempt any description of what followed. The Englishmen showed fight to begin with, retaining their posts with pertinacity; but they were soon borne down by multitudes, and were eventually chased to the boats which had brought them; and the net result of this assertion of civil authority was the loss of some lives, many persons being also wounded, while the enemy were elated with success.

"Well, brother," said Teetoo, speaking to Kharga Báhádoor, "if the English annalists record this day's fight truthfully, will they have much to boast of on behalf of their countrymen?"

"O, I am told," answered the Hindu Neoptolemus, "that they have a very significant motto of their own, which says that 'silence is golden,' and they will most probably keep quiet over the affair."

"I am particularly glad that the very first engagement has been such a victory for us," said Gholám Másoom. "Our men have smelt blood now, and that of itself should greatly strengthen us."

"Let us announce our victory to all the villages around us then in fitting style," said Miskeen Sháh. "It will now be an easy task to devastate them into submission."

The whole country for miles around the Ferázee quarters was now accordingly laid waste by Teetoo and his followers, and for some days continuously no efforts could be made to check their violence. This compelled the peaceful inhabitants to desert their homes, and all the tract about Nárkelberiáh was in a short time reduced to an untenanted wilderness. That this would be the unavoidable result of their outrages was forcibly pointed out to them by the Fakir; but he could not get himself to be heard.

CHAPTER XI.

THE FIRE PUT OUT, AND THE RUN FOR A SHAVE.

"We must call in the military now to our assistance," said the Magistrate, and he wrote down to Calcuttá for troops; and they made up a rather strong detachment there to put out the fire.

The party sent up consisted of one regiment of native infantry, a troop of horse-artillery, with a couple of field-guns, and some troopers of the Governor-General's body-guard, all placed under the command of Major Scott; and they pushed up by forced marches, and were before Nárkelberiáh by the 19th November.

"We are saved!" shouted the people of the country, as they emerged from their hiding-places to cheer and encourage their deliverers. "See how gallantly they march! These surely are not the men whom Teetoo will care to confront?"

"I hope not," said the oldest inhabitant of the village, who was also the general referee. "There is something going to happen this time which Teetoo and his men have not dreamt of."

"But, O, father!" said the son of the old man, "the force under the English is still much too small in numbers as compared with that of the Ferázees, and how do you know that the something you hint at may not be as unfavourable to us again as was the first affair?"

"No, boy, no; you needn't frighten yourself with any such fears. The body-guard and the artillery are something very different from a *posse* of chowkeydárs. Don't you see how well armed they are? Teetoo's men have no arms like theirs to fight with."

"O yes, father, they have lots of sabres, lances, and knives. The village barber, who knows a great deal more of the matter than anybody else, says that he saw a cart-load of arms with them only a few days ago."

"They may have four cart-loads of them, my son, and be no better armed notwithstanding," returned the old man; "for they have neither guns nor gunpowder, and that makes all the difference in the world. My grandfather was a camp-follower at Plássey, and could well describe how the English fought there and in other places with their guns. It is up with Teetoo this time, I say; and you will find the prediction verified in a very short time."

There was no fright, however, in the Ferázee camp as yet, notwithstanding the exultation of the villagers and their predictions. Teetoo had received timely notice of the approach of the English, and had raised the courage of his men to a high pitch by stimulants; and, well posted and commanded, they felt confident that, even if the odds had been against them as they were in their favour, they would still have been able to beat back their opponents in fair fight.

"Now listen to me carefully," said Teetoo to his adherents. "Our position is excellent, and we will await the approach of our enemies where we are. The main body of our troops will be under the direct lead of Gholám Másoom, of course; but it will be as well to have a strong reserve in charge of Miskeen Sháh."

The arrangement proposed was so good that it was cordially approved by all; but Kharga Báhádoor looked disconcerted that no particular mention was made of him, and asked the chief bluntly whether he was to stand by with his arms folded, looking at the rest while they fought?

" O, brother, your duty will be to fight along side of me and the Fakir," said Teetoo; " and our post will be in the van, ahead even of Gholám Másoom and the rest of them."

The compliment was very flattering, and Kharga Báhádoor was extremely gratified.

" I am very grateful, Meer Sáheb, for your kindness," was the only reply he made; and, becoming uncommonly excited, he drew out his scimitar dashingly, and marched up to the front.

The English troops advanced in their usual heavy style, and Teetoo was called upon to surrender before the fighting began.

"We are as ten against one," said the Ferázee chief laughingly in reply, "and who has ever heard of ten men submitting to one person, and why is such a foolish proposal made to me?"

" Ah, but notwithstanding your superiority in numbers, Teetoo, you know very well that the contest is not equal on your part. I ask again, therefore, whether you will yield or no?"

"I thought, Major Sáheb," replied Teetoo, coldly, "that you had come hither to fight with us. Instead of boasting like a woman had you not better get ready to repel our attack?" And, the Ferázee war-cry being immediately raised, there was a tremendous discharge of brickbats, as on the previous occasion, wherewith the fight was begun.

The English troops fired in reply, but their opponents found that the fire was ineffective. Major Scott, still anxious to prevent bloodshed, had directed a firing of blank cartridges only, just to intimidate the enemy; and, seeing that the volley was harmless, Teetoo raised the well-known cry of "*Gollá Kháddállá*," or, "We have swallowed up their bullets." This made his men distractedly courageous, and the shower of brickbats was renewed with yet greater energy; till a few rounds of actual firing sent the balls hissing and whistling through the air, and wrapped the rice-fields in a bluish smoke which was with difficulty seen through, while nothing was heard underneath but fearful shouts and groans.

"O, Heaven! how terribly the Ferángees shoot!" exclaimed Teetoo's army of cut-throats and coolies; and they ran pell-mell towards their fort with cries of fear.

The best fighters among the Ferázees were Teetoo, Miskeen Sháh, Gholám Másoom, Kharga Báhádoor, and the Fakir. Of these the first and third were shot down, while the other three were more or less severely wounded. Kharga Báhádoor had a regular hand to hand fight with a young English cadet, by whom he was smartly hit, upon which he raised his dagger with one hand while he seized his opponent by the throat with the other, and buried the flashing steel to the hilt in his chest.

"Down with them! Down with them! Slay! Slay!" was the shout raised by the Fakir; but there was no one to respond to it, all the men trying anxiously to get out of the battle-field and gain their fort or the plantations beyond it.

"It is trouble lost trying to rally our forces here," said Kharga Báhádoor. "Let us fall back on the fort while we can, and see if we may not be able to hold it against the enemy."

They did so accordingly; but down came the English there too, and it was astonishing in what short time the stronghold was attacked and stormed. It was a scrubby place at best, defended by the most trumpery fortifications, and swarming with disheartened refugees from the field; and the storming had only the character of a rush from without, answered by a shower of stones from within, the latter flagging in strength as the force of the former began to increase, after which there was a hand to hand struggle of the briefest duration, ending in a shout of triumph that drowned a cry of fear.

Over three hundred and fifty fighting men were taken prisoners by the assailants, the rest of the garrison scampering off across the fields, and dispersing themselves among distant villages and farms.

"The English are very demons in avenging," said the fugitives to each other as they fled, "and are sure to hunt us from covert to covert should we be unable to blind them. Let us fly to the barbers now and have our beards taken off."

"Yes, the devils are upon us, and we must elude them as we may;" and they ran frantically for a shave, not excluding even those who had fought to the last.

"Ha! Ferázee Sáheb, why this hurry to part with an appendage so respectable, and which has cost you the culture of so many months?"

"O, friend, you are uncivil. I am not a Ferázee, and never was. I kept a beard long before Teetoo Meer was heard of in this place: but, as the *goolmál* here is very great now, I am willing to part with it to prevent misconstruction."

" All right, friend, I am quite willing to believe what you say. But you know, of course, that we have raised our charge for shaving from one pyce to three rupees per head?"

"Monstrous! Surely you are joking."

" O, I was never more in earnest in my life. My next-door neighbour there charges four rupees per head, as you may ascertain by asking him."

The Fakir paid down the three rupees without making the inquiry suggested, and had his beard removed, after which he pressed on Kharga Báhádoor to leave the place.

" Where is now my bright-eyed dream?" murmured the latter to himself. "Would I could find and save her!" But he knew not where to seek for her, or how to help her; and he looked up listlessly towards the Fakir and asked him whither he wished to go, and how?

" To Boná Ghát, if your house would shelter us for a time."

"No, certainly not thither," said Kharga Báhádoor sharply, as if stung by a serpent. "I had no business to leave it in the manner I did, and must not bring danger to it by my return."

"That is very honourably resolved," answered the Fakir, "and I am not very sure either that your house could shelter us. Whither would you wish to go yourself?"

" O, I am for rambling all over Bengal and the North-West," said Kharga Báhádoor, without a moment's hesitation, " visiting the several *Tirthastháns*, or sacred places, in them; and I have already made up my mind to start within two or three hours."

"Good," replied the Fakir; "and I shall be ready to go with you by that time."

"How so? I mean to visit all those places which are held sacred only by the Hindus."

"And so do I," said the Fakir. "Have I not taken off my beard?"

CHAPTER XII.

THE REVELATION.

It is a grand sight where the Ganges and the Brahmapootra unite with each other between the districts of Pubná and Mymensing, which the conjoint channel effectually separates. The stream is deep, majestic, and flowing; and the broad lawns and rich plantations it passes through glow with a beauty the like of which can scarcely be met with in any place out of Bengal. The first junction of the two rivers is at a point called Bárni, a few miles above the present station of Goálundo; and by day and night, throughout every month of the year, devotees arrive here in motley bands to bathe in the sacred confluence. The shrine of Thákoor Lakshmi-Náráyana stands hard by, and adjoining it is a resting-place for pilgrims, where alms are liberally given to the maimed and the poor, the funds for the purpose being drawn from a large estate especially assigned for the maintenance of the idol by a pious lady of Pubná.

It was at this place that the two travellers from Nárkelberiah—namely, Kharga Báhádoor and the Fakir—arrived after an unpleasant and wearisome journey of more than two weeks.

"It is getting late already," said the first to the second. "Had we not better put up here for the night?"

"Yes, my son, and until we get better quarters elsewhere. We shall not be noticed here among so many pilgrims, and need not make ourselves conspicuous in any way;" and they groped on into the resting-yard, and stretched themselves out on the bare ground, in the same fashion as the other pilgrims, without mixing with any of them.

"Ought we not to change our names once more now at this place?" asked the first speaker again, the moment he saw that their movements were not much watched by the crowd around them. "I have a great mind to resume my old name to which I am naturally partial. *Kharga Báhádoor*[1] is an appellation that sounds like a malediction under present circumstances, and I am anxious to get divested of it."

"You think rightly, my son, for it is high time that we should drop our fighting names, and you will remember me henceforth as Bábájee Bissonáth, a *Kartá-Bhajá*, and not a Fakir."

"Why, that will do very well indeed, and then you will pass for an out-and-out Hindu easily."

"Ah! I was really so at one time, and there is no reason why I should not be so again. You don't believe me, but I speak in earnest when I say that I am not only a Hindu, but a Hindu Bráhman, a man of your own caste, by birth."

"If you were a Bráhman before, how did you come to pass for a Mahomedan afterwards, and a Ferázee to boot?"

"Listen then, and I will tell you my story.

"You must have heard of the Kartá-Bhajás of Ghosepárá, in the district of Nuddeá, a peculiar sect of Vysnubs who do not adhere strictly to caste rules and restrictions. The origin of the sect was with Aul Chánd, a foundling

[1] *I.e.* valiant wielder of the sword.

THE REVELATION. 83

discovered by a Satgope in his betel-garden. The child was then eight years old and of unknown parentage; but on growing bigger he declared himself to be a Bráhman, and an incarnation of Chaitanya. He proved his divinity by curing the blind and the lame, nay, by bringing back the dead to life; and it is from him that I draw my descent."

"That being so, do not the Kartá-Bhajás miss your absence at home? Who is the *Kartá* with them now?"

"Ah! you do not know the history of the faith, apparently. Aul Chánd was the first Kartá; but his children did not become Kartás after him. When he was taken ill and dying he asked for a cup of water which was brought to him by a Satgope named Rám Surn. Aul Chánd blessed him, and said that his spirit would take its next birth in the womb of Rám Surn's wife, and Rám Doolal, the son of Rám Surn, became accordingly the second Kartá, and not the son of Aul Chánd; and ever since the Kartáhood has remained in the Satgope line, while the descendants of Aul Chánd are simply Bráhmans, most of them priests by profession."

"Well, how did you accept your loss of position, then?"

"Very cheerfully indeed. We all of us became Karta-Bhajás, acknowledging the lead of Rám Doolál and his descendants, and, caring nothing for our Bráhmanhood, sat side by side with all castes, including Satgopes and Mahomedans, and took our meals with them. Love is the foundation of the Kartá faith, and caste is necessarily unrecognised by it, for caste presumes a distinction between man and man, which love will not allow."

"But all the Kartá-Bhajás do not reject caste surely, for I know that there are some of them in my zemindáry who are great sticklers about caste."

"Yes, and it was that which made me a Ferázee, and sent me out of Ghosepárá to Dowlutpore. I saw all the Hindu Kartá-Bhajás around me relapsing into caste and idolatry; I saw with grief the Dole and Rásjátrá celebrated in Ghosepárá itself. 'This, surely, was not Aul Chánd's faith,' said I. 'Why should not those Mahomedans who have become Kartá-Bhajás with us belong to the same brotherhood in all respects?' I consulted my own brother on these points; but we differed widely in opinion from each other. 'He was a Bráhman,' he said, 'as well as a Kartá-Bhajá, and would remain both.' I said, 'I am solely and wholly a Kartá-Bhajá, and to me a Bráhman and a Mahomedan are absolutely alike;' and, since the Hindu Kartá-Bhajás did not like this doctrine any longer, I went over to the Mahomedans."

"Then your brother is still at Ghosepárá, living in the bosom of his family, while you are wandering about the world as an outcast with me?"

"No; the family-property at Ghosepárá was sold, and the proceeds divided equally between us, when we disagreed on the point of faith to which I have referred. My brother is in your zemindáry; he is no other than the priest of Naggesur Mahádeva, whom you consulted before you joined our cause at Nárkelberiáh."

"Ha! then it was the two Kartá-Bhajás that put their two heads together to make a Ferázee of me? I wonder that your brother, differing from you in belief, accepted your suggestions in respect to myself so cordially?"

"O, he has a very great heart, though he is essentially a man of peace. His wish for the emancipation of the country is as unbounded as your own."

The compliment intended for Monohur was as ineffective as an ill-shot arrow. His suspicions had been excited, and he felt already that he had been ensnared.

"The fact is, the Ferázees were much too clever for us," said he, "and we were both taken in by them—both you and I. Is not that the real truth, Bábájee?"

"Only partially so, my son. The Ferázees did want your money to help them through their expedition. They had men in numbers, but no money to put them in motion. But I, as their agent, did not come to deceive you, for I had too high a respect for your house to think of harming it. I really hoped that the Ferázees would be able to break down the English power, and the help that my brother had received from your parents had made both of us very grateful to your family, and equally desirous to set you up as an independent Rájáh, not only over your own zemindáry, but also over the neighbouring estates."

A sudden flush spread over the face of Monohur as he felt that he had been entrapped only for his money's sake, and he sat upright and motionless for some minutes, with his faculties absorbed by the reflections that were called forth. But it was too late to get vexed over the matter now; nor could he well be angry with Bissonáth, since his motives apparently were perfectly disinterested. He shook off his stupor therefore with an effort, and reopened the conversation by changing the theme.

"And the girl you chose for me, Bábájee, what interest had you in her? Why were you so anxious that I should marry her instead of the heiress of Páithulli, whom my mother had selected for me?"

"Did you not like the girl I picked out for you?"

"So well, indeed, that it was a great grief to me that I could not find her out before our flight from Nárkelberiáh, for I had promised to restore her to her parents when the fighting work was over."

"If she did make such an impression on you, my son, my choice requires no further vindication. She is really a nice girl, and would have made a most excellent wife to you. My interest in her is that she is my niece—my sister's daughter."

"But she did not seem to recognise you as a relative in the least; she told me that she had no friends in the camp at all."

"She spoke according to her knowledge, my son. She was not aware of the relationship between us. To her, as to all else, I was simply a Ferázee and a Mahomedan."

"Were you able to extricate her from the power of the Ferázees before you left them?"

"Yes, that was the last act I did at Nárkelberiáh, within the two hours' grace you gave me before the starting time. She is now quite safe with her parents."

Monohur expressed his satisfaction by a sigh of relief.

"I should like very much to see her again," said he, "though I don't know if that will ever come to pass."

"It may; but you must not be impatient. We are now looked out for from every direction, and love and love-making must stand over for a brighter day."

CHAPTER XIII.

THE LOVES OF THE RIVERS.

THE collection of devoteés at Bárni was very numerous, and the demonstration next morning was so animated that Monohur could not but feel greatly pleased with it. The river, under a bright blue sky, was simply magnificent, and the emotion called forth by the fervour of the pilgrims was almost overpowering.

"Why, Bábájee, you don't seem to appreciate the excitement around us. Surely the scene must be as new to you as it is to me?"

"New to me? No, my son, life is new to you, but not to me; and I have visited this place before. I was for twenty years abstracted from the world, that is, before I became a Ferázee; and my wanderings during that period were very extensive, and enabled me to trace the Gungá from the ocean to its source."

"Indeed! Why, then, you must have been very happy in that way, at least, and I really envy you your good fortune, Bábájee. But is it not true then that the Gungá descends from heaven, as the sages tell us?"

"Of course it is; and we Sunyásis are able to trace the river only up to its earthly source, not beyond that. The Gungá, the Brahmapootra, and the Sindhoo all descend from heaven, coming down at almost the same identical spot, from which they separate to wander over the earth in different directions."

"Did you trace all the three rivers to that point?"

"No, we took up the line of the Ganges only, and could not trace it beyond Gángotri, its earlier course being concealed under a glacier or iceberg. The snow-bed we saw was about four *kos* long, one *kos* broad, and having a depth incalculable; and the cold was so intense there that we felt our bones freezing and cracking for all the fire we could keep ablaze."

"Well, and what did you see there?"

"O, the visible source of the Bhágirutty is a *cunda*, or cell, from which the water was seen to be perpetually oozing out, forming very small rills, about one hundred or so in number. These are called 'Weepers,' from the manner in which they fall and the noise they make in falling; and the *cunda* they come from is of the sacred lake named Mánosorobar, of which you may probably have heard before. The 'Weepers,' joining form a rivulet which dashes itself from rude mountains, with which nothing in Lower India can be compared in wildness and fear. The Jáhnavi, another mountain-streamlet, darts from glens that are, if possible, even more savage and terrific, after which the two currents join amid avalanches of snow. After this there is a succession of falls from rock to rock, while the whole scene around bristles with frightful precipices, cedar forests, and sharp, snowy peaks."

"What a magnificent sight that must be indeed! and what would I not give to have a look at it! You say that the altitudes you describe are terrific in their inaccessibility. But is there any real danger there to meet with?"

"Yes, there is. Large snakes abound in the mountain-gorges through which the river flows, and Rákshases are known to inhabit them."

"But why should Rákshases live in parts so remote and lonely? They can have nothing there to live upon?"

"The mountains are full of gold and silver, and these belong to the Rákshases who keep watch over them. There are wild animals there upon which they feed."

"And the Brahmapootra? Is the source of that river equally lonesome and wild?"

"I cannot speak of it from personal knowledge, my son, but I was told by other Sunyásis, who had prosecuted their inquiries along that line, that the Brahmapootra issues from the same *cunda* which sends out the Ganges, the direction taken by the stream being only different, and that the rocks around it are as wild as any, the torrent dashing headlong from them in cascades, till it forms into a regular river, called in different places by different names, as the Pákhiu, the Hladini, and the Sánpoo."

"O, Sunyási! lead me to the heights you have visited, and I shall be beholden to you for ever. Will you help me to see them?"

"It is not possible for me to do so, my son; I have become old now, and my limbs are no longer as flexible as they were before, and could not scale the precipices I have described; nor could you go thither, Monohur, without renouncing the prospects of home, affluence, and position, perhaps for ever."

There was a pause, which was broken by the Sunyási drawing the attention of his companion to the sound of the bell that was tolling in the shrine of Lakshmi-Náráyana.

"That is the bathing invitation, my son, and if you go

to the spot now you will hear another account of the rivers there from the mouth of the *Poorohit*, very different from what you have just heard from me."

"What is it? I should like to hear every account of the rivers, to be sure, though I am very unwilling to receive any from such a repulsive chatterer as the priest there. Don't you know the story yourself?"

"I do; I have heard it before, and will recite to you what I have heard.

"Many, many thousand years ago the Gungá, the Brahmapootra, and the Sindhoo were living beings—mountain-gods, not unlike the mountaineers to be yet seen at the foot of the Snowy Range. Gungá was a girl, the daughter of Himávan, the sovereign of the mountains, and her youthful playmates were Brahmapootra and Sindhoo, the former the son of Bruhmá, the latter the heir of a neighbouring chief. The children played and quarrelled, and made love, and grew up together, just as other children have done, and do to the present day; but when Gungá became of a marriageable age her parents had a difficulty in deciding which of her two lovers should marry her. The father favoured the suit of Sindhoo; but the mother liked the son of Bruhmá better, and Gungá was partial to her mother's choice. Old Himávan, however, refused to give way to the predilections of either wife or daughter, and though Gungá cried till her eyes were red, she made no impression on her father. Then said Gungá to herself—'Why stay here at all? I would rather wander all over the earth, and even end by drowning myself in the sea, than contribute to the disappointment and grief of Brahmapootra;' and she hid herself in the *cunda* for one whole night, the 'Weepers' representing the tears she shed.

"On regaining her composure Gungá prepared resolutely for her flight.

"'If I escape in my present form,' said she to herself, 'my father's people are sure to follow up and find me out. I shall change myself into a river and elude them.'

"She accordingly changed herself into a rivulet which ran down the slopes of the mountains and meandered at their base, till, after much floundering, she was fairly out of her father's domains, when she assumed the form of a full-developed stream to sweep adown the plains.

"Great was the grief at home when father and mother found that their only child was nowhere to be found. They blamed each other to begin with, as is usual on such occasions, and then sent servants after the fugitive in every direction, but all to no purpose. Sindhoo and Brahmapootra also started in search of the missing maiden, and emulated with each other in their exertions, forgetting their mutual dislikes and differences for the time.

"'How shall we go after her, brother?' asked Sindhoo.

"'No one can run faster than a river,' replied Brahmapootra, 'and if we stream down after her in that fashion, each taking a different route, one or other will surely be able to overtake her.'

"'Right!' said Sindhoo, and he rushed headlong through the western valleys, washing down rocks and tearing up trees by their roots; while Brahmapootra sped with equal vehemence towards the east, through gullies and ravines, sweeping out hills from his course. Fast ran the rival lovers in search of the missing fair, and the further they went the more furious they became in their flow.

"'You have taken a wrong direction, brother,' said the mountain-goat to Sindhoo, 'and should rectify your course.'

"'In what direction should I rectify it?' asked the impetuous youth; but the goat had commenced browsing on the hill-side and would give no reply, whereupon Sindhoo turned south-west, not doubting that that was the right way to pursue. Swifter and swifter flowed the river, and angrier and angrier it became every hour on finding that its swiftness was not crowned with success; and in this mood of mind it tumbled headlong into the sea.

"Brahmapootra had also made great haste in pursuing the course adopted by him, and was tearing right through untrodden slopes and swamps towards the land of the pig-eating Chinese, when the *Sunkochil*, or white-headed kite, told him that he was toiling wide out of the track.

"'Whitherwards should I go then?' asked he of the kite.

"'You should double back westward, and, after passing a hundred *kos* or so in that direction, should leave it for the south to overtake your beloved.'

"The bounding torrent doubled back at once with such force as to tear down a part of the mountain-ramparts of Assam, and then sped through the valley westward as vehemently as before, till the kite stopped him again above the Gáro hills.

"'Go downwards now, my son,' said he, 'through the fragrant lawns before you, and, if you run fast enough, you are sure to overtake Gungá before she drowns herself in the sea.'

"Such is the wild story that the priests here have related from generation to generation, to account for the junction of the two rivers at this particular spot, and the tolling bell even now commemorates the hour of their union, which is the most propitious time for bathing in the confluence."

"The tale is a singularly beautiful and poetic one," exclaimed Monohur, "and I was just endeavouring to jot it down in verse. But I am a more unapt scholar, I find, than I thought, and have not been able to follow you."

Bissonáth took up the leaf on which Monohur had been scribbling. Only three stanzas were written, which may be here translated and immortalised :—

GUNGÁ'S FLIGHT.

A FRAGMENT.

I.

Himávan, lord of mountains rude,
    Where hidest thou thy crystal bower,
Midst jagged rocks by thunders torn,
    O'er which the leafless cedars tower?
The home where Gungá laugh'd and play'd,
    Chasing the wild-goat o'er the steep,
Or shouting with the eagle's young,
    Or bounding with the torrent's leap!

II.

A vision bright has cross'd my eyes:
    Methinks I see the mountain-maid,
Beaming with looks of eager joy,
    Bursting adown the ice-clad glade;
Follow'd by hunters young and bold,
    Of noble mien and daring eye,
Fit lovers of a nymph so fair,
    Who for her love tumultuous vie.

III.

Sindoo, a stripling tall and fair,
  A neighbour's child the father loves;
Pákhiu bold great Bruhmá's son,
  The mother into rapture moves:
The maid herself no preference owns,
  For both she feels a sister's flame;
Or, if for one a stronger love,
  She does not know that passion's name.

    *   *   *   *   *

"Ah, I also could tag verses in my youth, Monohur," said the Sunyási, "illiterate though I be; but the fire has long died out of me, and, I may say, the penchant for the trade likewise. You too must leave by the poem now, I mean for the moment only, and make haste to bathe in the confluence as the other devotees are doing, or we shall miss the most propitious hour, and may give rise to suspicions also."

CHAPTER XIV.

A MYSTERIOUS LETTER.

A FEW days after the river-bathing at Bárni there was a great commotion in the little town of Comercolly, in the Pubná district, which lies on the banks of the Gorái, about thirty miles to the west of the sacred confluence. The crime of dacoity may be said to be one of the national institutions of Bengal, and, if the number of cases has since decreased, the state of things was very different some fifty years ago, when recognised gangs existed almost in every district, and threats used openly to be sent by them to houseowners that their houses would be attacked if security were not purchased by a money-payment, to be left at a certain specified place, generally the foot of a tree in some unfrequented part of the country. Almost all the attacks were projected in the open air, after which the conspirators invariably made a *poojáh* to Káli, their guardian deity, before starting on their expeditions. They always had their *massáls* and *láttees* with them; but swords, *koorális*, and guns were more difficult to come at, and were therefore less frequently used. The *láttees* referred to were very formidable weapons; usually, but not always, made of bamboos fresh cut and made smooth, and often encircled by large iron nails put in at irregular intervals, or bound by a heavy iron ring at the end. Armed with these clubs the robbers proceeded to the house they intended to attack, frequently in a large body, and some four or five hours after nightfall; and they always attempted to effect their entrance by the *khirkee*, or back-door, lest the main-door, being generally of tough make, should take a longer time to demolish. A continual shouting or yell was kept up to dishearten the inmates and their friends, and prevent their attempting any opposition, and, after having gained entrance into the house, a strenuous endeavour was made to get hold of the master of it, or its mistress in his absence, threats being held out to the captive that he would be burnt with *massáls* if full information of the property in the house were not given. Some general rules were also followed for self-preservation in making the attack, among which were: (1) that, if any of the party were known to the people attacked, such persons never went inside the house, but remained outside of it as pickets or *ghúntidárs* ; (2) that, immediately after the plundering was over, and before the plunderers left the house, all the lights with them were put out; and (3) that, until fear of discovery had entirely blown over, the property plundered was kept buried or otherwise concealed, while the plunderers themselves remained almost apart from each other.

The attack at Comercolly was on the house of a bankor named Bharat Coondoo, and was made by a party armed mostly with bludgeons. There were also some billhooks, or *koorális*, with them, to break open the doors and strong chests, and the firing of one gun or pistol was heard, which principally cowed down all thoughts of opposition.

"How many are there?" asked the master of the house of his son.

"O, sir, some thirty or thirty-five," said the latter in reply, "and the number seems to be increasing."

"What can we do then to prevent their getting into the house? Their hootings and yells hinder my making myself heard by the servants."

"The servants, sir! They have all bolted, and, I think, we also had better secrete ourselves."

"Do just as you like, then," said the old man tartly; "I do not move from this place, either for fear of the dacoits or in imitation of the servants." And, by the time the dacoits effected their entry into the house, the son was fairly ensconced within a *moorye*, or receptacle for grain, whither the women had fled before him.

The robbers finding the old man by himself laid hands on him to begin with.

"Where is your money, father?"

"Money? There is none in the house now. We sent down all our money to Calcuttá last week, after receiving that threatening letter from you."

"You are trifling with us, old man," said the chief robber, sternly, "and that may cost you your life. Our spies are everywhere, and we know that nothing has been sent out of your house to this moment. Will you come out with your money now?"

"I have told you already that I have no money here. How can I give you what I have not?"

The dacoits became very angry; but the old man stood erect and unshaken, and they were obliged to leave him to commence operations on his property. All the chests and almiráhs in the house were broken open, and their contents scattered about—including *thállas, kuttorás*, and clothing; but though they searched every nook and corner no money was forthcoming.

Getting furious from their ill success, they now touched the old man with their torches, and he was burnt in several places, but would not cry out in pain. Old Coondoo had a great soul in a small body, and even the robbers were affected by his uncomplaining anguish.

"Go out," said the women in the *moorye* to his son, "and try to extricate the old man from their hands."

"I can do nothing to help him," answered the wary youth, "but may aggravate his sufferings by attempting a rescue. I am best where I am, and will have leisure here to ripen my plans."

What plans he was ripening was never known. The old man still stood his ground without making any disclosures, and the dacoits, having collected together a large quantity of household goods, desisted from molesting him further, being anxious to get off with their booty. The lumber collected was almost priceless, and the plunderers on coming out of the house were twitted by their own *ghántidárs* on that score. But there was no time for recrimination now, as the villagers were turning out in numbers; and they decamped in a hurry to prevent their being pursued.

"You are a very brave chap indeed," said the villagers to the banker's son, when he came out from his hiding-place after the departure of the dacoits. "You could not, of course, think of standing by the old man since you were protecting the women?"

"Ah, I could not come out because my *láttee* was not forthcoming. What could I do among so many men without a *láttee* to strengthen my arm?"

"Why," said his better-half, "your *láttee* was where it is always kept, and is there even now. It did not, of course, follow you to the *moorye* to thrust itself into your hand." And there was a general laugh against the would-be hero at the happy repartee of his wife.

The villagers busied themselves greatly in going after the dacoits, but none of the persons implicated had been recognised, owing to their having put out their lights immediately after the completion of their crime, and there were no traces of them therefore to follow beyond some foot-marks, bits of cotton and clothes, broken *pettárás*, wisps of tow, and the like. All these were diligently tracked up, but only to the banks of the Goráí, after which there were, of course, no marks to pursue.

Situated almost on the brink of the river here, stands the temple of Chámoondi, or Káli, the guardian deity of Comercolly. It was built by a king named Bándeb, at a place where he had seen the goddess face to face. The king was fond of eating the *pábdá* fish, and retained a fisherman to procure it fresh for him every day. One day the man was not able to get it, which made the king very angry with him, so that he was compelled to seek safety in flight. Having escaped to the jungles he prayed to Chámoondi for protection, and she appeared to him and told him that he would get a supply of the required fish every day if he came to fish at a particular spot on the river-side that was pointed out to him. The fisherman acted accordingly, and everything went on smoothly afterwards for months.

"How are you able to bring this particular fish every day, in season and out of season?" asked the Rájáh's favourite wife one day, of the fisherman.

"O, mother, my life depends upon it. Your royal husband would kill me if I failed to do so."

"Ah, that I understand; but I want to know how you manage to do it. Where do you get the fish from?"

"I cannot satisfy your curiosity, mother, on that point; and you should not force me to speak of it, if only for your husband's sake."

This made the lady suspicious without abating her curiosity, and she set a servant over the fisherman to watch him. But the goddess Chámoondi was incensed that there should be any espionage over one favoured by herself, and, assuming a fearful appearance, she seated herself on the river-bank when the fisherman approached it. Both the fisherman and the servant were equally startled by the sight, and the latter ran back as fast as his fear permitted him, to apprise his mistress of what he had seen. He tottered as he approached her, and would have fallen down if the king, who happened to be in the apartment at the time, had not seized him by the arm.

"What is the matter with you, man?" asked the king in a rather displeased tone.

The servant had hardly breath to explain, but eventually succeeded in gasping out a reply. The tale was not long to tell, but was told so hysterically that it had to be repeated several times before it could be understood.

"I don't expect your majesty to believe in what I have said," urged the man finally, conscious of the strange character of the account he had given; "but your majesty may yet see the appearance for yourself, and decide if my story be true or otherwise."

"Yes, I must certainly assure myself on that point," answered the king, "if only to mollify the goddess, should she have really got offended with us;" and he went out with his whole Court to the river-bank to appease the deity by his submission.

Chámoondi was easily conciliated, and the fisherman was allowed to fish on the spot as before; and the grateful king raised to the goddess the temple that stands there to this day.

"I did not expect to find you here!" exclaimed Bábájee Bissonáth, who was performing his devotions at this shrine, and was somewhat taken aback by the sudden appearance of a half-masked man before him who seemed to have something important to tell him. "Do you want anything with me?"

"I have only this letter to deliver to you, or I would not have intruded."

"A letter? From whom?"

"Read it; I shall wait till you have done so."

The Sunyási glanced over the billet hurriedly and looked up with wondering eyes.

"You know what this letter speaks of?"

"I do."

"What is your opinion of the enterprise it refers to?"

"It has its risks; but the cause is good, and the men engaged in it are stout and brave."

"Ah! I have heard stories to the same effect before, and am only surprised at my own weakness in having suffered myself to be gulled by them. But I won't endanger you by detaining you longer. You had a hand in the dacoity here, I suppose, and must be eager to escape?"

"O, that is not a matter of much moment to me. You know that I cannot be easily taken. But if you have no further orders for me there is no need for my running any risk at all;" and shortly after the gallop of a tattoo was heard outside, though in what direction it went the Sunyási was not able to determine.

All the perpetrators of the dacoity had escaped out of the city by this time; but the Ghát Dároga was yet on the look out for them. He was watching the river with particular care, and, when on the third day after the event he saw a boat passing down with a number of men on board, his suspicions were easily aroused.

"Ha! they must all be in that boat, I fancy, for it seems to be very crowded;" and the boat being stopped twenty-one persons were found in it, having with them a pistol, a billhook, flints, powder, and shots for the pistol, and a number of *láttees*.

"Whither bound, friends? and on what errand?"

"O, we are going to take up a boat of ours which has sunk further down in the river."

"Take up a boat with *láttees*, pistol, powder, a nd shots?"

"There are goods in that boat, and some persons must be left behind to protect them."

"Ah, that is rather well-said. But are there no goods in this boat also? I must open your bundles to see. O goodness! what are these? Two silver *bállás*, a gold *hánslee*, a silver *bánk*, so many *thállás, lotáhs*, and *kuttorás*; a load of *dhotis* and *doputtás* also; and, what have we here again? a *gámchá* and a bunch of plantains even—I suppose for the happy few who are to watch over the boat that is to be recovered? They must eat something of course, if only to prevent them from falling asleep on their watch, and why not plantains?"

The Dárogá grinned, as policemen only know how to grin. The dacoits were all captured, all with the exception of their chief, who had escaped, none knew in what way. The property which had been carried off by them was also wholly recovered, owing to their having had no opportunity to secrete any portion of it; and all Comercolly sent up a howl of joy, and sang pæans in the Dárogá's praise.

CHAPTER XV.

HOOKED AGAIN.

IT was a late hour in the evening, when Monohur and the Sunyási came back to their lodgings at Comercolly, after having wandered all over the town in the sweltering heat.

"I am fearfully knocked up with fatigue!" exclaimed the former, "and would go to bed at once, Bábájee, if you have no objection to it?"

"But surely not without taking a morsel of food, my son?"

"O, I don't think I shall be able to swallow anything at present. I have had too much of excitement the whole day, and what I want now is rest and rest only."

"Then you won't sleep well either," said the Sunyási, "for sleep under excitement is sure to be visited by bad dreams. Come, let us sit in the open air awhile, till you have recovered your composure, and then you can eat or go to sleep as you like best;" and he spread out a mat on the grass before their door, on which they both lay down lazily, one at least being rather drowsily inclined.

"The sun was very hot to-day, Bábájee, and that accounts for my unwonted weariness. I was never before so excited or knocked up."

"Shall I give you a dose of medicine then to brace up

your nerves, or reserve what I have to say to you till to-morrow?"

"What do you mean, Bábájee? Have you got any news from home to tell me?"

"No, my son; but I have something else to speak of which the open air is the best place to reveal in."

"It must be about the dacoity here then, I suppose. Have you any further information in regard to it?"

"No, not much. What do you want to know about it? and how does it concern either you or me?"

"O, it does not concern us of course in the least; but I heard them say that all the dacoits have not been captured, though the Dárogá affects that not more than one man, if any at all, has escaped him; and I should like to know the truth about it."

"It is hardly a matter worth troubling our heads about, Monohur. Twenty-one men have been taken, and if thirty-five men were concerned in the business, as Bharat Coondoo's son asserts, there should be fourteen yet at large. I think, however, that the Dárogá is more likely to be right in his reckoning than the young Coondoo, who did not show himself anywhere while the plundering was going on. What I know for certain is this only, that the leader of the gang has not been captured."

"What makes you say that, Bábájee? How can you be certain on that point?"

"I have reason to know it, my son, because I met with the man at the temple of Chámoondi, and did not see him afterwards among the twenty-one men who were brought in."

"You met him? Why, you astonish me. What business had you with him, or he with you?"

"He only came to deliver a letter to me, and I may as well tell you that he is the Gháttál Báboo we know of, who helped us in the burglary at Boná Ghát, and took so distinguished a part afterwards as my scout in the Nárkelberiáh affair. But of course this is between you and me. Our knowledge of him must on no account be spoken of, or we shall be getting into trouble for matters with which we have no concern."

"I understand you, Bábájee, and shall be very careful. But what is this letter you have received through him?"

"It was about that that I wanted to speak to you, Monohur. It refers to another rising against the English power in another part of the country, and invites me to join it. Would you like to make one with me?"

"I would do anything to please you, Bábájee; and you know already that I have no penchant for the English name. But I have had no tidings from home for a long time, and I am really very anxious to go back to my mother."

"Ah, you hesitate to take part in such business again, I see, and I don't disapprove of your prudence certainly. I only thought you had devoted yourself to the good cause, otherwise I would not have asked you at all."

"You have misunderstood me completely, Bábájee, I assure you. Can I not go back to Boná Ghát for once only and then join you afterwards in the enterprise?"

"If you consult your own safety, my son, you should not go to Boná Ghát at all at present; and, as for the good cause, it will not wait for the best recruit. The time has not arrived for you to see your mother; you will be captured the moment you get there. You have only to decide whether you will go with me, or hie to the Tirthastháns by yourself alone?"

"No, no; if I cannot go to my mother I will not desert you. But must I not ask in what direction you go, and what this new scheme is?"

"You shall know all about it, my son. First read the letter itself, for it is very brief, and I shall then tell you everything more that I know on the subject yet."

The sleepiness of Monohur had left him a good while already, and he had a long conversation with the Sunyási in the night; and early the next morning the two travellers were seen going out of the town, equipped as palmers, just as they had entered it. It is hardly necessary for us to follow them through all their wanderings. It will be sufficient simply to record that they were seen about two months after at a place named Nirsá, on the Grand Trunk Road, in the district of Mánbhoom.

"We have now to go straight south to reach our destination," said the Sunyási.

"And a weary route it seems to be," murmured Monohur, "seeing that there is nothing but hills and jungles around us."

"Yes, my son, the route is a very dreary and monotonous one, as you observe," replied the Sunyási; "but, since we cannot make it more pleasant by our grumblings, we had best get onwards as patiently as we may."

"But night is approaching, father," said Monohur. "We must rest somewhere now at all events."

"Let us hasten our pace then, that we may reach the temple of Mudden Gopál in time," said the Sunyási, "for we shall get no other resting-place here I am sure;" and they hurried on till the temple of Mudden Gopál was reached.

It was a beautiful stone temple, situated on the side of a tank of great sanctity, and the lodging-huts for pilgrims were scattered all around it in numbers. The story current at the place is that the tank and the temple were both made by a Rájáh named Duryodhon, who was cured of leprosy on this spot. He had been a great sinner and was afflicted by a most inveterate type of the disease. The kobirájes and rojáhs consulted by him were unable to do anything to alleviate his misery, and his Tirthas to sacred shrines were equally ineffectual, though he visited many of them. At last, when he was passing this way, an old woman of the neighbourhood pointed out to him a small *cunda,* beside which an undistinguished round stone was quartered.

"Great, O king, is the might of Mudden Gopál, and if you dip yourself in that *cunda* there you may perhaps be wholly cleansed and healed."

The Rájáh tried the *ounda* accordingly, and the experiment was very successful, for he was completely healed within a few days; and, being grateful for the favour conferred on him by the deity, he amplified the *cunda* into a tank and built a stone temple on its side to accommodate the god. The god is no longer so undistinguished as he was in the past, for the round stone is now almost wholly encompassed by gold and precious stones; and the tank remains and has the reputation of being a cleanser of sins, though its miraculous ulcer-healing virtue has since been lost or exhausted.

"Well, we had better take up our abode in the hut at the foot of that rock there," said Monohur. "I see that the stone is largely sculptured, and should like to examine the figures carved on it by the streaming moonlight."

"I agree," said the Sunyási; "the hut occupies a secluded site, and will suit us nicely. The sculpture on the rock represents the story of Prahlád and Hiranya Kasyápa, which the temple-priest will relate to you for a *dumree*."

"As if you could not do it as well, Bábájee?"

"No, my son, not this night, surely; for I have to make many arrangements here before we proceed further, and must have some time to myself to get through my work."

Monohur cast a reproachful glance at the Sunyási by way of reply; but, his curiosity being excited, he did not tarry to waste more words with him. The figures cut on the rock, he could see, were those of a man-lion tearing to pieces the body of an *asoor* of tremendous size, in the presence of a boy of ten or twelve years; and the priest was already explaining the myth to the people who had congregated around him at the temple-door.

"The giant," said the priest, "had by his austerities extorted a boon from Mahádeva, which he regarded as equivalent to a gift of immortality. He would not die, said the deity's words of assurance, either by the hand of god, man, or beast; not on the earth, water, or air; not either in the day, or in the night. 'I am indestructible then,' said the daitya in his pride, 'just as much as the gods themselves;' and this made him insufferably arrogant. He now spoke of the gods with contempt, and especially of Mudden Gopál, because his son, Prahlád, was devotedly attached to the worship of that divinity. The father tried to school his son to a different faith, and, failing in that, endeavoured to do away with him. He was hurled down from a hill, but was uninjured; placed on a burning pyre, but the fire would not scathe him; thrown into the sea, but the waves threw him back on the shore; trampled over by an elephant, but without being hurt in the least.

"'How hast thou escaped such trials, boy?'

"'By the favour of Mudden Gopál, my constant protector.'

"'Where is he then? I see nothing before me but a ball of stone.'

"'He is everywhere, and present at all times.'

"'Shall I find him in this crystal pillar?' asked the king, pointing mockingly to an architectural ornament of his palace which stood nearest to him.

"'Yes,' said the boy, 'for nothing is or can be without him.'

"The tyrant shattered the pillar with one stroke of his battle-axe, when out darted from it a terrific figure, bearing the general semblance of a man, but the face and foreclaws of a lion. Hiranya Kasyápa was seized by the monster, placed on his thigh, and torn to pieces. The assailant was neither god, man, nor beast; his victim was destroyed neither on the earth, sea, nor air; he was torn to pieces at twilight, which is neither day nor night."

"But, O, sir!" exclaimed Monohur, who now remembered having often heard the story in his childhood from his mother, "was it not Vishnu who assumed the form of a man-lion to destroy the infidel?"

"Yes, my son; but you must not get confounded by names, for the gods have each a thousand names, and Vishnu and Mudden Gopál are one."

CHAPTER XVI.

THE FOREST RISING.

THE Jungle Mahals embrace a wide expanse of territory, of some sixty miles in length and eight in breadth, lying between the Bengal district of Midnápore and the semi-independent State of Rewáh. The soil is rocky, and overspread with thick forests, which are well-nigh impervious in several places. The Zemindárs are called "Rájáhs" by their ryots; but their ancestors were all freebooters, and the ryots their banditti. Peace was a thing unknown among them, for they were always either quarrelling with each other, or raiding into the countries contiguous to their own. So long as they were in power they were strong enough to keep all outside depredators in check in their direction; and it was not till they were weakened by their internal feuds that the Mahrattás were able to raid into Bengal.

One of the most troublesome of these robber-chiefs was the Rájáh of Dhulbhoom, whose territory was contiguous to Midnápore. The rule in Dhulbhoom had always been for the son of the *Pát Ráni*, or the Rájáh's first wife, to succeed to the *Ráj;* but the practice was set aside by the British Government when it decided, on the death of Rájáh Vikram Náráyan, that his eldest son, Rughoo Náth Sing, who was the son of his second wife, should succeed to the estate. The *Bhoomij*, or the people of the Bhoom, did not accept this decision loyally, and gave audible expression to their discontent.

"What business has the British Government," they cried, "to interfere with our laws and customs? Can we not defend them like men, and should we not do so?"

"Will you swear loyalty to me, then?" exclaimed Lakshman, the son of the Pát Ráni, who was seated in their midst at the foot of a tree. "If you do, and obey me, behold I am ready to oppose tooth and nail, and break down, the English power."

The Bhoomij swore fidelity and obedience to Lakshman with great eagerness, and he was easily persuaded to believe that they were prepared for action, which in reality they were not. It takes a long time for grumbling and discontent to develope into treason; but this the aspirant chief did not understand.

"You are going to expose yourself to great danger, if not to certain destruction," said an old, white-headed priest to Lakshman. "First be sure of your men before you declare yourself."

"They have sworn to obey me, and I have pledged myself to fight for our independence. What can either do more? God will not abandon us in such a cause, and a priest, of all others, should not endeavour to dissuade me from it."

The attempt was a mad one, but Lakshman's heart was on fire, and he was unable to control himself; and so the foresters rushed recklessly into the abyss of danger without any preparation adequate to the occasion. The result was as might have been expected. Very few of the Bhoomij adhered to their chief to the last; and an interval of great anxiety was followed by a surprise, and

Lakshman, being run down, was captured and thrown into prison.

"He has been severely wounded, and cannot survive long," observed several of the people now in dismay.

"That is truth indeed, and the greater the shame on us that it is so," replied many others; and they all began to regret that they had not joined the cause heart and soul, as they had promised.

The men got infuriated when Lakshman died; and Rughoo Náth Sing, the Government nominee, dying a short time after, there was a general and well-matured rising throughout the Bhoom in support of Gungá Náráyan, Lakshman's son. The ostensible cause of this fully-developed rebellion was the oppression practised on the ryots by Mádhub Sing, the Dewán of Rughoo Náth, who had undertaken the management of the *Ráj* during the minority of Rughoo Náth's son. Gungá Náráyan decided on overturning the administration of Mádhub to begin with, and seven thousand foresters stood arrayed on his side.

The same old man who had before dissuaded Lakshman from hurrying heedlessly into rebellion, was now similarly at the elbow of his son.

"O, my son," said he, "take heed what you do. The English are sure to uphold the Dewán's authority, and, if they capture you, will they not repeat on you the treatment your father received at their hands?"

"Be it so," said the young man, proudly. "Our fate is with the gods. But the son of Lakshman must not hesitate at such an hour to avenge his father's death if he can."

"The young chief is right," roared out the Bhoomij by whom he was encircled. "Let us, at least, smoke out

Mádhub from his lair, and offer him up as a sacrifice to the shade of our deceased master, in whose capture he was chiefly instrumental;" and they went and attacked Mádhub in the *Rájbáree*, and got hold of him.

"What shall we do with our prisoner now?" asked Gungá Náráyan of the vengeful spirits around him; and some suggested that he should be put into prison, others that he should be blinded, others again that he should be decapitated.

At this moment the mother of Gungá Náráyan, Lakshman's widow, came out to the spot, with dishevelled hair and the face of a Rákshasi, and in a peremptory voice demanded to be heard.

"I am a soldier's widow and a soldier's mother," said she, "and have come out to make a request to you which you must not refuse. The English have no business to be in our country, far less to interfere with and upset our time-honoured customs and institutions. How happens it that they are able to do so with impunity? It is not that they are really stronger than we are, but that our gods have got offended with us for our neglect of them. Carry your captive, then, to the hills, before the shrine of Ránkini, and drench her temple-floor with his blood. When the gods are propitiated you will easily drive the pale-faces from your fatherland."

The proposal was received with a burst of applause, and the victim was carried uproariously to the shrine of Ránkini. Gungá Náráyan smote him with his battle-axe, after which all the other chiefs who had joined him pierced the victim successively with their spears, by which they all became equally implicated in his death; and over the blood of the slain they swore to free Dhulbhoom from the English yoke.

The country was now at the mercy of Gungá Náráyan; and he took formal possession of the palace of his ancestors, from which he was proclaimed Rájáh, which of itself brought him a considerable accession of strength, while his agents went out far and wide to collect together all the disaffected people of Bengal, for one united effort to sweep out foreign domination from the land. Among the recruits thus brought in were Kharga Báhádoor and the Sunyási, and by them stood the old priest before spoken of as having dissuaded both Lakshman and Gungá Náráyan from committing themselves into treason, but who was now as enthusiastic in the good cause as any other person present, although he could barely stagger about where the rest were stalking with loftiness and pride.

The Government authorities were now seriously alarmed, and preparations were made in haste to put down the insurrection. Three regiments of Native Infantry and eight guns were sent to operate against them, under the lead of Capt. Williamson, a young officer of great promise. But the difficulties they had to encounter were many. There were no roads to go by, and the cart-tracks, which were the only roads, were in some places mere ruts, and in others so overgrown with jungle that it was more easy to get lost among them than to thread them out successfully; and it was with much trouble, therefore, that the guns and ammunition could be moved forward.

The insurgents were in great spirits. They were commanded in chief by Gungá Náráyan, assisted by a council of leaders which included both the Sunyási and Kharga Báhádoor. The youth and handsome appearance of the latter made him a great favourite with the wild jungle-races, and his reckless daring was spoken of with praise even by their veteran chieftains. The force mustered together was not less than fifteen thousand in tale, and Gungá Náráyan was in daily expectation of being joined by another equally strong party from Jushpore. It was an honest expression of opinion, therefore, of Subadár Rahamut Khán to Capt. Williamson, that if he did not attack the insurgents quickly he would not be able to defeat them easily; and Capt. Williamson made every effort to act in accordance with the advice.

The English forces were hurried through the forests to confront the enemy, and came up to a pool of water remarkable for nothing in particular but a high curtain of shrubs around it. In advance were Subadár Rahamut Khán and Capt. Williamson, who peered cautiously about them as they went along, and in a short time they were near enough to discover, through the gaps of the jungly screen, the disposition of the insurgent army on the other side of the pool. The bronzed countenances, short beards, and dark, staring eyes of the foresters gave them a strange, and not unwarlike appearance; but they betrayed no discipline to speak of, and were miserably armed, and most of them were seen lying down, as if much fatigued, on the ground.

"They are savage to look at, Subadár," said Capt. Williamson, "but I don't think they will stand to fight with us."

"It is not likely that they will," replied the officer addressed; "but still our best course is to fall on them suddenly, so as to surprise and startle them, and then they are sure to disperse, without waiting for a second attack."

Both Capt. Williamson and the Subadár were, however, mistaken. The Bhoomij were indeed taken by surprise, but showed no wish to fly, and the fighting was maintained with an intensity of bravery which their opponents had certainly not expected, and by none more so than by a party of youthful warriors acting under the personal direction of Kharga Báhádoor.

"They have stolen a march on us," cried that young leader, "and have taken us unawares; but let each man do his duty boldly, and the disadvantage will be quickly remedied." And his followers, thus encouraged, renewed the struggle with great zeal and energy.

But the fight was still unequal, and to a considerable extent one-sided, as it had been, in fact, almost from the commencement, owing to the absolute impossibility of silencing the English guns; and Gungá Náráyan, who had been watching the exertions of his men with great anxiety, saw that they were being beaten back almost at every point.

"All is not over yet, but shortly will be," said he, "unless we can stop the firing of those infernal machines. The enterprise is a dangerous one. Will you undertake it, Kharga Báhádoor?"

"You honour me much by asking, and I appreciate your kindness."

"But do you appreciate the danger of the attempt, likewise? I must not wheedle you on to an attack without pointing out the peril of it."

"I know how to die, and you have warriors enough to replace me."

"I deny the latter statement emphatically, my young friend: but hasten if you must go; there is no time to lose."

Kharga Báhádoor did go up against the guns with

some thirty men; but, though the onset was dashing, their efforts were fruitless. They were beaten back again and again every time they rallied, and their final repulse led to the utter rout of the forest army, which filled the mind of Gungá Náráyan with despair.

The consequence of the defeat was the desertion of the chiefs by almost all their followers, which obliged them to take refuge in the hills.

"Will you submit now?" asked the Sunyási of Gungá Náráyan, who was seething in white rage.

"Submit? Never! Let them catch me in the toils and kill me."

"Why not go to the Larká Koles then, and try to raise them? They like the English rule as little as we do."

"You say well," said Gungá Náráyan, suddenly buoyed up with new hopes. "I should not fall without another effort surely."

CHAPTER XVII.

REBELLION IN THE KOLEHÁN, AND HOW IT WAS EXTINGUISHED.

WITHIN a week after the defeat at Dhulbhoom, Gungá Náráyan, with the remnants of his party, had repaired to the Kolehán, and had lost no time in opening the necessary negotiations with its native chieftains.

The Koles are a numerous people, occupying all the country from the jungles of Rámgurh and Házáreebágh to the confines of Gángpore and Sirgoojáh. They are naturally very inoffensive, but are exceedingly impressible, and get easily excited, if any attempt be made to oppress them. The tribal divisions among them are many, the Larkás being held to be among the most valiant. The quarrel of these with the British Government was that the authority of the Rájpoot Zemindárs over them, which they had always repudiated, was upheld by the Government, which had led to their own *Mánkis,* or chiefs, being displaced to make room for Sikh and Mahomedan adventurers, who held many of their villages in farm. This was regarded as insufferable tyranny by them; and Gungá Náráyan had no difficulty in inducing them to make common cause with him against the English power. There was, however, one peculiar obstacle to get over which required much tact to deal with, as being nothing more or less than a question of precedence. The Larkás had their own leaders, the

Mánkis, and would not accept the command-in-chief of Gungá Náráyan.

"My brother is welcome amongst us," said the Kole spokesman to Gungá Náráyan, in a perfectly friendly tone, "and we are very willing indeed to join him against the common enemy. But a Larká never receives orders from any but his own chief; we shall march under our Mánkis only."

"But there must be a directing head somewhere, my friends," expostulated Gungá Náráyan. "Separate, distinct commands would inevitably lead to confusion and discomfiture."

"Then why not make one of our leaders the chief? The Larká is a terrible warrior, and he despises the barkings of the English cur quite as much as my brother can."

"I know," replied Gungá Náráyan, "that the Larká is strong and valiant. But, O, my brother, the white men are sorcerers, and require artifice as much as valour to subdue them; and your tribe is too honest and open-hearted to circumvent their wiles and deceit."

The Larká was pleased, but would not give up the point of contention so easily, and there was a short silence before he replied.

"My brother is a great warrior," said he, "and we have the greatest confidence in him. But he must prove to us that he is fit to lead us in war before we submit to accept his command. We are at feud now with the Thákoor of Kharsáwan, a Rájpoot forced on us by the Government. The fellow is wily, as our brother says the English are. Let my brother lead us against him, and when he is able to defeat and humiliate him we shall willingly accept his lead against the English power."

"That is a very fair offer," exclaimed Kharga Báhádoor. "Let us demolish the Thákoor of Kharsáwan first. We shall have ample time afterwards to make a joint move against our foreign oppressors."

But the conquest of the Thákoor was easier to plan than to achieve. His fortress was too strong to be taken by a rabble army, and he refused to move out to give them battle.

"The Thákoor is a great chief, and has a wide-spread renown. Why does he remain cooped up within stone walls then when his enemies are calling on him to come out to meet them?" asked Kharga Báhádoor of the Sunyási.

"The Rájpoot is indeed as powerful as you say, my son; but he is knowing also. There is no need for the exhibition of his valour at present. He expects to weary us out here before he will take the trouble to attack us."

Kharga Báhádoor looked discontented and vexed. He had anticipated an open fight, for which he was ready at all times; but there seemed to be no chance of coming to that immediately. The Bhoomij were crowding at the foot of the fort, but the fort was too careless to observe what was going on at its base.

At this moment a window of the edifice was thrown open, and obscured by the burly figure of the Thákoor making its appearance there to hold a parley with his enemies.

"Ha! foresters and barbarians!" exclaimed the chief, "what mean ye by mustering here in such numbers at the foot of my fort? And what is it ye want of me?"

"Our first demand of you," said the irascible Gungá

Náráyan, "is that you surrender your fort to us, and yourself with it."

"Indeed!" replied the Thákoor, with a scornful laugh, "do you really ask so little of me? And may I inquire why I should surrender myself or my fort to you so complaisantly?"

"Because you cannot do otherwise," cried out the Sunyási. "We have the means of capturing both if you resist."

"Try to do so then, by all means. My castle is surely worth fighting for to me."

"Do you refuse to surrender then?" asked Gungá Nárayan in a peremptory tone. "We want a definite and straightforward reply."

"Well, I may say that I do; may I not?" observed the Thákoor, sneeringly in return. "Don't you see that I need do nothing but close this window to defend myself against your terrible resentment; and has any warrior ever surrendered himself, or his fort, under such circumstances? Be off, ye dogs, from my place, or I will pelt ye off with stones."

Saying this he closed the window as abruptly as he had opened it, which left his enemies no alternative but to attack the place. But the valour of the Bhoomij and the Koles made no impression on the rock-walls of the fortalice; and, though they went round and round on all sides, they could discover no inlet that could easily be broken into. A chaos of rocks, surrounded by dense masses of virgin forest, begirt the castle on every side, and the assailants seemed almost entangled within the labyrinth into which they had penetrated.

"Well, what are we to do now?" asked Gungá Nárayan of his counsellors in despair.

"Nothing immediately," answered the Sunyási. "Let us rest here for the night as well as we may. To-morrow morning we must get ladders ready to scale the rocks with."

"That is indeed," exclaimed Kharga Báhádoor, "a very happy thought! And then we shall get into the fort and settle with the garrison easily."

"Yes, when we are there," replied Gungá Náráyan, rather peevishly. "The idea is a good one, and ought to be worked out; but it will not be a very easy matter to give effect to it, I fear."

They lay that night on the uplands and irregular meadows that surrounded the fort, but got up with alacrity at daybreak to carry out their plan. The morning was faultless, except that it was unusually cold, and the trees were roaring to the north-wind. The ladders were prepared quickly, there being no lack of timber or osier-bands at the place; but it took them four good hours to fix them, after which several of the stout Larkás began to get up by them, and were accompanied by Gungá Náráyan and the other chiefs. But even the women and children of the fort turned out now to repel the assailants; and they showed great adroitness and activity in pouring down brickbats and stony fragments on them.

"Good!" exclaimed the Thákoor, who superintended the defensive operations in person; "this scaling should cost them dear at any rate, and, if they are able to get up eventually, why, we have enough of warriors here to receive them."

"It is very improbable, my son, that they will reach us," drily observed an old woman, who was trying to unfasten a huge mass of rock from its base, almost at the side of the chief; and, succeeding in lifting out the mass, she dexterously directed its descent right on Gungá Náráyan, whom she had especially marked out for destruction. The fall of the rock drowned both the roar of the wind and the yells of the attacking party, and a fear fell on the latter when they saw their chief lying crushed beneath its weight.

Everything was now in confusion, both in the fort and out of it, and the invaders ran off in different directions, not knowing whither, and scarcely understanding wherefore. Kharga Báhádoor, the Sunyási, and some of the Mánkis endeavoured to rally the fugitives, but in vain.

" It is only the loss of one man," exclaimed the first, " and surely we have other warriors here to replace him."

But the palladium of the Bhoomij was gone, and they showed no further appetite for the fight; and the Larkás, who had not been able to effect anything against the Thákoor hitherto, took it for granted that he was not to be conquered.

" I send you the head of Gungá Náráyan," wrote the Thákoor of Kharsáwan to the English commander. "Will you make me a Rájáh now, as I have so long besought the Government, or will you leave me to become one ? "

They made him a Rájáh Báhádoor by return of post; and, the confederacy against the Government having broken up, Bissonáth and Monohur were obliged to assume their old names and decamp.

" Whither now ? " asked Monohur of his guide.

"To the Tirthastháns you spoke of. Men in our circumstances have no other refuge to fly to."

CHAPTER XVIII.

A MOTHER'S DISTRESS.

LEAVING the discomfited warriors to follow their solitary wanderings the reader has now to return with us to their old homes, which the march of events had not hitherto allowed us to revisit.

It was a long time before the mystery of the burglary in the Zemindár's house was sufficiently explained to be understood by his mother. The hints of the Surburákár, that Monohur was probably himself at the bottom of the whole affair, had staggered, but not convinced her, for a mother does not so easily surrender her own impressions of an only son. But things began to look very ugly when Monohur was nowhere to be found. Why did he not come home from his morning excursion, as before? Where could he be lurking? Had anything happened to him? The mother's heart was torn with anguish and misery by her doubts and fears; and bitter, bitter were the complaints she made of the unkindness of her son.

"Why was Monohur harassing her in that manner?" asked she. "Why was so much weight laid on her shoulders? Why was she alone to be so miserable while others equally placed in life were so happy?"

As we all complain in our misery, regarding ourselves to be the most unhappy of all beings, so complained the heavy-laden mother of her fate.

"Every body has deserted me!" cried she in her agony; "else would not Monohur have left me and evanished from my sight. I wish I could die now, for I have nothing more to live for. O God, have pity on me, for my burden is getting much heavier than I can bear!"

Her repinings were at their height when the Surburákár approached her apartment one morning to announce something that had happened which he considered it of importance for her to know. He looked embarrassed as he entered the room, for he was doubtful how the information he had to communicate might affect a mind already overborne by its fears.

"But there is no help for it," murmured he to himself. "She must be told of everything as it turns up, that under present circumstances being by far the best course to follow;" and he stood his ground firmly to do his devoir.

"What is the matter, Nilkant?" asked the lady, almost starting from her seat the moment her eyes fell on her Surburákár. "What do you mean by gliding into my room in that pondering mood?"

"O, mother, I come only to announce that our servant Seeboo Sing, who was endeavouring to escape from this place, has been captured by one of our chowkeydárs, with a bundle on his head."

"Has he been caught with any portion of the property that has been missing? and does he know where Monohur now is?"

"I had no time to make any inquiries myself, lady. The chowkeydár is bragging so much of what he has achieved that no one else has any chance of being heard. But they are bringing up both the captor and his captive hither, and you will know everything from their own lips presently."

The chowkeydár's story, relieved of its verbiage, was this:—A comrade of his, named Mirzá Shebán Beg, had occasion to proceed from Thánnáh Ghyeghátty to Jágooleá, and took a coolie to carry his baggage. They started together and drank spirits freely at the different grog-shops on the road, and Shebán Beg became so much the worse for it that the chowkeydár, in passing by the same road a short time after, saw him lying on the way-side naked and insensible. As the baggage and the coolie were not there he went forward in search of them, and, after a hard run, came up to a man who was carrying a bundle on his head, who, on being challenged, dropped the bundle and made off towards the rice-fields to effect his escape. But the chowkeydár ran like a greyhound after a deer, and soon caught him by the throat; and here were both the greyhound and the deer.

"Was the bundle dropped by the man identified with the baggage of Mirzá Shebán Beg?" asked Nilkant.

"No; for the man I got hold of was not the coolie engaged by my comrade, but the Zemindár's servant, Seeboo."

"Well, what did he say to you? Did he say why he was running away?"

"He uttered a tissue of mere lies and contradictions, saying successively, that the bundle on his head did not belong to him; that it did belong to him in one way, having been confided to his keeping by the person to whom it belonged; and that he did not care to tell anything more about it to me."

"All this has nothing to do with our affair, Nilkant," said the Zemindár's mother impatiently. "Does Seeboo Sing now say why he was running away hence, and where his master has gone to?"

"O mother!" said the chowkeydár, taking out the answer from the Surburákár's mouth, "I was coming presently to those very points, for I opened Seeboo's bundle by force on finding his answers to be so evasive and unsatisfactory, and what should I see in it but several silver articles which could not possibly have belonged to him, such as a silver tumbler, a silver *recáb*, a silver *pándán*, and the like. 'To whom do these articles belong?' asked I of him, and he answered, 'To my master.' 'How then come they to be in your possession instead of being in his house?' 'He has left them with me.' 'Wherefore should he have done so? He has plenty of places in his own house to put them in.' 'He is not in his own house at present, and that is the reason that I also am going away from it.' 'Where is he now then?' 'How can I say? I was not asked to watch his movements.'"

"Ah, Nilkant, all this is perfectly unintelligible to me. The refusal of the man to answer the most important of the questions that were put to him seems to me to be more fearful even than his revelations. I don't want to ask him anything myself; I don't think I could endure even to see him. Take him away with you, and try to get out of him any tidings he may have of Monohur. I don't want to know more about the lost property. It comprised the savings of many years, and was meant to give my son a fair start in life. But, since—since— there is so much mystery about its disappearance, I don't want the veil to be removed. Only let me know where Monohur is at this moment, and how he is to be brought back."

Seeboo Sing was removed from the ante-room of the lady's apartment, and Nilkant, an old Zemindár's man, knew better how to deal with him than any mere chowkeydár. His children, Gooná and Chooliá, a boy and a girl, were brought out of his house by order of the Surburákár, and were placed before him tied together by the hair.

"Shall we plunge both these children together in the Bhetná, Seeboo, or will you tell us the little—very little—that you would not tell to the chowkeydár?"

"What is it that you want to know?"

"Where is the Zemindár now, and the bulk of the property that was stolen?"

"What do I know, sir? How can I tell?"

"To the point, Seeboo, if you want to save your children. You know me of old, and I shall surely consign them both to the bottom of the river if I don't get a prompt and truthful reply."

"Why then, the Zemindár is with the Ferázees, and his property with him. They want to fight the English, and the Zemindár has had to find the money for the enterprise."

"You can go home now with your children, Seeboo. I have no further questions to ask."

And with a heavy heart the Surburákár went back to his mistress's apartment, to impart to her the awful news which he had himself long previously anticipated.

"The boy has gone clean mad then!" said the poor mother with a sigh from her heart; and she sank on her cushion shivering convulsively, and remained for some time in a state of utter unconsciousness.

The explosion of the Ferázee affair was known all over Bengal within a few days after, and this forced the lady to get up from her bed to have her son searched for in every direction; but all her endeavours were fruitless, for he was not to be found. From this time everything went wrong with her; she heeded nothing; took no part even in her zemindáry affairs, which she had always diligently attended to ever since her husband's death. For whole days she would sit down at one place, almost without moving; and, as the prospect of seeing her son became more and more remote, the gloaming of her mind deepened, and, from having been at one time a most active and intelligent specimen of her sex, she soon dwindled down into an almost imbecile state.

"You are just killing yourself, lady," said Nilkant, "and without any certain cause. My impression is that Monohur, having got free of control, has rushed forth to see the world; and I am certain that he will return to us as soon as he gets tired of his whim."

"That would be a hopeful anticipation indeed if I could persuade my mind to accept it; but, O, Nilkant, my fears will not allow me to do so."

"But why, why should you allow your fears to master your judgment? Be as strong-minded, lady, as you showed yourself before under a yet greater affliction. Never was there more need for strength than now, for your senses are reeling."

"I know that, Nilkant. My fears are killing me."

"But what is it that you fear? Let me only know what shape your alarm has taken and I shall be able to judge whether it is really so well-grounded as you seem to suppose?"

"This then," answered the lady, getting up from her seat: "Monohur has been seen with the Fakir, Sunyási, or whatever the man may really be, after the explosion of the Ferázee revolt. We all know that, for the most part, these Fakirs and Sunyásis are monsters of the worst type. They affect to be incarnations of the Deity, but are in truth incarnate fiends. Monohur has money with him, and poisoning has become a recognised system now all over our country, as Thuggism is in the North-West. What so likely then but for this same Fakir, or others acting at his instigation, to give that potion to Monohur which, by depriving him of life, would enable them to get off with his wealth?"

"I assure you, lady, that your fears are groundless. You well know that I never had a liking for the Sunyási or Fakir before; but I have since ascertained that he bears a most excellent character, and has a large share of sound common sense, notwithstanding that his principles are misdirected. He is, in fact, the brother of our priest at the temple of Nággesur Mahádeva. He will do no harm to Monohur, though, when going wrong himself from an error of judgment, he will, of course, carry his *protégé* along with him. As for money, Monohur has none with him now; all the wealth of Boná Ghát was spent in maturing the Nárkelberiáh revolt. But, even if he had money with him, the Sunyási is too wide-awake for either poisoner or Thug to operate against them."

"I trust it may be as you say, Nilkant. I could die peaceably now if I but saw my Monohur's face once more."

"Then live upon that hope, lady. There is no reason to conclude that Monohur will not return to us again."

The mother's heart beat fast, and she tried to reason herself into the same belief with her manager, but could not. A presentiment of evil had come over her which she was unable to shake off, and she sank back to her seat with a groan.

CHAPTER XIX.

INUNDATION, FAMINE, PESTILENCE, AND DEATH.

The inundation of 1833 will long be remembered in the annals of Bengal for the distress caused by it in several places, and especially in various parts of the district of 24-Pergunnáhs. The floods originated with the heavy rains in the Sub-Himálayan ranges, which were largely supplemented by continued wet weather throughout the country. In 24-Pergunnáhs in particular there had been incessant rain for not less than three months, whereby all the lowlands in it were laid under water, which the river-channels, already suffering from their own accessions, were utterly inadequate to carry off.

The rising of the rivers was very rapid, while some of them were affected besides by a peculiar bore, called the "Harpa," which carried away everything before it, drowning large numbers of men and cattle, and scavenger animals, such as dogs and jackals. This was especially the case with the Bhetná, and the sufferings caused thereby in Boná Ghát and the surrounding country were fearful. The alarm was quickly raised when the bore was seen to be coming; but it came on quicker than the villagers could fly, and whole families were swept away by it from their homes. In some places the water rose to the height of seven feet above the ground, and the people who were able to save themselves did so by occupying the upper branches of large and strong trees, the roofs of *puccá* houses, and the *chuppurs* of straw and tiled huts; or by floating on rafts, canoes, and boats, where they were able to catch them. The danger was so great that the most noxious animals and reptiles were rendered inoffensive by it. The cobra warmed itself by nestling close to the suckling mother; the wolf looked askance at but dared not molest the goat and sheep standing by his side. The horrors of the visitation were further augmented by a tremendous hurricane, which lasted a whole night, and uprooted many of the trees on which the poorer families had taken refuge; and, unforeseeing such contingency, many unfortunate people were killed at the very moment they were congratulating themselves on their escape from the inundation. In almost all places whole families were without food for some three or four days, and when the waters did subside, the impossibility of finding anything to live upon forced many persons to commit suicide. "I am going to seek for food for all of us," was the plea put forth by many a father when bolting away from his family to avoid seeing the distress he could not relieve; and many a mother, tormented by the cries of her starving progeny, became so frantic as to destroy them, and then dashed out her own brains, not to survive those who were dearest to her.

The mother of Monohur had a particularly heavy time in connection with these sufferings, as being sore at heart at a juncture when she was called upon to do justice to the oppressive responsibility devolving on her. Many a battle is fought in private life which leaves but little trace for the careless chronicler to note upon, and such a battle had she to fight, and did fight with a stout and bursting heart. She applied herself to the duties of her position with an assiduity and singleness of purpose that called forth the honest praises of everybody who had an opportunity of knowing what she was doing.

"Give everything to everybody liberally, Nilkant," said she to her Surburákár. "Stint not. All, all we have, is to be given away to those who are suffering. O, Monohur, where are you at this moment? Who shall assure me that some monstrous 'Harpa' has not swept away my son to the sea?" And in the midst of her largehearted charity would the poor, forsaken woman be thus overcome by her fears, and lie down for hours as one bereft of motion.

"Rise, lady, rise! be what you ever were; be equal to the occasion which demands the husbanding of all our energies. The country is not threatened with famine alone; large gangs of men are moving through it armed with clubs and hatchets, breaking open and looting whatever they can lay hands upon, and the police are powerless against them."

Without a murmur, if not without a pang, would the lady rise forthwith after every such call, to work as bravely and unflinchingly as before, leaving, even on the Surburákár, the impress of a superior mind by the lucid and appropriate orders she gave him to carry out.

"If we have robbers now to contend with, Nilkant, you must get our men together, and employ even the plunderers themselves in our service, and pay them, and feed them, and bid them protect our ryots from depredation. The greatness of our ancestors was given to them in trust only. In the day of their trouble the poor have a right to our protection and assistance, and must have both." And well did the afflicted lady, drying her tears, follow up her words by her acts, by protecting the hapless, and setting up all those who had broken down by rendering timely assistance to them in rebuilding or securing their houses, drying up their grains, and providing supplies of other food and clothing.

Dreadful were the troubles which were thus encountered and overcome; but there were more yet to pass through. After the waters had subsided, after lawlessness was put down, after the immediate demands of hunger and nakedness were supplied and satisfied, there came forth another enemy more difficult to contend with than either inundation or famine. Disease in the shapes of cholera and fever set in, both of the worst type, and originating apparently from rotten crops and fetid slime; and they were so widely spread in a short time that the few who were not attacked could do little to relieve the many who were. Even against this enemy did the lady of Boná Ghát fight most willingly and courageously to begin with, sending out kobirájes and medicines in every direction, and assistance of every description that was wanted. But the excitement was too much for her enfeebled frame. Unsoothed in mind and unrefreshed in body she had laboured so strenuously as to get thoroughly exhausted; and she was now stricken down by a fever which bereft her of what little strength had hitherto remained to her.

"You are looking very ill, lady; you have over-exerted yourself, and must take rest—rest both of body and of mind."

"Rest! what rest? If you mean sleep, I can get none of it; or, if there be any at times, it does not refresh me."

"Nor will it if you continue to torture your mind as

you have done so continuously. O, lady, remember that, if anything goes wrong with you, everything will go wrong with the household and the estate."

The lady raised her eyes towards the face of her Surburákár, as if she wished to understand the meaning of his words fully.

"Ah, you are trying to frighten me, Nilkant; but nothing surely has gone wrong with me yet. It is only the cramped atmosphere around us that chokes me. O, that we had a breath of fresh air now to dissipate this suffocating closeness!"

"No, lady, I would not alarm you for the world. But you look pale, and your eyes are restless, and, if you are not suffering from illness, you must be suffering from exhaustion."

Her eyes had the weary, hopeless, and restless expression which tells clearly of a heart that is comfortless and breaking; but, besides that, there was also an unaccountable pallor on her face, unaccountable if she had really no illness to complain of, as she said.

"I have no bodily ailment to speak of, Nilkant," repeated she once more. "I feel weaker surely—much weaker indeed than I have ever felt before; but have we not worked harder for some time now than is our wont? and does not that account for the loss of strength fully?"

She maintained over and over again that nothing ailed her; but the evidence of her face was unmistakable, and became more and more striking day by day, till the fever developed itself with delirium, which was at times so wild that they had the greatest difficulty in keeping her to her bed. The one only idea that haunted her now was that her son was hiding himself from her, and all her struggles and ravings were for reaching him.

"He is not dead. It is not so bad as that. He has been wheedled away from me. He is willing to come back now, but they will not allow him. I see him frequently passing by me; but a dense cloud comes invariably between us which I cannot penetrate. O, Nilkant, why hast thou removed my son from me, my handsome and noble-hearted boy? Why won't you allow him to come back to his mother's arms?"

"Be calm, lady; be patient, for the love of God, and I will tell you all I know of him. I am labouring day and night to bring him back to you; and he shall come back if you will only bear up till I am able to bring him hither."

The face of the lady was now illuminated by an unutterable expression of gratitude, and, while her heart beat rapidly with expectation, the delirium she was suffering from was checked momentarily, as if by magic.

"Have you heard of Monohur lately, Nilkant? Have you got any certain tidings of his whereabouts yet?"

"Yes, lady; they are vague scraps only at present, but still the tidings are such as should reassure your mind. You were afraid lest he should have suffered from the inundations that visited us, but my informant writes that, when last seen, he was in the high and dry lands of Western Bengal, and not in any of the countries which were flooded."

"But in what direction was he going? Could not any of your messengers overtake him?"

"No; for as yet he is ahead of my men, who are only following in his trail; and the tortuous line he is tracking makes it impossible at times to keep up the pursuit."

A thick, impenetrable cloud was forming in the western sky, and the Zemindár's mother looked intently at it, as if her eyes would pierce through its inky veil to seek for her truant son.

"O, Monohur! even in the land beyond yon cloud will my spirit seek for and find thee. Nilkant, I am dying."

"Dying!" exclaimed the Surburákár, as he hastened to take hold of her cold hands to feel for her pulse. "Ah, poor lady! she is gone already—killed by her son!"

The lady was dead indeed; but she had not taken off her eyes from the western cloud. Her soul had leaped out in that direction, and the eyes were gazing fixedly as before.

CHAPTER XX.

THE ZOHUR STONE.

THE station of Suádi is situated on the plateau formed by the sand-hills of Gángpore, and is full of caves and natural excavations, which were largely used as hiding places by the local chiefs and their families during the height of the Mahrattá inroads. The retreats are very secure, the paths leading to them winding through tangled grass-plains and round large boulders, and not being easily threaded; and one of the caves—namely, that which is the largest—has the reputation of having been occupied by Káma and Sitá during their residence in the forest, whence the latter was carried off by Rávana. The general belief on the spot speaks also of the excavations as extending subterraneously so far as Tálcherá, on the banks of the Bráhmini river; and it is pretended that, even to this day, the underground zigzag is passable from one end of it to the other, and is actually traversed by those who are not afraid of its loneliness and gloom. The population throughout the tract consists almost entirely of mountaineers and woodmen, nominally divided into septs, but not materially differing from each other either in race or character. They have, in fact, a legend amongst them that they are all descended from a common progenitor, the father of seven brothers who came to this part of India from the mountains of the North, and became divided by a trifling accident. They were all hunters when they came; but the head-dress of two of them having got entangled in the jungles they were passing through, these were sundered from the rest, and, while the latter followed the chase, the former, vexed at the obstacle that had hindered them, took out their knives to cut down the thickets, and became wood-cutters from that day.

The place is wild and unfrequented, and not without a spice of romance about it, and the people in it are wilder still, though perfectly unsophisticated and exceedingly warm-hearted. Every stranger is an uninvited guest with them, and, once a guest, they cannot harm him ever after on any account. It is said that a murderer having at one time found a refuge here with the parents of the man he had murdered, had all his wants supplied by them, though the father of the murdered man had recognised the slayer of his son. They shared their simple meal with him, and gave him a bed to sleep upon, and it was not till he had started on his journey the next morning, and was at a fair distance from their habitation, that his host ventured to stop him.

"There is a blood-feud between us," said he, "and I cannot allow the murderer of my son to pass further without settling the account between us. I could not, of course, accost him to this end while he was my guest."

"Can you do so now, old man? Have I not eaten of your rice and salt?"

The would-be avenger of blood hung down his head, and was obliged to admit the claim; and the murderer passed on without being further interfered with.

Such was the retreat and such the men among whom

Monohur and Bissonáth had taken refuge after their escape from Kharsáwán. They inhabited one of the caverns to which we have referred, and, being equally well liked by the woodmen and the mountaineers, had all their wants fully and freely supplied. The character and appearance of the Sunyási commanded the respect both of the young and the old, while the youth and manliness of Monohur made him perhaps a yet greater favourite with all of them. What the Sunyási was especially esteemed for was his knowledge of charms and medicines, which induced even the patriarchs of the septs, who yet retained the pride of their traditional high birth fully, to regard him as a superior being, and to salute him with becoming deference.

"Our place of refuge is singularly lone and unpicturesque, Bábájee," exclaimed Monohur, "but I nevertheless feel very pleasant and comfortable in it, and am loath to believe that we could have done better anywhere else under our present difficulties."

"You are right, my son, for our retreat is a very secure one; but still must we depart from it as soon as we may, that is, as soon as the hue and cry after us has subsided."

"Why, wherefore should we leave it in such haste? Are you getting tired of our cave of freedom already?"

"Yes, indeed I am; for I want more freedom than a nook like this can ever give us. Our sphere of action is far beyond these brown thickets and bare rocks, and we put up with them so long only as we must."

They were both seated near the opening of their cave, with their backs against the stone, and were busily engaged in pruning a climbing clematis that threatened to monopolise the whole place. At this moment a respectable woodman approached them in a hurry, and it was apparent from his short and quick breathing that he had run over a great distance to come to them.

"What brings you here in such haste, friend? Have you any tidings for us?" asked the Sunyási, somewhat in alarm.

"No, sir; but my wife has been bitten by a serpent, and I have come to you for help."

"She is not dead yet?"

"No, not quite dead, but very nearly so. The last sparks of life are yet lingering."

"Where did the serpent come from? Do you know where it burrows?"

"O, sir, she was bit in the woods, and we cannot say where the serpent came from, or where it is now to be found."

"Well, that is unfortunate, for the best cure for a serpent-bite is to compel the reptile to suck out its own poison from the wound."

"Can that be done, Bábájee?" asked Monohur, wonderingly.

"Yes, to be sure; that is, if the charm for forcing the reptile be known—not otherwise. The next best course is to find a substitute for the serpent; and I will let you have one."

He drew out a bag from his side, and, after fumbling in it for a time, picked out a blue stone very like a small knotted serpent in shape, and having a rough mouth.

"Just give a little milk to this serpent of mine. Put it in a can of milk, and it will drink eagerly for itself. When it ceases to do so take it out of the can and apply its rough mouth to the wound. Don't get alarmed if it sticks there. If the poison be strong it may adhere for half-an-hour or so; but when it has sucked it up fully it will let go its hold of itself. Dip it then again in a fresh can of milk, and you will see the poison exuded into the can."

The man took the stone home, though with a despairing heart.

"There is little chance," said he to himself, "for a little plaything like this to bring back the life that must be nearly out by this time; but I shall do with it as the wise man has told me, if only out of respect for him." And he did as he was told before a large circle of sympathising friends.

They gave the stone milk to drink, and it sucked it up with a fizzing sound, which surprised the simple spectators greatly.

"Don't you be very uneasy yet, brother," said a relative of the despairing husband, encouragingly. "It is not a mere inert stone that we have here after all. It has drunk for itself, and, having got filled, has ceased to drink. Let us put it to the wound and see how it acts."

It was put to the wound accordingly, and stuck to it with a most stubborn bite.

"Will this cure her?" asked the husband, still partially in doubt, but now hoping more than ever.

"What makes you think otherwise?" remarked a third man. "The Sunyási has never deceived us, and if ever there was a wise man in the world it is he."

"Hush! see she is moving," pointed out a fourth bystander; and then the mystic stone came off as if its work were done.

It was dipped into a fresh can of milk now, and began to exude a thin, slightly-greenish oil, which was well understood by all to be the poison it had sucked out; and within a short time after the woman who was bitten, and who had hitherto been insensible, sat up.

"This is a greater marvel than was ever seen or heard of in these tracts before," was the remark of the oldest of the foresters; and so in sooth it was, for the wild residents of the plateau had never heard of the Zohur stone.

They came to return the stone to the Sunyási, but not on that errand only; they also came to worship him.

"Why, what does this mean, friends? What is this you are doing to me with offerings of flowers and libations?"

"Mahádeva drank poison in the days of old, on its being churned out of the sea, and his throat is therefore stained blue. You are surely an incarnation of the deity?"

"I—I, an old sinful man, stooping with age and infirmities, is it me that you are come to worship as an incarnation of God? No, no; give praise only to Him to whom it is due. He has not left us unprotected against the evils of life. Every earthly malady has its cure, every poison its antidote; though all the cures and antidotes be not yet generally known to us. This stone, that has worked such a marvel before your eyes, is to be found in abundance at the foot of the Himálayá Mountains, which abound with serpents. Your progenitors came from those regions, but the virtues of the stone were not known to them. They have been since discovered, and no recluse comes back from his Tirtha now without bringing handfuls of these bits with him. As I have some more of them with me I shall make a present of this one to you, that you may remember me when I am gone. It will always effect the cure you have seen, whether I remain with you or not."

They liked both their stranger friends, and were really sorry when they saw them making preparations to depart.

"Don't you like to stay with us?"

"O, friends, we have work elsewhere to do. Our home is different from yours—we are sojourners here only; and our stay with you must terminate."

Very sincere was their grief in parting with them. The fact is, the Sunyási had made himself very useful to his simple-hearted entertainers. He had regulated their households, adjusted their differences, and become a referee with them on all subjects of importance; and, having got used to his assistance, they could ill do without it.

"Charming people these," said Monohur. "They are easily satisfied, and seldom unhappy."

"Yes, indeed; but what bounds their aspirations would not bound ours; neither you nor I could be happy after their fashion; and, as the pursuit after us has sufficiently slackened in force now, our departure hence is well timed."

"But whither do we go then, Bábájee? If there be no more danger to fear, can we not take any course we choose now?"

"Let us get out from this mess of hills and forests first. We should strike out for the high-road to Pooree, I should say, to begin with, and, that attained, we shall know how to shape our course afterwards, according to circumstances."

"A very good idea!" exclaimed Monohur. "Let us strike out for Pooree by all means. There must be a great deal to see there to be sure."

CHAPTER XXI.

THE EMISSARY AGAIN, AND A STEP-MOTHER'S STORY.

WE are not in a position to say how Monohur and the Sunyási departed from Suádi—that is, whether by the subterranean passage to which we have referred, or by the common road. It is only known that within a short time after they were seen at Dhenkenel, which stands at a distance of about fifteen miles from the Pooree road, and that they were then walking rather leisurely, and the Sunyási somewhat silently, notwithstanding that his companion was prating much about the beauty of the landscape around them. Their path lay through extensive meadows and woods, without ever crossing a barren or deserted spot; and there was a fragrance in the air liberated from the thousand nameless shrubs which covered the ground as they trampled over them. Monohur's rapture was unbounded, and he gave emphatic expression to it; but there was no corresponding response from the Sunyási, who had already fallen into a reverie.

"How can you be so absorbed in your thoughts in such a delightful place as this, Bábájee? Don't you observe the remarkable contrast it presents to the rocky wilderness which we have so recently left behind us?"

"I do, my son, I do. I can no more help admiring the scenery than you yourself. But the old have many things to brood over, and many entanglements to unravel with which the young are not usually troubled, and you must not be surprised therefore to find me either absent-minded or inattentive occasionally."

"I did not mean to complain of your inattention, Bábájee, in the least. I was only anxious that you should relax your mind a little to enjoy the soft beauty of this spot before we had passed out of it altogether. If our affairs are getting involved, should I not know how they actually stand?"

"O, it was not exactly our affairs that I was thinking of, Monohur, but of matters with which we have no concern at present, though we may possibly become connected with them by-and-by. If we do get mixed up with them at all you shall, of course, know everything about them in time."

The steps of the speakers were now suddenly arrested by a voice that seemed to issue from the ground. It called on the Sunyási to stop, and he did so unconsciously, drawing Monohur closer to him. They were fleeing from danger and death, and their fear was natural; but it was only a single man that had accosted them, and he was easily recognised.

"You here again?" exclaimed the Sunyási, in surprise, on seeing the Ghátttál Báboo standing before them.

"Yes, I have been sent to ask if you have made up your minds yet to come over to us."

"Sent from Bánpore do you mean?"

"Yes, from Bánpore."

"Are you going back thither?"

"I am; and I have been told to take you with me if you would come."

"We can't accompany you immediately for many

reasons, of which one only need be named. Being here we must proceed to Purushuttom first."

"What answer shall I make then to those who have sent me?"

"Say that they may expect us at the eleventh hour, when the mine is ready for explosion, but not till then."

The man disappeared from the road-side as suddenly as he had sprung up, and was lost among the surrounding thickets and brambles. Monohur had seen him distinctly, but was so taken aback by his abrupt appearance that he had not been able to speak to him. He now asked the Sunyási to explain to him the mystery of his appearance there, and understood, of course, that it was intimately connected with the matters his companion had been so intently brooding over.

"Ah, yes, it is now time to disclose everything to you, my son;" and the account he did give was extremely satisfactory.

"The Gháttál Báboo is not worth following indeed," said Monohur, when the explanation was ended, "but should we not hasten to the trysting-place now, since our appearance there is so anxiously waited for?"

"No, my son, not immediately. It was this eagerness of yours that I was afraid of, and that made me move in the matter so cautiously. We will not disappoint those who expect us. But I would give them time to bring their disaffection to an issue before we have anything to do with them."

"I agree with you in the abstract, Bábájee; but it does appear to me to be more creditable to be among the first on the spot to ripen a good project, than among the latest, to share in what others will have ripened for us."

"O, my son, this business is theirs far more than ours, and there is no reason for our risking the dangers of an immature scheme, should they be unable to ripen it."

"Are you in doubts about the enterprise at all then?"

"No, not at present; but, seeing how we have fared in our previous undertakings, we cannot, I think, be too careful in catching the bait a third time, though I do not dissuade you from doing so cautiously."

Monohur did not quite relish the over-care and delay which the Sunyási's suggestions involved; but he could not, of course, think of pulling different-wise from him; and they went down the path in silence, slackening their steps somewhat, as if to enjoy more fully the invigorating tranquillity of the place.

"The sun is fast going down, Bábájee, and we have not secured a safe place yet for the night," observed Monohur, breaking the muteness after a time.

"That was just what I was thinking of," replied the Sunyási. "We should not be longer on the road now, and are besides tired enough to need rest. But I am afraid we must proceed a little further before we can find suitable quarters for us."

"I have no objection to go as far further as you wish, Bábájee; but there are high words going on in that hut over the hedge—somebody is threatening there that he would beat some woman or child to death. Had we not better look in to see what the difference is about?"

"Wherefore? What have we to do with the quarrels of other people, my son? But perhaps you are right, Monohur. We may possibly be able to prevent mischief if it be threatened, and at the same time probably secure the shelter we seek."

The hut they approached belonged to a family of

Goárs, or Goáláhs, a common class in Orissá. The quarrellers were man and wife. The husband was a middle-aged man, named Dabrá, and the woman, his second wife, was called Bhago. Though Dabrá had re-married after the death of his first wife, he loved his son by the latter—a boy of twelve years—far better than he loved his new wife, and this Bhago was unable to endure. Father and son had just returned from ploughing, and the boy being hungry had asked for food. His stepmother had thereupon given him a dish of *Khichree*, or *Chow-Dallia*, as they call it, and had directed him to eat it in the kitchen.

"How can I eat it in the dark?" said the boy; and, unmindful of her order, he had taken out the dish into the compound where there was light yet to see.

"There is something yellow in the middle of the dish," observed the boy, looking at the platter intently; and, having taken a mouthful of the *Khichree*, he added that it was bitter, and spat it out. His father coming up gave the remainder of the dinner to a dog that was near, and the animal had no sooner eaten of it than it was seized with convulsions and began to roll upon the ground.

"How, bitch? What did you dare to give my son to eat? Shall I not thrash your life out of you for attempting to poison him?"

The woman protested at first that she had given nothing harmful to the boy; but, finding that she was not believed, she became as clamorous as her husband, who at last brought out a thick cane to thrash her with. It was at this juncture that Monohur and the Sunyási entered their hut, which the absorbing nature of their altercation had rendered them incapable to observe.

"I will kill thee, bitch, with this stick," exclaimed

the infuriated husband; but Monohur caught hold of the cane before it could descend, while Bissonáth, availing himself of his sacred character, came forward with a benediction on the house in regular Sunyási fashion, and deprecated the anger and violence of its owner in the mildest terms.

"Hear me out first, Thákoorjee!" said Dabrá, "and you will be aghast at the crime which the woman had attempted."

But the woman denied the charge that was brought against her, when, to her confusion and the triumph of her accuser, the proof of it was made manifest by the death of the dog.

"Don't try to deny your guilt, woman," said the Sunyási, "but rather be thankful to Heaven that your attempt has not succeeded. And you, friend," added he, turning to her husband, "must not retaliate, for your wife seems now to be with child. Listen to a story which I will tell you, which almost sets forth your own case in different words, and it may be that you shall be able to shape your course aright after you have heard it.

"A man married a second time after the death of his first wife, as you have done; he loved his second wife, but his son by his first wife was not less dear to him. In time the second wife gave birth to a son, just as yours will within four or five months; but the husband loved his first son best of all.

"'This must not be,' said the wife to herself. 'There is a Rákshasi in the forest who is related to me. I shall send my step-son to her, and she will eat him up.'

"She called the boy to her, and told him to go to her aunt in the forest. 'Carry this basket of sweetmeats to her and remind her of me, and bring me word how she is.'

"The boy was pleased with the mission intrusted to him, being anxious to secure the good graces of his step-mother, and went off as directed with speed.

"'Are you my step-mother's aunt?' asked he of the Rákshasi, on arriving at her place.

"'Yes, that am I. What have you got for me?'

"'O, all these presents here, and she wants to be remembered with love. Now say what I am to tell her from you, for I must go back quickly against my father's return.'

"'Not quickly, my child; you must first eat and drink here. Sit down for a while and amuse yourself, while I get things ready for you.'

"The boy pressed hard to go, but found that he was detained and fell crying. The Rákshasi had feasted that day already, and had reserved him for her next meal.

"'What are you crying for, boy?' asked a little ringdove that was perched on the nearest tree.

"'I can't go home; I am detained.'

"'Knowest thou what for? Thy step-mother's aunt is a Rákshasi, and you were sent here that she might eat you up.'

"'How shall I escape then?'

"'Take this twig, this leaf, and this wisp of straw that I have brought for you. The doors will open when you touch them with the twig, after which you are to run for your life. If the Rákshasi discovers your escape, and pursues you, throw this leaf before her and a river will intervene. If she crosses the river and threatens to overtake you, throw the wisp of straw at her and it will become a dense forest which will effectually cover your flight.'

"The boy took the gifts the ringdove gave him, and

while the Rákshasi was asleep he touched the doors with the twig and they flew ajar. He ran out as he had never run in play, and had already cleared half the distance home when he saw that the Rákshasi had awoke and was coming after him. He was much agitated and frightened, but remembered to throw the leaf at her, and it became a wide river. The Rákshasi thereupon flung herself into the stream, and began to swim over with the celerity of an otter. The boy had run fast in the meantime, and was very near home; but the Rákshasi had already crossed over, and was bounding recklessly after him. He now threw the wisp of straw at her, and, while she vainly attempted to penetrate the forest that arose between them, the boy reached home.

"'Whence, boy?' asked his father of him angrily, for he had been awaiting his return with impatience.

"The boy related the story of his adventures faithfully, upon which the father got so angry with his wife that he took up his hatchet to kill her. But the dove that had helped the boy out of his danger was now sitting on the thatch of their hut, and came forward as peacemaker between man and wife.

"'Your wife has borne you a second son, and you must not kill her. Make her a necklace of betel-nuts, and she will live in the house as a cat;' and the second wife, converted into a cat, lived purring and snarling all the rest of her life, without being able to do any further harm to her step-son."

"How am I to dispose of my wife then to make her as harmless for the future?" asked Dabrá of the Sunyási.

"Excuse her the offence she has committed, and she will remain bound to you for ever; and you, woman, if you try to harm your step-son again I shall have your body, and the body of the child in your womb, covered with leprosy by my imprecations."

"O, father, I shall never think of injuring my step-son any further, since you have saved me. Don't, for heaven's sake, curse the child in my womb."

CHAPTER XXII.

JAGGANÁTH KE JAI!

HAVING patched up a truce between husband and wife, the travellers had little difficulty in making good their quarters with them for the night; and, in fact, the proposal that they should do so came from Dabrá himself, though in a rather ungracious way.

"It is not the custom with us," said he, "to receive guests at this late hour. But we have given you so much trouble with our affairs, and you have been so long delayed thereby, that it would scarcely be kind now to send you away; so you may as well put down your wallets where you are, and rest here for the night."

"So be it," answered the Sunyási, stopping the reply of Monohur, who was about to refuse an asylum so ungenerously offered. "We are pilgrims only, and will not require much attention from you or your family; and we go out very early to-morrow, as time is of much value to us."

But Dabrá, though rough in manners, was not naturally an inhospitable man. He had a young wife at home, and did not care therefore to receive strangers indiscriminately at night; but, having allowed the pilgrims to stay, he attended to all their wants cheerfully, while Bhago, grateful for the service they had rendered to her, was particularly assiduous in performing those functions which women are always best able to discharge.

"After all, Bábájee," said Monohur, "these people are not really so churlish as they appeared to me at first, and we would have acted foolishly indeed had we refused the shelter they have given us only for the words in which the offer was made."

"Just so, my son. Wayfarers, like ourselves, should never quarrel with mere words. If we had refused their offer we might have been faring worse elsewhere at this moment, or perhaps not have found any shelter anywhere at all."

They ate and slept well there in the night, and were up very early next morning, ready to depart.

"I pronounced a blessing on the house when I entered it," said the Sunyási, addressing Dabrá and his wife, "and will bless it again in departing from it. Do you live in concord and peace evermore, my friends, putting up with each other's infirmities, and frequently forgiving each other, which is, I assure you, the only way of living happily on the earth."

They were out of the house the next moment, and, directing their steps towards the main road to Pooree, came up to it at about a mile beyond the town of Cuttack. There are passengers on this road day and night throughout every month of the year, though more so during the festival seasons than at other times; and every village on the road-side has its pilgrim encampments. The parties vary in number from thirty to three hundred men, and nearly ninety per cent. of the pilgrims are females. They are collected by *Pándás*, or touters, who visit every part of India to bring them together. These allurers do not go about preaching like Peter the Hermit, but simply seek the women in their retirement when their husbands are away from home, and there work both on their fears and hopes—fears as regards their future salvation, hopes connected with their worldly happiness and exaltation. The bait thus held out is irresistible. Young women are easily induced by the very novelty of the journey to undertake it; widows snap at the idea of looking about them in the world with avidity; while barren wives, unfortunate mothers, and all in distress of mind are easily persuaded to proceed in person to the "Lord of the Universe,"[1] and pour forth all their sorrows before Him. The women hooked, the men follow like so many sheep; and at the time of the great festivals the stream of pilgrims is literally continuous.

Monohur was astonished at the number of men he saw on the road, and the variety they represented.

"O, Bábájee! where do so many people come from? Is all India on the move at this season of the year?"

"Yes, my son, almost all who can afford to do so, and many even of those who cannot afford the expenditure take advantage of the festivals to run over to Pooree; and by far the greater portion of them come from our own province of Bengal, and, next to it, from the North-West. The number is so considerable, in fact, that it frequently causes an artificial famine where the pilgrims halt; and you will find high prices the rule throughout their line of march."

Monohur gazed on the crowd with extreme surprise, for he had never in his life seen such numbers on the move before. "Jagganáth ke jai!" "Purushuttom Swámi ke jai!" were the only cries bawled out by the passengers as they trudged along, each party distinguished from the rest by some striking peculiarity of its own. The white-dressed

---

[1] *Jaggat-Náth*, or *Jugganáth*.

and diminutive females from Bengal moved with slow and languid steps, but yielded not to any in the fervour of their faith; more bravely jogged on the females of Upper India, dressed in all the colours of the rainbow, though their rags were coarse, dirty, and full of vermin; while mixed with both were to be seen bands of Sunyásis covered with ashes, and some of them completely naked, all armed with stout staffs for extorting that charity which might otherwise have been refused to them.

Generally, all the passengers were on foot, but, occasionally, covered waggons were seen carrying the women of the higher classes, whose smiling faces were ever and anon visible through the canvas parted by curious hands. At greater intervals came down trains of *pálkis* carrying over the rich ladies of Calcuttá and its immediate neighbourhood, the good-natured inmates always keeping the sliding doors of their prison-house partially open, that they might see and be seen by the other travellers on the road. More rarely still passed caravans of elephants, camels, and led horses taking down north-country Rájáhs and their seraglio, the latter carrying on their flirtations under the very nose of the chuprássis set over them.

"I thought that the journey would be fatiguing, Bábájee, but find it on the contrary to be exceedingly pleasing."

"Of course you do, for you have no knowledge of its disagreeable side yet. There are many disadvantages connected with it which, I hope, it will not fall to our lot to encounter."

"Disadvantages? I can scarcely conceive what they can be."

"Want of food, want of water, mortality; all these are

felt by those who have to make a continuous journey for months almost for the first time in their lives, and are not accustomed to privations as we have become. In their onward journey they have funds with them, and perhaps do not suffer very much, except in the purse; but on the return journey, when their purses have got lightened, they suffer so much as to die off by thousands every week."

"Why, that is horrible to think of," exclaimed Monohur, as the brightness of the picture he was painting got clouded. "How many come to Pooree then annually, and how many out of them die on the road?"

"I really don't know. I doubt if there be any data anywhere to show that. But it is said that at this Car festival, that we are proceeding to witness, somewhere near a hundred and fifty thousand men will be congregated, of whom not more than three-fourths will ever get back to their homes."

Monohur was almost terrified into silence, and avoided further conversation until late in the evening, when he heard some pilgrims complaining of an extortionate ferryman who had fleeced them.

"How is that, Bábájee? Are not the ferry rates fixed? I have often seen you to part with ferrymen on the best terms, without complaining that you were cheated."

"O, my son, I am a man of the world as well as a Sunyási, and put up cheerfully with impositions which it is not in my power to prevent. The rates, as you say, are fixed, and, what is more, they are always posted up at a prominent place near every ferry. But look at the bulk of pilgrims before you, and say how many of them you think can read and write. How, then, are they to dispute the demands made of them?"

"But you can read and write, Bábájee; why have you never complained of the imposition which, you say, it was not in your power to prevent?"

"Have we not always been fleeing for our lives? Even if it were otherwise, who would wish to leave his occupation or business, or to postpone his journey, to prosecute an extortionate farmer?"

"And this, of course, emboldens the fellows to wrench out whatever rates they choose?"

"It does; and they vary their demands only according to the head-force of the men they have to deal with, of which they are excellent judges."

Monohur felt that his bright picture was, one after another, losing all its roseate hues. The downright realities before him, deprived of the unreal lights in which he had hitherto viewed them, now looked as ugly and frightful daubs; and his uneasiness was yet further augmented when he heard a short while after that, on the previous day, there had been a case of poisoning on the road.

"This is what I could never have dreamt of," exclaimed he. "How in such a frequented road can any attempt to poison be made?"

"O, nothing is easier," answered the Sunyási. "When people who don't know one another, have to eat and sleep almost side by side at so many places, what so easy for the poisoner than, under the veil of fellowship, to mix *dhatoorá*, arsenic, or aconite with the food of his fellow-travellers?"

"But, surely, the chances of escape, after commission of the crime, are less in a crowded road than elsewhere?"

"They ought to be; but as the effect of *dhatoorá* is only giddiness or partial stupefaction to begin with, that is often attributed to mere weariness, and passes unnoticed till the poisoners have had time to place a considerable distance between themselves and their victims."

"Ah! your pilgrimages, then, are productive of frightful atrocities and crimes, Bábájee. The gain per contra must be great indeed to tempt so many to prosecute them under such risks with so much enthusiasm."

"The gain? Of course the gain is great, my son. Don't you know what it is? '*Rathay Báhmana dristay poonar janma nabidatay!*' 'He that has seen the Dwarf³ face to face at the time of the Car festival has no further births to pass through!'"

A brisk walk brought our travellers to the city of Pooree, where, lost in the great wave of pilgrims, they put up for the night openly with others, without any fears or misgivings.

"You may rest here in peace with us," said the Pándá who found accommodation for them, "musing on the Great Creator whom you shall see in the flesh to-morrow; and, if you are not niggardly in your charities, nor in your offerings to the Deity, there is no reason why you should not secure a straight and easy path to heaven."

"O, priest," said the Sunyási, "I am but half a beggar by trade, and possess little indeed, of the treasures of the world, and this youth is my *cheláh*, or disciple, having, at present at least, no other person to befriend him. But what little we have with us we shall certainly pour out freely to secure our salvation; and we shall do it in such manner as you yourself may direct."

The Pándá was fully gratified, and left them with a smiling face, to speak in the same sense to the many other pilgrims he had brought together on the same errand, and to the same spot.

³ An *Avatár* of Vishnu.

CHAPTER XXIII.

THE MINE READY ONCE MORE.

THE night was passed pleasantly, the pilgrims sitting up to a late hour to listen to the story of Jagganáth, which was narrated by the Pándá for their edification.

"In the golden age the Lord of the Universe was worshipped in Orissá by the name of Nilmádhava, or the Blue God, and dwelt in a large forest near to the seashore. His reputation was so great that a puissant Rájáh of Oujein, named Indradyamna, came with a large following to see him. But the god was wroth at his ostentation and pride, and said—'Thou surely shalt not see me till I have cured thee of thy self-esteem;' and the blue stone vanished from the forest it had inhabited, and was nowhere to be found.

"'Gone!' exclaimed the Rájáh, in blank dismay. 'Evanished, just when, after years of anxious thought, I had come out hither to see him! O, merciful Heaven! why was such grievous disappointment reserved for me?'

"Sore, sore grieved the Rájáh, that his heart's wish could not be gratified. Hot tears ran thick and fast from his eyes, and he sobbed almost like a child. For years and years he had thought of nothing but how he should approach the deity, and this, the sole wish of his heart, was now hopelessly frustrated.

"'Build him a temple,' said the priest of Nilmádhava,

'and the god will surely come to inhabit it. You have wealth, position, and honour; how can he meet such a man in the forest, under the hedges, where men in rags and tatters only come to seek for him?'

"The king snatched up the idea with great eagerness, and a grand temple was built on the sea-shore within the shortest time. But still the god came not, and the Rájáh clasped his hands vainly in despair.

"'O, king!' said the priest to him once more, 'if your faith and love be really so great, and worthy of the deity you seek, build him a city round the temple. How can he inhabit a temple built on a waste?'

"'I shall certainly do so,' said the king; and they had not to wait long before a large city arose around the wild spot where the temple had been raised, and a large and glorious city it was, even this city of Pooree.

"But the god was still as obdurate as ever, and even his priest knew not what further suggestions to offer.

"'Must we go back, then, without seeing him?' asked the Rájáh's wife, in a plaintive voice of complaint.

"'Not so, my beloved!' said the king decisively. 'I have read the Veds and the Puráns, and know how to perform those austerities which it is not given even unto the gods to disregard or repel;' and he sat down to perform *Homs* and *Jagyas* which shook the deep foundations of heaven.

"'This man will surely force me to reveal myself to him,' observed Nilmádhava, in a cogitative mood. 'He has thought for nothing else in his heart but me. How is such a devotee to be gainsaid?'

"Thus compelled to appear the god made himself visible to the king in a dream, in the form of a Neem-wood log, which was decked with all the insignia of

Vishnu. The Rájáh awoke with irrepressible feelings; and the block of wood seemed as if it were vanishing before his eyes, and lo, it was gone!

"Sore, sore grieved was the Rájáh again that it was only a dream; but when he spoke of the vision to his courtiers and servants, and when the news of it was carried far and wide, the response came quickly that just such a block of wood as that described by the king had made its appearance on the sea-shore, having been thrown up by the tide. The Rájáh now cried out in an agony of joy—'O, my heart's wish! O, Saviour of my race! hast thou descended to me at last?' and all his retinue were set to draw up the wood from the beach, and were helped by the labouring population of the place with great enthusiasm.

"'There it is up at last!' exclaimed the king with ecstasy, 'the emblem of the deity that has been sent down to us from heaven!' and his wife and relatives joined him with eager voices to raise the song of exultation and love.

"'O, king!' said the priest of Nilmádhava, 'it behoves you now to give this shapeless wood a form. You have built a temple for the deity. Will you set up this log in it as it lies?'

"The mandate of the king went forth thereupon to collect carpenters, and a large number of them were brought together to work out the wood. But they could make nothing of it, for their instruments broke, and made no impression on the wood.

"'It is surely the obstinacy of the god again,' said the Rájáh's wife, 'that is still endeavouring to disappoint us. O, king, you must resume your austerities, for we cannot leave our work half done.'

"The king accepted the well-judged advice with alacrity, and his *Homs* and *Jagyas* were resumed, which forced Vishnu to come down personally in the form of an old carpenter to accomplish what was wanted.

"'Wilt thou work out the wood, sayest thou?'

"'Yes, king, if you will allow me.'

"'But you are too old. Younger men have tried their strength on the block in vain.'

"'I was sent for, and have come, and surely I shall be able to do what I have come for. Know you not, O, king, that Providence works impossibilities by the weakest hands?'

"'You have pronounced a wholesome truth, old man, and for that saying's sake I shall intrust the work to you, and if you can shape the wood tastefully I shall reward you even beyond your highest expectations.'

"The old man worked with a willing hand, and the three beautiful figures of Jagganáth, Balarám, and Subadhrá were quickly made, and great was the pleasure of the king when he heard of the carpenter's success.

"'Fetch me the artist now,' said he, 'and I will clothe him in purple and gold, and he shall have a seat on my right hand, for he has satisfied the dearest wishes of my heart.'

"But the carpenter was no longer to be found; he had vanished the moment his work was completed, vanished together with his implements.

"There was surprise on every face now, and most of all on that of the king, when, lo! a voice was heard to speak out to him from heaven.

"'O, blessed king! thou hast opened the gate of salvation to all mankind. Ask what boon you want, and it will be granted to thee.'

"'Be it this then,' said the devout worshipper, 'that there be no second birth for me! Let Thy servant escape the vicissitudes of transmigration for ever, since he has seen Thy salvation!'

"'The boon asked for is granted,' answered the same voice from heaven, 'not only to thee, but to all who shall come to the same spot, to worship the same three deities, with the same singleness of heart that you have shown;' and for more than thirty thousand years have people from all parts of the world poured to this place to secure the promised immunity."

The story was very interesting and instructive, and prepared its hearers fully for the devotion they had come so far to render.

The next day was the day of the Car festival, and Monohur and the Sunyási got up very early therefore to visit the temple, to worship the symbols of their salvation before they were removed for being placed in their cars. The worshippers were both of them devout Hindus, albeit, one of them had passed at one time for a Mahomedan and a Ferázee, and they approached the idols with the greatest enthusiasm and joy; and all the rites enjoined by the Shástras, which were indicated to them by the Pándá, were gone through with reverential precision.

"Now is the last and crowning desire of my heart fulfilled, and my errand in this world accomplished!" exclaimed the Sunyási, in the fulness of his heart; "I am quite ready to lay down my life now, for my work is ended!"

"This is heaven surely, to see God face to face, as we see Him before us!" responded Monohur, with equal fervour and devotion.

At this moment a band of Pándás rushed suddenly

towards the idols to carry them off to the cars, and the shouts of "*Jai* Jagganáth!" "Jagganáth *ke jai!*" were reiterated and prolonged with such deafening roar both from within the temple and from the outside of it that they could be heard from a great distance—even from a distance of three or four miles. The scene now was intensely exciting, though all that was clearly visible, even to the foremost beholders, consisted only of the overwhelming offerings of flowers to the idols on their being seated on their cars, and the by no means inconsiderable offerings of coins to the priests who stood in charge of them. The crowd was immense, and began to increase more and more every moment; but there was never an unkind word or angry look exchanged between the myriads who composed it, though they trod on each other's toes so frequently and mercilessly. Everyone tried his best to have a pull at the cords by which the cars were to be drawn, but it was a great misfortune to many that the tackles were too far away from them to get at. It was scarcely understood generally, except by hearsay, whether the cars were drawn at all or not.

"Did the cars move perceptibly?" asked an old woman of Monohur, who had been in the thickest of the crowd.

"Yes, but a few cubits length only."

"Why were they not drawn further?"

"To prevent deaths by accident, for several persons had laid themselves down purposely near to the wheels to get crushed under them."

"Ah, that must be the sweetest way to heaven!" exclaimed the woman devoutly. "Would I could get in further to throw myself under the wheels!"

"Is such immolation pleasing to the deity, Bábájee?"

asked Monohur, turning round to the Sunyási with a woeful face.

"I do not believe so, my son, though the Pándás maintain that it is."

"Must not some further attempts be made to draw the cars again to-day, after removing the deluded devotees from the places where they have managed to prostrate themselves?"

"No, not to-day, I am told. But they must be taken to the Gandichá Mandir, before the *Poonar Játrá*, and better arrangements for the forward movement will certainly have to be made by to-morrow or the day after."

"O, Bábájee, should we not stay here a few days then to witness the end of the festival?"

"No, my son, we have no time for that; nor is it at all necessary that we should so delay ourselves. We have had a full sight of 'Báhmana in his car,' which is all that is required for the purposes of salvation; and have had a pull at the cords besides, which is the utmost felicity that a longer stay here could give us. There is pressing business for us elsewhere, and we must on no account lag longer at this spot if we can help it."

While thus speaking to each other Monohur and the Sunyási were both endeavouring assiduously to extricate themselves from the crowd, and eventually succeeded in doing so after the lapse of about half-an-hour. Their hearts were still full of the thoughts which the divine presence had called forth, and of the "peace on earth" and "good-will to all" which is the synopsis of every religion; and they were yet loath to depart from the temple-grounds, the more so that the dictum had already gone forth that that was to be their last day there.

At this juncture their attention was drawn and their

steps directed towards a nook of the court which represented the love-bower of Subadhrá, where a number of Ooryáh girls were dancing, and singing the love-songs of the gods to the sound of a lute which was being played upon by one of themselves. They were only children of ten and eleven years, who, too young to get into the crowd, were thus enjoying themselves apart from all others; and, being all of them more or less lovely, they aptly represented the fairies of the grove. Their naked arms and feet glittered with ornaments of silver and gold, which made a tinkling sound as they danced that blended charmingly with the music of the lute. Monohur gazed intently at them, and heaved a deep sigh as the fay of Nárkelberiáh came back to his mind. But the thought was dispelled as quickly as it came. There was a third man dodging the footsteps of the pilgrims as their very shadow, and Monohur almost started back on seeing him. This made the Sunyási also turn round to him, and, finding that it was the Gháttál Báboo again, he addressed him almost in an angry tone.

"What is it that you still want with us? Have I not given you our answer already?"

"The answer was delivered to those who sent me, and I am bid to tell you again that you are urgently waited for."

"How could you have gone to Bánpore and returned thence in so short a time, friend?"

"O, the means were given to me, and are at your disposal at this moment, if you will avail of them, for life and death are in our speed."

"Then speed back to your employers yourself, and say that we come. But it will not suit us to go with you."

The man said nothing in reply, and when the Sunyási raised his eyes again towards him he was gone!

"Need I ask what this means, Bábájee?" exclaimed Monohur, his heart beating rapidly, and fully anticipating his companion's reply.

"It means that the mine is ready, my son, and that we must hasten to set fire to it."

CHAPTER XXIV.

THE CHILKÁ LAKE, AND THE STORY OF THE SERPENT'S ROCK.

"What is that billet there, Bábájee, that you are reading so intently?"

"A missive from the camp, my son. We are asked to report ourselves at Burkowl, which stands on the western bank of the Chilká Lake, which you have often so eagerly wished to visit."

"O, how glad I shall be surely! And you will take me to all the little rock-islands on the lake that I have heard you speak of?"

"I don't know whether we shall have time to visit *all* of them; perhaps not. But we shall certainly see a good many of them, and there are shrines on some at which I am anxious to perform my devotions."

"Agreed!" said Monohur. "Let us hasten then towards the trysting-place;" and his heart became as glad as that of a butterfly at the prospect he was permitted to muse upon.

The journey was begun the next morning, and the country they passed through was very fair and pleasing. But the curiosity of Monohur had now been sharply excited, and, though he frequently looked round on the meadows with rapture, he talked a great deal more than ever, always asking for information on all points connected with the lake.

THE CHILKÁ LAKE, ETC.

"Do not be angry with me, Bábájee, but I would fain know all about the Chilká beforehand, if you will humour me;" and the Sunyási was obliged to communicate as much as he knew of it himself, which was not very much to be sure.

"What is the distance of the lake from this place? How long will it take us to reach it?"

"About two days at most, going by easy stages. The distance of its upper extremity from this point is not more than eight *kos* or so."

"And then we shall be on the lake at once?"

"Right upon it, my son."

We may as well describe the lake ourselves, which will materially shorten the account the Sunyási gave of it.

The Chilká is a shallow inland sea, lying some fifteen or sixteen miles to the south-west of Pooree, and is separated from the ocean by a long sandy ridge nearly two hundred yards wide. It is about forty miles in length, and has a width varying from five to twenty miles. Throughout its entire extent it is more or less shallow, the depth varying from three to six feet in low water, and from five and a half to ten feet in high water; and it has a single narrow mouth for its outlet into the Bay of Bengal. In the hot months its supply of water is derived entirely from the Bay, and is necessarily brackish. But in the rains the rivers come pouring into the basin, and, by expelling the salt water from it, turn it into a fresh-water lake.

The scenery around the lake is very varied, the north of it being a level country, and having sedgy banks, while on the west side it is walled in by lofty mountains, in some places ascending perpendicularly, and in others thrusting out gigantic arms or projections of rock into the water. The southern boundary is made of hills, which form the natural frontier of Orissá in that direction. Where the hill-ranges abound the lake is dotted with rocky islands, on some of which the ruins of a few ancient edifices are yet to be seen. Most of these buildings were temples of Mahádeva in the past, but have for several centuries been appropriated to the worship of Jagganáth, Balarám, and Subadhrá. The fact is that all the temples in Orissá, erected by the princes of the Kesari Bangsa, were originally dedicated to the worship of Mahádeva, and only came afterwards to be assigned to the worship of Vishnu on the elevation of the Gungá Bangsa to the throne. The most sacred shrine on the lake, however, is one consecrated to neither Siva nor Vishnu, but to Nág Panchánan, or the Serpent Deity; and this was the place that the Sunyási was especially anxious to visit. We shall leave it to him, therefore, to give the history of the shrine.

"We have come to the Chilká at last," exclaimed Monohur, as he caught the first glimpse of it on the second day, "and there is certainly a wild kind of beauty in its loveliness, notwithstanding that it looks so still."

The lake was as smooth and level almost as a billiard-table, not the slightest ripple being seen on its surface at this time.

"We have certainly come to it in very quiet weather," replied the Sunyási; "but it may not preserve this mood long, for it does not take much time here for the winds to arise and get angry."

"Ah, I am sure the lake will be kind enough to remain undisturbed while we are on it, if only to oblige me," said Monohur smilingly; "and see, Bábájee, there is a boat coming towards us already, as if intending to take us up into it."

"Your eyes are very good, indeed, Monohur. The people are all quite on the alert here I see, for there is no mistake but that the boat is meant for us."

"I trust, Bábájee, we proceed in ease, visiting all the islands we may pass by?"

"We shall do that certainly, nor be long delayed on that account, the islands being small bits of rock merely. But we must proceed carefully, passing by unguarded posts, and avoiding the salt-chowkeys, of which there are a good many here."

They entered the boat the moment it touched the shore, and were rowed over swiftly and cautiously, the *Mánjee* giving his orders with a calm energy that showed clearly how alive he was to the dangers of the duty he had undertaken.

"Well rowed, my children!" exclaimed the Sunyási; "we are speeding very swiftly in the absence of a breeze. Now take care that you do not omit to touch all the islands on which there are relics to worship;" and Monohur's wish was fully gratified, as almost all the islands they passed by were visited.

"Your skill in doubling the rocks was great," observed the Sunyási, addressing the Mánjee with a satisfied air. "Do you belong to this place by birth?"

"No, I am from Bengal, from the banks of the Megná, and have been brought hither by your own man, the Báboo from Gháttál."

"Ha! Is that it? How then have you been able to master the currents of the lake so quickly, when, as I have been told, they cross and recross in a most hazardous way? You seem to be quite at home in every part of the lake."

"O, sir," answered the Mánjee, "a man who has to live by his own exertions must either be at home everywhere, or be nothing at all at any place."

"You speak truly, my son," said the Sunyási, "but still is it very difficult to acquire such dexterity as you have shown when not to the manner born. Whither are we drifting now?"

"To the Serpent's Rock. Is not that the last of the islands you wished to visit?"

"It is; and I am very thankful to you for having remembered my requests so faithfully."

The boatman and the Sunyási were well pleased with each other, and the shrine of Nág Panchánan was quickly reached. It was found to be in a very decayed condition; but Bissonáth knew of its sanctity, and tarried in it longer than elsewhere over his devotions. The god worshipped was represented by a black stone serpent of enormous size; and Monohur looked at it with unfeigned surprise.

"This is the most curious representation of the Deity I have ever seen, Bábájee," he exclaimed, addressing his companion the moment his devotions were over, "and you certainly must know some legend or other about it?"

"Ah, I understand; you want me to relate the story to you, and I have no objection to do so, since we have no other work to engage us here at present.

"Many, many hundred years ago, when the rivers had just purified the lake, an elderly woman went to fetch water from it, accompanied by a daughter seven years old. The child fell into the lake, and rolled down into a depth from which the woman was unable to extricate her. The mother wept loudly and bitterly, and called on all the gods to save her offspring, when out came an enormous serpent from the bottom of the lake.

"'If I can save the girl from the water,' said the serpent, 'wilt thou give her in marriage to me?'

"The mother said—'Ay,' little dreaming that a serpent would ever insist on the completion of such a promise.

"The serpent thereupon dived back into the bottom and brought out the child.

"'O, mother,' said the girl, 'the serpent was telling me that you have betrothed me to him. How could you do that?'

"'Foolish girl, it was only jestingly proposed and agreed to. What can a serpent want to marry you for?'

"Years went by, and the girl grew up, and many men sought her hand, for she was very pretty to look at. But, just when the mother was about to select a proper husband for her, out came the serpent from the bed of the lake and entered her hut.

"Both the mother and her daughter were terribly frightened.

"'Why do you look so afeard? I come only to claim my wife.'

"'Your wife?'

"'Yes, mine. Did you not promise her to me?'

"The mother hung down her head without being able to give a distinct reply; but she felt that the promise had to be fulfilled, and the girl was married to the serpent.

"'But my child cannot live under the water with you,' said she in an expostulating tone to her son-in-law.

"'Ah, that is not necessary,' answered the serpent. 'She can remain with you, as now, and I shall visit her here;' and the serpent came nightly to his wife, transforming himself into a man as long as he remained with her.

"'Well, how do you like your husband, child?'

"'Very well, surely,' was the daughter's reply; and she explained to her astonished parent that in bed he always assumed the form of a man.

"'Why don't you try to find out his secret then? He is perhaps a god or other supernatural being in disguise.'

"The girl promised to do so, and on the very next night the serpent found his little wife sulky and silent when he came to her.

"'Why, what is the cause of this mood, my love? What are you distempered for?'

"'I am your wife, and you say you love me; why then do you conceal anything from me? To this moment you have not told me who you really are. You show yourself as a serpent and a man by turns. There must be some mystery in that. Why should I not know what it is?'

"The serpent was not well pleased that his wife should have become curious about his appearance so soon. But he loved her intensely, and was unwilling to speak unkindly to her.

"'If there be a mystery in my life,' said he, 'why should you be so anxious to know it when it may possibly grieve you to do so, or fill your mind with fears? It may be that I have some very important secrets to keep, which you will not probably be able to cherish as carefully. Is it not enough that you know that I am a man in reality, and that I love you tenderly?'

"'No; how can that be enough to one who loves you more than she loves her own self? If you have any great secrets to keep, though you may not share them with others, you ought surely to share them with me; and I am certain that I shall be able to preserve them quite as carefully as you do. What is not comfortable to me is to suspect that I have not your whole heart, that I do not even know who you really are; and it is particularly painful to me to be twitted by everyone as a serpent's wife, when in reality I am no such thing at all.'

"'Ah, that name you must bear for the present, for my sake, my love. I will not hide from you that I am really a man, as you see me now, and a prince of the Nágá race; but the time has not come for either you or me to reveal it to the world. I have a great enemy in Vikramáditya, the King of Oujein, who is *Sakádwisha*, or the foe of our race, and I am obliged to hide myself from him in this disguise, which a god has permitted me to assume. But the day of vengeance is coming, and people will not twit you long as a serpent's wife. And now you must love me very dearly, for you know the great secret that I had hitherto kept wholly to myself.'

"The wife was satisfied, and her mother also; and the Nágá's secret was well kept between them. A few years later Vikramáditya was defeated and killed by Saliváhana, after which the serpent's wife had the satisfaction of being widely recognised as the conqueror's queen. Another and more generally accepted account, however, makes Saliváhana the son of the marriage between the serpent and the girl, the former being taken for the god Nág Pancháuan, to whom this shrine has ever since been dedicated."

CHAPTER XXV.

THE NEW REBELLION.

BÁNPORE is the extremest southern pergunnáh of Pooree, and is situated on the western side of the Chilká lake. It consists of two large fertile valleys, and is bounded on three sides by hills and jungle, and on the fourth by the lake, and forms part of the estate of Khoordáh, the Zemindár of which is the hereditary custodian of Jagganáth. The pergunnáh was divided in the past into *Seemás*, or *Mahals*, to which were attached *Dulbehrás*, or *páik* leaders, holding from sixty to one hundred beegáhs of jyghere land; *Bissoees*, or sub-leaders, holding from forty to eighty beegáhs of land; *Náiks*, or village headmen, holding from ten to twenty beegáhs of land; and *Páiks*, who held smaller jygheres at one time, but to whom such allotments came afterwards to be refused, which made them disaffected. The people throughout this part of the country and the contiguous districts had at all times been unfriendly to the British *Ráj*, and there had been several previous risings in Goomsur and Khoordáh, of which one in 1817 was the most violent.

The chief concocters of the rebellion of 1836, to which we now refer, were three persons, named Lochun Bissoee, the son of a rebel pardoned in 1817; Pánchoo Náik, a wealthy middleman of Rorung; and Kirtibás Pátsáhánee, the *dulbehrá* of a decayed castle named

Gurh Arung, who was persuaded by the first and the second to join their cause. Besides these there were some factious Zemindárs and their hirelings from Bengal, who had come over especially to plan the revolt; and it was by their advice that the wild Ooryáh races were mainly guided.

The castle of Arung stood in the centre of a cluster of cliffs, at a short distance inland from the borders of the Chilká lake. It had a half-ruined and singular appearance, the singularity being principally attributable to the construction of the building in parts and at different periods, without any attention to architectural uniformity. At the foot of the castle was a large table-rock which was selected as the site for a general meeting just before the revolt broke out. All the disaffected Khonds and *páiks* of Arung and the surrounding country were summoned to muster here with their arms, and did so with alacrity; and the chiefs we have named moved backwards and forwards among them to incite them to action, encouraging the impassive and extolling the bold.

"The men are all in excellent spirits," said Kirtibás, speaking to Pánchoo, who was distinguished by a bow in his hand decked with rattles of gold. "You had better take advantage of their temper and get yourself proclaimed as their king."

"That is a post of honour indeed," replied Pánchoo, "but of danger also, and might well make one pause before committing himself."

"You must not shrink from the danger though," said Lochun. "We are playing for a high stake, and must play out the game as bravely as we may."

"Why should not Kirtibás or you then accept the royal post?" asked Pánchoo.

"Because the people will not have us, and we have no money to support the dignity of the office."

"There must be no hesitation now," observed the Gháttál Báboo, "or the expedition will come to an end before it has started."

"There is no hesitation, sir," answered Pánchoo proudly. "Deliberation is not hesitation, and it is always right to appreciate the danger we embrace. I have made up my mind now, and you may announce to the people that I have assumed the *Ráj* of Bánpore under the royal name of Surn Sing, and that I require their assistance to put down the British power."

The announcement was made, and was received with tremendous cheering; and a rebel force of about four hundred men was mustered at once on the spot, and began to increase hourly, till by the evening of the second day it was nearly doubled. Among the chiefs who came forward were several of the old Goomsur rebels, and at their suggestion the insurgents proceeded at once to Bánpore to take possession of the place.

"Wherefore to Bánpore?" asked a *dulbherá* named Prithá. "Is not the British power rather strongly posted there at this moment?"

"O, no!" said the Gháttál Báboo. "The sepoys and burkundauzes there, taken together, do not exceed some eighty or a hundred men. But they have firearms with them."

"So have we," said Lochun. "Let us go and attack the Police thánnáh to commence with."

"Forward then to Bánpore!" cried Pánchoo; and they marched pell-mell, uphill and downhill, and through cane-brakes and jungles, to get to it.

The thánnáh at Bánpore was a little fortified place,

rather well situated on an elevated platform. Its walls were of no strength to speak of, but there was a broad and deep ditch beyond them, which had to be crossed, and the crossing was disputed by the thánnáh guard, who turned out in numbers to receive their assailants.

"Bring out your muskets," said the Dárogá to his men, "and shoot at the knaves bravely!" and three shots were fired by the Dárogá himself, which forced the Khonds and *páiks* to fall back at first in some confusion.

The repulse, however, was only a momentary one. The sepoys under the Dárogá were raw recruits merely, and utterly unskilled in the use of the muskets they held in their hands; and their firing was so badly aimed that the insurgents were easily reassured by their chiefs to return to the charge.

"Press on! Press on!" shouted Kirtibás, rushing himself at the same time into the thickest of the fight, and dealing lusty strokes with his battle-axe on every side; and Pánchoo and Lochun bringing up their best-trained soldiers to his support, the ditch was soon crossed, and the thánnáh captured, the guard, with the Dárogá at their head, betaking to their heels.

"The day is ours, friends!" cried Pánchoo, exultingly. "Shoot at the mean-spirited hirelings while they are running for their lives."

"Let us rather push up our success in other directions," said Lochun, "that the whole country may submit to us simultaneously;" and they followed up their advantage accordingly for two whole days and nights. As there were no opponents, however, to fight with, their strength was mainly exercised in the destruction of houses and other property; and, after the thánnáh and salt-chowkey premises were burnt down, they fell on the houses of the people and of the foreign residents of the place, and destroyed them without pity or remorse. They also extorted large sums of money from the merchants to make up the funds required for prosecuting the war; and their physical strength was at the same time largely augmented by the *budmáshes* of the country joining them in hopes of plunder.

"We had better proceed to Burkowl now," said Pánchoo, "which will place a wider extent of country under our command;" and this being generally agreed to they went thither in state, the Rájáh being conveyed in a *pálki* which had been procured for him, while Kirtibás and Lochun accompanied him on horseback, and the rest of the chieftains on foot. The bustle and excitement throughout the march was great, and the reception at Burkowl was as warm as could have been anticipated. A large additional force of *páiks* joined them at this place; and, flush of money and men, the insurgent cause was looking very hopeful at this time.

"Well, Sunyási, give us your *ásirvád*," said Pánchoo, the moment he saw him. "You have come very late to join us."

"Don't say that, Rájáh, or you will make us truly sorrowful. The enterprise has only just commenced; nor have we been idle here either, for all the men who are joining you at this moment are of our raising."

"O, we knew of your arrival betimes," remarked the Rájáh, "and were watching what you were doing. Kharga Báhádoor's reputation as a soldier has travelled before him, and he should have the lead of the troops you have raised."

This was cheerfully agreed to, and very great was the assistance rendered to the general cause both by Kharga

Báhádoor and his companion. But their efforts were spent in petty skirmishes only. No real opposition on behalf of the Government was ever attempted at Burkowl and the surrounding country; and it was torture alike to Kharga Báhádoor and the Sunyási to see the strength of their little army wasted in acts of mischief and oppression. All the bungalows of the Salt Department were burnt to the ground, to which the Sunyási did not especially object, his antipathy against the Government being deep-rooted; but, when the village non-combatants in Burkowl, Munrájpore, Chárpádán, and other places were wantonly attacked, he strongly protested against the outrage, and was warmly backed up by Kharga Báhádoor.

"This will never do," said both of them together. "If we act like vultures and cormorants, swooping down upon everyone indiscriminately, the whole country will be rising up against us to befriend the English power."

"Let them do so then," said Kirtibás, "and we shall put down the country and the English power together. Woe be to him who attempts to quench our ardour, or to misdirect its operation, at this moment."

"Would I had understood these savages aright," murmured the Sunyási, regretfully; "they do not seem to be fit for the work they have undertaken. This is a mere renewal of the Ferázee game played out from Nárkelberiáh, and every outrage thus committed is sure to hurry on the day of retribution."

There was, however, no time now for reproaches and regrets. The fighting went on as the *páik* chiefs wished it, and opposition, where offered, was effectually put down. The despoiled inhabitants of the country saw the destruction of their effects in blank dismay, and for some time sought only for any possible means of escape.

Despairing of this they began to become venturesome; but they still relied more on their brains than on their arms for relief.

"O, Rájáh, you have become the ruler of our country, and should not hunt down your own subjects in this fashion," said a village spokesman, addressing Pánchoo. "We can help you both with men and money if you will only spare us our homesteads."

"Where be your men and money then?" said Lochun, speaking on behalf of Pánchoo. "Why are they not forthcoming at once?"

"They are not here, chiefs, but at Bheempore. We thought you would wish to risk an attack on Pooree, which alone can give you a decisive advantage over the English, and have sent forward our warriors to wait for you on the road, to join you promptly as you march up."

"Let us press on to Pooree then," said Lochun. "There is no need for trifling away our time in this place further."

"You must not be so eager as that, though," said the Sunyási. "The Government forces are now assembling at Taughy, and we should not go forward to meet them till we are sure of our allies."

"We are perfectly sure of them," said Pánchoo. "There is no reason whatever to doubt that they are well attached to the good cause."

"But I do suspect them," said the Sunyási, "and will be so bold as to say so. It looks as if they have laid a trap for us, to ensnare us."

"Ha! art thou afeard, Sunyási?" cried Lochun grimly, looking him straight in the face. "If not, why this unseemly agitation when there is so little occasion for it?"

"I have fought before, chief," replied the Sunyási,

"and boldly too, though I am so much older and weaker than you are; and I hope to fight again, even where you will fight yourself. But this I will say, for the occasion demands of me to do so, that that chief is not worthy of command who thinks counsel a proof of cowardice."

"No quarrel among friends and brethren here," shouted Kirtibás; "no excitement of any sort till we are baited against the enemy. Forward! forward! The Rájáh desires every warrior to push on."

"But we are at the crisis of our fate," said Kharga Báhádoor, "and if we are betrayed by this hurried movement we shall be hopelessly undone."

"No, no," said Kirtibás, "both you and the Sunyási are much too suspicious, as all Bengalis are. Let us press on to Bheempore, and, with the additional men awaiting us there, we shall have but to stretch forth our arms to secure the possession of Pooree."

They did move on to Bheempore, and, as had been feared by the Sunyási, fell into the snare laid for them, being inclosed all at once by a large body of men who had been lying in wait for them there. Pánchoo and Kirtibás were the first to be captured; but Lochun fell fighting bravely, resisting his assailants to the last.

"Down with them!" cried he. "Down with the fiends incarnate who have betrayed us! I at least will kill as many of the cowards as I can. Let those who wish to do likewise follow me."

Saying this he rushed forward to attack the human girdle that encompassed them, for he was a bold man and true, and had never known a fear; and he was closely followed by the Sunyási and Kharga Báhádoor.

"Strike, and strike deep, Kharga Báhádoor. I am wounded and dying, and can do no more. O, Sunyási!

excuse me my intemperate words, and avenge my death if you can."

The struggle was now hopeless, from the mass of fresh enemies that came against them from all sides; and, seeing that it was useless to prolong it, the Sunyási broke through the multitude around him, dragging Kharga Báhádoor with him.

"Come away, Kharga Báhádoor, come away. We can be of no further service here, and have really not a moment now to lose;" and they had barely time to escape from the spot, while most of the other chiefs who lingered there were captured, at the same time that word was sent to the British authorities to come over and take charge of the prisoners.

"This game too is lost," said the Sunyási to his companion in flight, "and the avengers of blood will be after us once more. We had better resume our old names again, and fly."

"Is there any way out of this untoward place?"

"We must find one, my son, and may as well start for the forest-country through Nyágurh."

When the English forces came down to Bheempore the principal rebels had all been arrested by the people, and no difficulty was experienced in tracing up and capturing their aiders and abettors. In all ninety-two persons were brought to trial and punished, the Rájáh and Kirtibás, with some old Goomsur rebels, being transported for life, while the subordinate chiefs were sentenced to various terms of imprisonment. The *paiks*, or ryots, were allowed to settle down as peaceful inhabitants, which put out the last embers of the rebellion; and the people of Bheempore were handsomely rewarded for the loyalty they had displayed.

CHAPTER XXVI.

THE BEDIYÁ DOMES.

"WE must have cleared a good distance, Bábájee, in five days," said Monohur, after the lapse of that interval since their departure from Bheempore. "Am I wrong in my reckoning in thinking that we are safe from pursuit by this time?"

"Well, I am not quite sure of that yet," replied the Sunyási, "and dare not think that we shall be altogether out of danger till we are able to overtake the encampment of the Bediyá Domes, located somewhere further in the forest."

"But how do you make out that there is such an encampment anywhere in this place?"

"By seeing Bediyá Domes every now and then passing and repassing us. Have you not observed them?"

"Yes; and you think they have an encampment hard by?"

"I am sure of it. They do not move about the country as isolated passengers."

"And do you think we shall be secure from pursuit among them?"

"If they admit us into their company, which, however, is very doubtful. They do not care to mix with other people; nor are other people very anxious to have anything to do with them. They are pilferers and dacoits by profession, and have very disgusting habits besides; but once with them we would be safe from the pursuit of the police, for the police are afraid to approach them."

" Why so ? "

" Because the men use their knives very freely on the smallest provocation, and the women bespatter their assailants not only with abuse, but with filth of every kind."

" How should we prevail on them then to allow us to take up our quarters with them ? "

" Ah, that must be left to the chapter of accidents. We cannot prearrange for that."

The supposition of the Sunyási was correct, for it was soon found that the Bediyá Domes had encamped in the forest half-way between Nyágurh and Duspullá, and it was about mid-day when our fugitives overtook them there. They did not, however, come forward at once to join them; it was absolutely necessary that they should keep away from them at a distance, till they could find some likely plea to introduce themselves.

" I fear I am no match for the craft of these slippery fellows," said the Sunyási to himself, almost losing hope from delay. " How to make a favourable impression on them, such as would induce them to extend their protection to us, I really cannot conceive."

Just at that moment they heard an uproar in the encampment, caused by a young vagrant having wounded his brother's wife with a hatchet. This family had a shed of their own in the encampment where they lived and messed, and here the girl had been quarrelling with her mother-in-law, when her brother-in-law came in.

" What are you quarrelling with mother for ? "

" What is that to you, you brute ? "

"Darest thou to abuse me, vixen? And won't I break your head for it?"

"Will you? Take this then to begin with;" and she gave him two smart blows with the broom, with which she was sweeping the ground.

The young man, greatly angered, took up his axe, which was at hand, and struck his assailant on the right shoulder, which felled her to the ground.

Monohur was the first to rush in to assist the girl, but was sharply repulsed by her, severely hurt as she was.

"Who are you? And why do you interfere between us?"

"You are hurt; let me bandage the wound, or you will lose much blood."

"But why should it concern you whether I am hurt or not? Is it not my own husband's brother who has struck me?"

"He had no right to strike you, surely?"

"Of course he had. My husband strikes me every day, and why should not his brother strike me occasionally now and then? It is you who have no business with us, or to be amongst us at all;" and this appeared also to be the opinion of the Bediyás generally, who looked with no kindly feelings towards Monohur.

It was now that the Sunyási came to the fore.

"I am a doctor," said he, "and this young man," pointing to Monohur, "is my pupil. We have no occasion to intrude upon you, indeed, as the girl has properly observed; but, if you will allow us, we shall be glad to heal the rather distressing hurt she has received."

"If you can do that you are welcome," said the brother-in-law of the wounded woman, who was already sorry for what he had done; and this saying being approved by a nod from the elders of the tribe, the Sunyási moved forward to exhibit his knowledge of pharmacy.

"We shall try our best by all means," said he, and, taking the girl by the hand, he went through his task with an easy confidence that made everyone expectant and hopeful.

The wound was bandaged with a piece of thin cloth which was ordered to be kept wet, while the doctor muttered charms to his patient in a sing-song tone. In the meantime Monohur was despatched to collect some wild herbs which were named to him, and, these being found, their juice was squeezed out and the wet cloth saturated with it. The wound was superficial, though it had bled much, and the vegetable juice closed it in a short time to a considerable extent, at the same time that the pain was also much allayed; and the Sunyási and Monohur made good their quarters among the Bediyás on the force of this introduction.

"If you have any articles of value with you," said the girl to her doctor, "you had better trust them with me, or otherwise you will surely miss them before the night is over;" and the Sunyási, who fully understood the significance of the advice, gave up his purse to her keeping.

The contents of the bag were searchingly examined by the young woman.

"Why, you are poorer than I imagined," said she at last to the Sunyási. "I took you for people well to do in life. Are you really so penniless as this purse indicates?"

"At present, yes," answered the Sunyási. "The luck has gone against us in all our speculations, and we are exactly in the condition you find us in."

"Ah, that is not my business, but yours. I asked only to be certain that you kept back no part of your money with you, for that, you must understand, may be very dangerous to you."

"I understand it fully, my child," said the Sunyási. "We have nothing with us now but our clothes."

The girl nodded her belief in what he said, hid the purse under her garment, and strode away.

"Will she return the purse to us, Bábújee, do you think?"

"She may. If she does not we shall not be greater losers than if we had attempted to keep it with us, for, in the latter case, we would have run the double risk of being robbed and of having our throats cut in the bargain."

Their doubts respecting the girl's honesty were, however, unfounded. She was very faithfully disposed towards them, and grateful for the service they had rendered her; and she did all in her power to make their stay with the tribe as comfortable as possible. A canvas-covered hut was assigned to them, in case they wished to make use of it; and all their other wants were met to the extent their circumstances required.

"All our hopes are blasted, Bábújee," said Monohur to the Sunyási, despondingly, as they sat by each other before their hut, as the guests of a vagrant tribe. "My *penchant* for a soldier's life has brought nothing but disappointment to me."

"The most successful life, my son, is only a tissue of disappointments. We must try to rise superior to them."

"What for? Have you any especial object yet in view for me? Are there any more enterprises to undertake, any laurels yet to gain?"

"Possibly, yes; probably, not. But we must go on steadily as if there were, and, if you have the best species of courage in you—patience—you may yet fight your way to success."

"Ah, you speak, Bábájee, as if you expect another call from the Gháttál Báboo soon. Do you?"

"No; I am not aware that there is any game now on foot anywhere in which you or I could take part; nor am I very certain that the Gháttál Báboo has been able to effect his escape from Bheempore, though I wish heartily that he may have done so."

"I do not anticipate otherwise," said Monohur. "He has hitherto succeeded in eluding all traps and dangers, and has always been wandering over the country in what manner he chose; and, judging from our own escape, there seems to be no reason to suppose that he should have failed in what we were able to achieve. But who is the man, Bábájee? He carries a peculiar expression about him; a face with a story in it, if I may say so. Does he not?"

The Sunyási nodded assent, and said—"Yes, there is a story connected with the man, though I don't know that you would care to listen to it, for it has not much of novelty in it."

"O, that does not matter, Bábájee. If it does not involve any betrayal of secrets or confidences I would certainly wish to hear the account, for I cannot get the thought of the Báboo out of my mind."

"Very good then; I shall give you the main points of his history as briefly as I can.

"The Gháttál Báboo is a relative of the Rájáhs of Gháttál, whom you may have heard of, but is not owned by them as such. The family lived originally at Duttopookur, near Baraset, where they were at one time in great power. It was represented by two brothers, named Rádhá Mohun and Bipprodáss, at the time that Áli Verdy Khán was Nawáb of Moorshedábád. The brothers quarrelled for a trifle—the possession of a *Debálaya*— which was separately claimed by each—and, Rádhá Mohun retaining it forcibly, Bipprodáss went over to Áli Verdy, and made some very secret revelations to him which tantalised him. The annual profits of the zemindáry, he said, exceeded fifty times the kházáná that was paid to the Nawáb; and, on the Nawáb proceeding to inquire into this point, Rádhá Mohun fled to evade the investigation. Áli Verdy thereupon seized all his property, and carried off his women; but, as Rádhá Mohun was a better administrator than Bipprodáss, he was eventually recalled and restored into favour. Rádhá Mohun continued his residence thenceforth at Gháttál, the place to which he had fled, and in course of time the family property at Duttopookur was lost. The Gháttál Báboo represents Bipprodáss's branch of the family. He went to Gháttál in the hope of ingratiating himself with his rich relatives there, but they refused to have anything to do with him for his extraordinary ways; and he has been a wanderer ever since in search of that good fortune which so many seek for, and so few are able to find."

"Poor man! I feel very much for him; perhaps the more so that my *Adaysto* seems to be very akin to his, and our chances of eventual good fortune nearly equal in degree."

"And yet it may be that both he and you may alike meet with good fortune in the end, my son. I shall tell you a story of *Adaysto* that I heard many years ago.

It will, at least, help us to while away a half-hour or so of idleness here."

"Say on then, by all means, and I shall give you as patient a hearing as your tale may deserve. I trust it may have the effect of lulling me to sleep."

The reader will find the story in the next chapter, which he may read through or skip over as he likes.

CHAPTER XXVII.

ADAYSTO.

It is wasting words to say that the Sunyási was fond of telling tales, and had a happy manner of doing so, and that Monohur was equally fond of hearing them, particularly when they were related by his companion.

"There were two brothers," said the Sunyási, "one of whom was rich and the other poor, and they lived side by side of each other, one in extreme affluence, the other in extreme poverty, without the latter asking for help, or the former offering it to him.

"Said the wife of the poor man to her husband: 'Why don't you go to your rich brother and ask him to assist you? Don't you see that even his servants fare better than we do?'

"'Ah, silly wife,' said the poor man, 'the rich have no poor relations. There is a gulf between me and my brother which cannot be crossed. If I go to him he will perhaps disdain to remember that he has, or ever had, a brother, and that would be an additional grief to us.'

"'Why not try him once before coming to such a conclusion? One should not hesitate to seek the aid of his own brother in distress as you do. If you were not ashamed to apply for his assistance I am sure he would not feel abashed to acknowledge the claim.'

"Well, the man went to his rich brother, if only to please his wife; and he went straight up to him, and bluntly spoke of his misfortunes. But the rich man met him with a contemptuous look, and would scarcely listen to him patiently; and the few words he said were cold and cutting as steel.

"'What I have, brother,' said he, 'I have earned myself. No one has helped me; I did not seek for the help of anyone. Had you worked as hard and lived as carefully as I did you too would have been equally successful. You need not waste your time here, for I have nothing whatever to give to you.'"

"Ah, I dare say," said Monohur, "that the Ghâttâl Bâboo received some similar rebuff from his Râjâh relatives before becoming the outcast he now is."

"Possibly he did. In the story that I was telling the poor brother raised his hand with an effort to wipe away the sweat which bathed his brow, and was barely able to stammer out a remonstrance.

"'What you say, brother,' said he, 'is not wholly applicable to me. I did work hard, very hard indeed, and lived most carefully also; but while fortune smiled on you she always showed me a frowning face.'

"'That is ever the excuse of the lazy and the improvident,' returned the rich man with a scornful smile. 'If you are really so unlucky there is the less reason for you to cross my threshold, since ill-luck is said to be infectious. Why don't you get away now? I have other business to attend to.'

"The poor brother turned round with a burning face, and groped his way out of the house without answering a word; but he was unable to return home at once, and slunk away towards the forest with tears in his eyes.

"'What are you crying for?' asked an old woman he met with.

"'Ah, you won't understand me. I am crying because I am so miserable.'

"'But why are you miserable?'

"'Because I am so poor. I have nothing at home to eat; and my wife and children there are starving.'

"'Why don't you work—work hard, and work late?'

"'I do; but my ill-fortune thwarts me.'

"'Then shake off your ill-fortune, man. Go, and do as I bid you. A few paces further on in the forest you will find an old and decayed tree. Break it down and take the wood home and sell it. It will give you food for the day at least, if it does not yield anything more.'

"'Thank you,' said the poor man; 'I shall do as you direct. Why, indeed, should I not be a wood-cutter to find food for my children?'

"He went up to the tree with greater alacrity than he had gone to his brother's house, and found it to be an old and withered trunk, but not very large to carry.

"'What am I to cut it with?' asked he of himself, as he remembered that he had no cutting instrument with him. 'But, never mind, I will break it down, and take it home bodily on my shoulders. It will certainly get me a few pyce for the expenses of the day.'

"He exerted himself to break down the tree, but it came up by the roots; and lo! there was a black polished stone beneath, with a ring attached to it to lift it by.

"'Ha! what can this mean?'

"He pulled up the stone by the ring, and went down to a vault below and found untold riches there—gold, pearls, and precious stones—and felt that his ill-fortune had dismounted from his shoulders, for they had suddenly grown lighter.

"'Good heavens! Whose can all this wealth be? Would I do right in taking away any portion of it, since it is lying unused and useless here?' asked he of himself.

"'Whose, but yours,' the riches before him seemed to reply. 'Your very own! Why do you stare at us in that witless way? Take us away with you from this place.' And he did take up as much of them as he could conveniently carry, and went home after replacing the stone where it had lain before, covering it up with the tree he had broken down.

"'Stop! stop!' cried a voice from the vault before the stone was fully replaced, 'you must not leave me behind you.'

"The poor man got alarmed, and closed the stone the more securely after him, hurrying home with what he had obtained. It was his ill-fortune that lay buried underneath the black stone.

"'We have enough now,' he whispered softly to his wife, 'to live upon in ease to the end of our days, and this should keep us in content.'

"'To be sure it should. But how have all these riches been obtained?'

"'You shall know all. I think an angel from heaven has given them to me;' and he narrated the story of his good fortune to her very faithfully, not omitting to speak of the debate he had in his mind before appropriating the discovered wealth, and how it was silenced.

"The poor man now became a rich man, and people wondered how it had happened. His brother in particular became very envious, for the once poor man was now the richer of the two.

"He came to his brother and asked him how he had managed to become so rich.

"'O, by following your advice, brother, by working hard and living carefully.'

"'Really?' answered the once richer brother incredulously. 'Nothing more than that? Surely you are not telling the true secret to me?'

"'Nay then, my brother, if you must fain know the truth, it is simply this: It is Heaven's will that I should be what I am, and not the result of any act of my own. It was Providence itself that directed me to what I have secured.'

"Getting no other answer from his brother the envious man went away in a huff, and, still wishing to know the secret, he set his wife to find it out from his brother's wife; and, as women will blab, the latter made a clean breast of everything she had heard herself, except about the strange voice in the vault, which she forgot to speak of.

"'Now we shall secure the rest of the riches easily,' said the envious brother to himself, 'and be the richer of the two again;' and he went into the forest, driving a bullock before him.

"He discovered the stone where his sister-in-law had described it to be, and opened it, and, laying upon his bullock all the treasure he found in the vault, was preparing to come away. At this moment he heard the mysterious voice crying out: 'Stop! stop! You must take me with you, to be sure.'

"'Who are you, then, and where are you? I cannot see you.'

"'It does not matter. You will feel me as soon as I am at your side, and I shall be a constant friend to you, and will never part company with you;' and he felt as if a blast of air waved over him, and finally settled on his shoulders.

"The wealth was brought home, and the envious man was now much, very much, richer than his unenvying brother; but somehow or other his expenses increased greatly from his becoming vicious in his habits, till he was ruined by the very riches he had obtained.

"The tables were now turned, and he had to go to his unenvying brother for help.

"'O, my brother, I come to beseech assistance from you in my need.'

"'Why, what has brought you down so low?'

"'My ill-fortune.'

"'Your ill-fortune! Ah, she has shifted her seat then from my shoulders to yours. I shall not send you away empty-handed from my door, my brother, as you did me from yours. But take care you do not leave your companion behind you when you go.'"

"I wish," exclaimed Monohur, "I could dismount my ill-fortune from my shoulders as easily, Bábájee, as the poor man in your story was able to fling off his; but mine seems to be too firmly seated to be so summarily dislodged."

"O," said the Sunyási, "our affairs shape their own course, and in good time even your ill-fortune will have to get down, whether she likes it or not."

"Let us hope that it may do so soon then," replied Monohur, "for I am drifting into despair."

It was late in the night when the tale was finished; but Monohur was still restless, and could not sleep.

What made him the more uneasy was a deep wailing voice that came from a Bediyá shed far at the end of the encampment.

"O, Bábájee! I am distressed and cannot sleep. Who is it that is crying so bitterly, and what is she crying for?"

"You need not heed the cry at all, Monohur," said the Sunyási. "It comes from a foolish woman, simply because she has not seen her son, a grown up boy of fourteen or fifteen, for a week. The boy went out on a pilfering expedition from which he has not yet returned, and the woman is so silly as to lament for him as if he were dead, to the utter disgust of the elders of her race, such grief being altogether opposed to the Bediyá creed."

"Ah!" exclaimed Monohur, "if a son's absence of seven short days so vexes a vagrant mother, how very distressed must my mother now be in not having seen me for nearly seven years? I must start for home this instant, Bábájee, to see her."

"O, Monohur, what fancy is this? Is it, can it be necessary to remind you that even now we are fleeing for our lives? And can you think of moving in a direction in which you are sure to be captured by enemies who will never think of sparing you?"

"I must take the risk, Bábájee, for I have resolved to see my mother. Go to her I will, and at once. But I don't say that I shall not come back to you again, if I can do so. The rains have begun to fall, and for the next three or four months your progress towards the Tirthastháns will not be great. Before the expiration of that time I trust to be at your side once more. But you must not attempt to dissuade me from going back to Bouá Ghát forthwith; for I have decided on doing so."

"This is what I had feared," thought the Sunyási within himself; but the crisis had come, and it was useless discussing further about it.

"If you must go—go with a stout heart, my son," said he, "and may Nággesur Mahádeva take you under his especial protection, for very much will you require his support."

CHAPTER XXVIII.

HOME, AS MONOHUR FOUND IT.

THE wish to return home had arisen, and Monohur stopped not to think of the dangers that were risked. He had to go back, and would do so regardless of consequences, for the desire to see his mother had grown into a pain; and the journey was undertaken with feverish energy, though the weather had already become wet and nasty, and the way to retrace was so long.

It was a hurried start, unaccompanied by any disposition to loiter on the road; and the penitent son moved on as fast as *dooli-dáks* and boats could carry him, his spirit rising as he passed through well-remembered districts and villages that brought him nearer and nearer to his native place.

"We are tired of pushing on at this rate," would his bearers frequently remonstrate, in the vain hope of being able to induce him to go by easier stages. He did not feel the tedium they complained of; he could not imagine how anyone could tire on such an errand as his; and he hurried forward more and more vehemently, till, after a continuous journey of twenty odd days, the familiar trees of Boná Ghát arose before him.

But there had been many changes at the place which quite surprised and staggered him. The village was before at all times a busy one, but the life that should have pervaded it was now wanting. The grounds were all overgrown with nettles and long grass, and bore a subdued and joyless look; and even the famous mango-grove, which used always to be kept so scrupulously clean, presented the appearance of an impervious jungle. The roads and temple-squares, too, instead of being thronged with passengers, as in the past, were nearly vacant; and the people who were seen in and about them did not even recognise their Zemindár as he passed by them.

"My features must have undergone many and great changes within the last few years," thought Monohur, "which probably accounts for their not recollecting me. But how is it that I cannot recognise any of my ryots, and why—why has the place become so desolate and weird-like?"

He alighted from his *dooli* almost immediately after entering the village, and, dismissing his bearers, proceeded homeward on foot.

"The evening is beautiful, and a mile's walk ought to brace up my nerves," murmured he to himself. "I am coming back to those who have missed me long, and should make the best appearance among them that I can."

What his feelings were as he came nearer to his house we shall not attempt to describe. He had met with no kind faces in the streets, but had still hoped to find plenty of them at home. How great was his dismay then, when, on approaching the big white building of his fathers, he saw that its doors and windows were closed, and a settled gloom reigning over it and its surroundings. Not a living creature was visible anywhere—neither servants, nor horses, nor kine; the place had, in fact, all the appearance of having been deserted, perhaps ever since the time he had left it; and he stood alone by the scenes of his joyous boyhood, staring blankly at a gate that would not open to receive him.

"What can this mean? Where are they gone? Had any great calamity befallen the family?"

He ventured to knock at the gate at last, and, after a short delay, a shrill female voice asked from within what was wanted.

"Open the door and you will know," answered Monohur.

"To whom shall we open it?" asked the same piercing voice again.

Monohur gave his name.

"Ah! Come back at last?"

"Yes," said Monohur, "and I am quite confounded to find the house all shut up, with its grounds overgrown with jungle, and its gate rusty and locked."

The door was now opened, and two or three women were seen passing and repassing, among whom Monohur recognised the withered face of an old aunt, now looking more withered than ever. She was a tall, thin woman, with dark tangled locks, hollow cheeks, and a sharp nose; and her eyes, which were at all times brilliant, were now sparkling like fire.

"O, aunt, where is my mother? Where are our other relatives and friends?"

"They are all in the house, and will be soon coming forth to greet you. Don't you fret, my boy, for their delay. You must be hungry. Satisfy your hunger first, and you shall see them presently."

Monohur was puzzled and knew not how to understand her. He looked again and again at her face, but that afforded no such information as he wished for. She had set before him some sweetmeats on a silver *recáb*, and alongside of it was a silver tumbler to drink from, but this was empty.

"O, aunt, give me a little water first to drink, for I am very thirsty."

The aunt was standing at some distance from him, and extended a hand at least four cubits long to pour out water into the tumbler from a *lotáh* at her side. The young man was terribly frightened; he could scarcely breathe: but even at this extremity he made a mechanical effort not to betray any terror on his face. He affected to drink the water given to him, but did not; poured out some of it to moisten his face with, and then said that he would go to wash himself in a neighbouring tank, by which time he hoped to see his mother there, and to get hot rice and curry to eat, which he would prefer to sweetmeats.

"Yes, boy, come back quickly. Your mother is coming, and everything you want will be immediately ready."

He started when the words "your mother is coming" were mentioned, and saw a shade as of his mother advancing towards him, and he felt a gentle breath pass across his cheeks. He approached the phantom with an agony of love, even though his knees were tottering in fear; but it retreated as he advanced. He followed it to the extremity of the room, but could get no further. A low, hoarse moaning, hardly louder than a whisper, was all the sound that came to him from the shade, and, as Monohur bounded out of the house by one strong effort, it vanished before him with a sigh.

In the deadly terror that possessed him Monohur ran off he knew not whither, but stopped on coming up to a *moodi's* shop at the nearest crossing, though his knees were still striking against each other.

"Did not that old house there belong to the Zemindárs of Boná Ghát?" asked he of the shopkeeper, whom he could barely recognise as one of his former tenants.

"Yes; but they have all died within the last five years."

"All?"

"Ay, all; with the exception of the heir, who slunk off from the house with a Fakir some seven years ago, and has never since been heard of."

"Then who occupy the house at present?"

"No one, unless it be the spirits of the dead, for the house has got a bad name."

"But how came it that all of such a large household have disappeared at once?"

"O, don't you know that there was a fearful inundation in these parts, followed by a yet more fearful epidemic some five years ago? Not that house only, but the whole village, and a great part of the country to the east of us, were depopulated by them. If you had ever seen Boná Ghát before these afflictions came you would have appreciated at once the frightful character of the changes they wrought."

Monohur did not want to know more. There was a rush of contending feelings in his mind that almost unsettled his brain. The mother that had so loved him was dead, and the thoughts of her brought with them a burden of reproach. Was life worth living now? He went off from the shop, and walked to and fro by the lovely banks of the Bhetná.

"O, mother! dearest mother! if I ended my life here

by throwing myself into the stream would I meet with you in the shadowy land?"

The words had hardly passed out of his mouth when he seemed to feel again as if a sweet breath passed across his cheeks, and, looking steadfastly before him, he beheld once more the shadow of his mother gazing at him with sorrowful and pleading eyes.

Monohur approached the apparition boldly as before, with a fixed and reverential look. But it retreated again before him, crossing its hands on its bosom and looking upwards to the sky. The pale moonlight revealed the figure most clearly to the son, and the next moment it was gone! Monohur continued to gaze at the lovely light for some time, in the hope of seeing the shade again, but it did not return.

"I shall not stay in this village to-night," muttered he at last, speaking to himself; and he left it as fast as he had come to it. A Byrági lived in a hut at the foot of a banyan-tree on the outskirt of the village, and he resolved to lodge with him for the night. The man was well-known, though rather more feared than loved, for he dealt with unorthodox arts; but Monohur had been too long the disciple of Bissonáth to be afraid of him. Great, however, was his surprise on seeing him perched on the revetement of a bridge which he had to go by.

"What are you doing here, Byrági? I was going to meet you where you live."

"Ah, I am enjoying the moonlight here. What did you want with me?"

"A night's rest only," said Monohur, "for I do not know where else to seek for it."

"Then come and sit here for a while, and we shall have a pull at the *hookáh* together before we go home."

But Monohur did not smoke.

"I am weary, Byrági, for I have been on foot for a long time to-day, and I must go to sleep at once. You can come home when you like. May I not occupy your place till then?"

"Of course you may—that is, if you are not afraid to sleep alone. Would you miss me if I did not come?"

"O, come by all means; but you will find me fast asleep after the smallest delay."

Monohur proceeded towards the Byrági's hut at a rapid pace, but was not pleased to find a small crowd before it when he reached the spot.

"What is the matter here?" he asked.

"O," said one of the throng, "the Byrági is dead."

"Dead! When did he die?"

"This afternoon, and the body is yet lying on the floor;" and while Monohur looked at the body his legs tottered visibly. Surely there was the very same man lying stark dead before him whom he thought he had met and conversed with a few minutes before on the revetement of the bridge!

He did not speak a word more with anyone, but ran off to the temple of Nággesur Mahádeva and fell prostrate before the deity, beseeching his protection. There was no one in the temple at this hour of the night; but he felt no fear on that account, for he was conscious of being in the presence of one who was fully able to protect. When the imagination is disturbed and reason staggered if not overthrown, how is it that nothing can restore calmness to the mind but faith?

Long, long did he lie prostrate on the ground, wrapt in speechless devotion. He saw no more apparitions floating before him, no shape nor shadow but the placid pillar of stone that represented the deity. At last he felt a flower fall on his body, as if thrown towards him, and he arose and picked it up. It was the very same flower he had seen at the top of the Lingam when he entered the temple, and he received it as a direct assurance from the god himself of the protection extended to him. The withered flower was carefully fastened by Monohur to the Tulsi bead-chàin which encircled his throat; and he went out sharply again from Boná Ghát, to overtake the Sunyási in his wanderings.

CHAPTER XXIX.

THE PARAMHANGSA.

DURING the time that Monohur was escaping by forced marches from the Cuttack forests to Boná Ghát, the Sunyási was not idle, but was following almost the very same route though a little more circuitously, till he found that he had reached Sátgáon, or Saptagrám, a village in the district of Hooghly.

"I confess I don't see what I can do now besides staying here for the return of Monohur, who cannot possibly remain at home after all that has happened there since he left it," said he to himself in a self-communing mood. "The country is yet in a disordered state. Why not tarry here then for him, since I have got a friend hard by whose character would be my best protection?"

The village of Sátgáon was at one time the mercantile capital of Bengal, and is mentioned as such in the Puráns, where it is also spoken of as a celebrated place of worship, the seven villages of which it was originally composed having been especially consecrated to the seven Rishis of the Shástras. From seven it came gradually to comprise as many as a hundred villages, but what remains of it at the present day are some twelve or thirteen huts only; and its condition was barely a little better when the Sunyási visited it. The celebrity of the place at the time was more directly derived rather from the residence in it of a

Paramhangsa, a man of high character and great learning, whom Bissonáth had met in his wanderings, and with whom he proposed now to remain till the return of Monohur.

It was a July evening, and the Sunyási was walking with a half-filled wallet slung over his shoulder, a *chádur* passed over his head to protect it from the weather which was by turns hot and rainy, a small *cháttá,* or parasol of mat, kept in position by being tied to the wallet, and a staff of rather thick dimensions in his hand. He was evidently exhausted, and the accumulation of mud on his feet bore evidence to his having travelled a long distance that day. The beauties of an autumn sunset were yet in the sky; but they had no charms for the wayfarer, for he was anxious to reach his destination before the setting in of night.

"My son," said he, addressing the first peasant he met with, "can you direct me to the residence of the great Paramhangsa who lives somewhere about this place?"

"Are you a stranger, father, that you don't know where he lives, when even Rájáhs and Zemindárs are well aware of the road?"

"Not altogether a stranger, indeed," said the Sunyási in reply; "but it is several years now since I was in this village before, and I don't think that the Paramhangsa had settled in it then."

"Ah, that is too true," exclaimed the peasant, "for the holy father has come hither amongst us but a few years only. I am going towards his *Tole* this moment myself, and if you will come with me I shall be glad to show you the way."

The Paramhangsa was a celebrated character at Sátgáon, a man of really extensive acquirements and spotless fame. He was an old man of splendid, though decrepit appearance, who had given up all that was best in him in the search after Truth. His wanderings in particular had been wide and varied, and had contributed not a little to the establishment of his reputation. The river-banks of India are sacred ground, and to follow the course of a river from its source to the sea and back again by the opposite shore to its source is called its *Pradakshina;* and this the good man had accomplished by several streams. His holiness had necessarily made a great name for him; though what had established him at Sátgáon was rather a peculiar *Máhita* he had exhibited, which is not uncommon among the recluses of the East. The Jaggatpore Zemindárs had, several of them, died childless, and this had created a great alarm in the family.

"Is the zemindáry to go down, decade by decade, by adoption? Cannot the curse of sterility be removed from our women?"

They had consulted the Paramhangsa, and he had advised them to change their place of abode.

"I shall find out a site for you where you will surely prosper;" and proceeding to a retired spot some six miles to the west of Sátgáon he had there burnt a lock of his hair and scattered the ashes on the ground.

"Behold, I have purified this spot for you. Live here and multiply:" and they had built there a big palace to live in, and had multiplied and prospered; for the ladies of the family had borne children in due time ever after, and the children were all healthy and robust.

"Surely this man is a saint! What should we do for him?" asked the Zemindárs.

"Is he a saint or a god in disguise?" inquired the women, with unaffected devotion.

"Whatever he be we must not leave him uncared for in his age," observed both the Zemindárs and their wives; and they offered to establish him at Sátgáon in their immediate neighbourhood, to which the sage having assented the *Tole* was soon raised, at the front of which he was always to be seen, morning and evening, with a rosary in his hand and his eyes fixed reverentially on the sky.

But a new saint, like a new doctor, has to make himself known to the public at large by some exploit or achievement of even greater moment than such Máhita as the Paramhangsa had shown. The high encomiums and profuse bounty of the Jaggatpore Zemindárs went a great way in securing for the good man the veneration of the mob; but it was necessary that he should establish himself in the estimation of more competent judges by giving proof of his reading and wisdom; and the opportunity for doing so was very soon offered. Envying his good fortune another *Sádhoo*, or holy man, came to his place a short time after him, with the scarcely hidden intent of entangling him in a religious debate. He was received by the Paramhangsa with kindness and respect, but the latter was taken quite aback when the stranger proposed to hold a learned disputation with him.

"A disputation with me? Why, I am old and feckless, and rapidly hastening to my rest. What honour will you gain by vanquishing me?"

But the new-comer was not a man to be thrown off from his purpose so easily.

"O, I don't aspire to the distinction of overcoming you, my brother," said he. "It would be presumptuous in me to do so, for your fame fills the whole earth. I have come hither simply to receive instruction from your lips."

There was a pause now between the two Sádhoos, but not the least discomposure on either side.

"Well," said the Paramhangsa at last, "if you will have it so I have no option but to accede to your wish. Shape your questions then as you list, and I shall try to answer them as best I may."

From the commencement of this prelude there was deep silence in the *Tole*, the pupils of the Paramhangsa waiting in breathless expectation for the debate. But it was too learned even for them to understand, for the questions asked by the new-comer were clothed in the rugged and obsolete Sanskrit of the primitive ages, by which he expected perhaps to surprise and intimidate his opponent. What was the wonder of the challenger then when the Paramhangsa, looking him steadfastly in the face, gave his answers slowly and deliberately in the ancient Chaldean dialect. The Sádhoo received the replies with fear and astonishment, nay, it is said that he became insensible, as if struck down by a spell.

"Revive him, my children," said the Paramhangsa to his pupils, and they sprinkled water on his face till he was able to sit up.

"Well, brother, have I answered your propositions aright?"

"Be merciful, father!" exclaimed the new-comer almost in fear. "You are infinitely my superior in every respect, both in holiness and learning; and I beseech you to receive me among your disciples."

After this the reputation of the Paramhangsa was in every mouth, and crowds of people came to him from great distances to salute him and receive his benedictions.

This was the man to whom the Sunyási was conducted, and whom he met with at the threshold of his *Tole* counting his beads.

"Well, brother! Is it me you seek? If so, you are welcome."

"Yes," said the Sunyási, "it is certainly to you, master, that I have come, though you do not seem to recognise me."

The Paramhangsa was gazing steadfastly at the face of his visitor, and the Sunyási, appreciating his difficulty, took off the covering from his head.

"Ah! my old friend, the ardent companion of my travels among the Snowy Mountains, do I see you face to face again? Excuse me that I was not able to recognise you at once, for I am getting infirm from age. I can never sufficiently acknowledge your kindness in having come out so far, and to such an out-of-the-way corner as this, to inquire after me."

The Sunyási bit his lip to hide his uneasiness.

"Do not give me credit, master, where no credit is due. I have been wandering over a great part of the country on my own account, and have but accidentally come upon you here."

"Ah! wandering about yet, my brother? Give glory to Him then who has given you health and strength to do so. Have you finished any other *pradakshinás* besides that of the Ganges in which we were engaged together?"

"No, master; I have been detained in my own country mainly for the last ten years; but my business in it is now ended, and I may possibly start on fresh journeys if I can get fit companions to tramp with."

"But you cannot be thinking of any long distant expeditions now, my brother, for you are getting stricken in years, though perhaps not quite so disabled yet as I have become. Why not settle down now at some place as a teacher of youth, as I have done?"

"Could I accept the responsibility conscientiously, master? You are learned, I am not; I have followed *Karma* and *Bhakti* all my life, but in *Gyán*, the highest phase of religion, my portion is but small."

"Say not so, my brother. Stay with us, and we can gain knowledge from each other by mutual communication. The process is not difficult, though it may seem so to begin with. If we do not get disheartened we are sure to advance. Will you remain here with us to this end?"

"I shall remain with you willingly, master, if you will allow me; but I stay only to wait for a friend whom I expect here shortly, and my after-course will depend more on his wishes than on mine."

This was agreed to, and Bissonáth stayed with the Paramhangsa, whose *Tole* was crowded with students. The Sunyási was a pious man in the main, though worldly-minded, and the questions that occur to every reasonable mind had often occurred to and distressed him. "What am I?" "Whence come?" "Whither bound?" "What is the actual relationship between soul and body, between material and immaterial natures?" "What is the character of the Being who has made us?" But he had received no light to assist the gropings of his mind, even though he had sought for it so sedulously, first, by becoming a Kartá-Bhajá, and then by converting himself into a Ferázee. The light and opportunity were now offered him, and he was a devout listener to the instructions that were imparted, and to the discussions that were carried on. India has a hundred races, a hundred dialects, and, it may be said, a hundred religions; but these religions are so connected with, and in fact so melt into, each other that they seem and are generally accepted as one. No one was better competent than the Paramhangsa to explain both their divergences and their agreement, and from the lips of none could such instruction come with greater gentleness and grace. The burden of his instructions was briefly this : "Whence are we ? From God. Whither bound? To God. But God is a complete entity, which we are not. Soul and body, matter and spirit in unison cannot be complete, and necessarily cannot approach that which is. The aim of life, therefore, is progress simply, progress out of matter, for that union with the Universal Spirit, which finishes the scheme.

"This, my brother, is the essential doctrine of all the schools of philosophy which are orthodox, and of the Upanishads on which those schools are based. The differences between them are mainly on minor points, and of no great moment in any case."

CHAPTER XXX.

THE SHÁSTRIC SCHEME.

THE Sunyási's knowledge of the Shástras was very indifferent, but the Paramhangsa, sheathed in the armour of benevolence, was never weary of listening to his doubts and inquiries, nor spared any pains in giving whatever information and explanation he stood in need of. Bissonáth, on his part, received every interpretation from the lips of the sage with the most respectful attention; and it was a real comfort to the instructor to find that all the faculties of his auditor were, for the time at least, absorbed in the instruction imparted by him.

"O, master, I am very ignorant of these matters, and am afraid that you must begin even from the beginning, with the axioms and postulates of the Shástras, to enable me to understand their teachings aright."

"I would have been very much surprised indeed, my brother, if your inquiries had been otherwise shaped, for no one can understand any subject thoroughly without tracing it up from the commencement. You know of course that the Shástras are divided into two parts, the *Sruti* and the *Smriti*—the orally-delivered and the written, the former coming direct from God, the latter derived from the mouths of sages and handed down to us by tradition. Of the former the chief divisions are: the *Mantras*, the *Bráhmanas*, and the *Upanishads;* the first being prayers and hymns of praise addressed to the heavenly powers; the second, prescriptions for conducting sacrifices and ceremonies; and the third containing all the essential and secret doctrines which lie below the surface of inquiry. The essence of the first is *Bhakti*, of the second *Karma*, of the third *Gyán*; and it is on the last that all the schools of philosophy are based."

"But the schools of philosophy, master, though based on the Upanishads, are erring; are they not? They are often diametrically opposed to each other, or seem to be so."

"As human institutions they are erring. They were founded by men like ourselves—the *Nyaya* by Gautama, the *Vaiseshika* by Kanada, the *Sankhya* by Kapila, the *Yoga* by Patánjali, the *Mimánsa* by Jaimani, and the *Vedánta* by Vyasa; but as vehicles of true instruction they are all of them eminently useful, and I have found personally that the Upanishads, read with their assistance, are more easily appreciated and understood."

"How more easily understood when the schools have differed so widely in their beliefs?"

"The difference in belief between the schools is not, as I have said before, intrinsically so great as is usually supposed. The leading principles maintained by them, divested of their verbiage, are very nearly the same."

"And the Smritis, do their teachings also accord with those of the Upanishads?"

"I cannot say that they do not," said the Paramhangsá, "though at first sight it may seem otherwise. The Smritis comprise the *Vedángas, Dharma Shástras, Puráns,* and *Itiháses*. The religion of the mass is necessarily a religion of accretions, and apparently the Smritis seem to advocate different kinds of belief; but the principle at bottom is

THE SHÁSTRIC SCHEME.

in every case the same, though exhibiting different phases of the Truth."

"O, master! has Truth, can Truth have different phases then, like other ordinary things?"

"Why not? It cannot but have different phases when seen from different stand-points and with different eyes. We see it through different media, and therefore in different lights. When we come to *know* Truth we shall find that it is one; and those who *know* have certainly realised this."

"What then is true in this, Mohásoy—One God, or three gods, or thirty-three, or thirty-three millions, these being the different phases in which the subject has been considered?"

"The truth is One God; its phases merely are multiform. The Triad of the Veds are Agni, Surjya, and Indra; but when you put the three names together you find them to make one term only—God. Similarly, the total number of deities enumerated in the Veds is thirty-three, the explanation of which is that three and eleven are mystic numbers in the Sanskrit, and multiplied with each other, make up the aggregate returned."

"But why was such multiplication necessary?"

"To suit the understanding of different minds. That which made one three, increased the number to thirty-three, and eventually to thirty-three millions, which simply denotes that, the Deity being interminable, His attributes are uncountable. The Triad of the Veds was changed for the Trimurti of the Puráns when it became necessary to give to each attribute of the Deity a visible form. The functions of the Triad were also now distributed; but even that, my brother, did not make them distinct. One was called the Creator, another the Preserver, the third the Destroyer: but their attributes remained interchangeable; each was still first in place and last; their distinct representation simply singled out the three principal *Goonas* of the Self-Existent."

"And the incarnations and minor deities?"

"Were compromises made to render the religion acceptable by all."

"I understand your explanation then to mean that the different names of the Universal God, however numerous, are nothing more than the manifestations of His several attributes separately symbolised. If so, why were there strifes and contentions between the worshippers of those different names?"

"Ah, the strifes and jealousies are but proofs of human passions and frailties, not of antagonism among the attributes severally worshipped."

"But are not the Puráns themselves antagonistic to each other, and do they not teach that antagonism which you attribute to the passions and frailties of human nature only?"

"Have I not said that the Puráns were delivered by human authors? Of the eighteen Puráns, six—namely, the Bruhma, Brahmánda, Bruhma Vaivartha, Markandaya, Bhavishya, and Vámana—extol the glories of Bruhmá; six others—the Vishnu, Bhágavat, Náradya, Garura, Padma, and Varáha—glorify Vishnu mainly; while the remaining six—namely, the Saiva, Lainga, Skanda, Agni, Matsya, and Karma—are especially devoted to the adoration of Mahádeva. But it must not be supposed that any set of them is exclusively appropriated for the exaltation of one particular deity. There is a constant interchange of courtesies and compliments between them. They were all based on one foundation, and, even though presenting multiform aspects outwardly, had really but one cause to advocate and uphold."

"Well, besides the Veds and the Puráns and the schools whose teachings were based on the Upanishads, have there not been other teachers also in the country who carried great authority with them even when explicitly disowning the authority of the Veds?"

"Yes; for, though they ignored the Veds, they did not disown the great and only Truth which the Veds were the first to make known. There was a war of races in the country, owing to the Kshetriyas, who at one time occupied the first place, having been afterwards forcibly ousted from it by the Bráhmans. The Bráhman schools of philosophy came thus to be called orthodox, while the Kshetriya schools were characterised as unorthodox by their detractors; but the doctrines enunciated by some of the latter, and by Buddhism in particular, were too pure to be rejected, too true to be denied."

"You admit then the soundness of the Buddha faith?"

"Who dares deny it? No philosophy, not even that of the Vedánta, can boast of a sublimer or purer creed: the best phases of Vedantism and Buddhism march together, while the *Karma* code of the latter is perhaps superior to any that has ever been enunciated. The main precepts of that code are divided into two broad divisions of 'prohibitions' and 'injunctions.' The primary prohibitions are:—'Kill not,' 'steal not,' 'commit not adultery,' 'lie not,' 'drink not strong drink.' The primary injunctions are:—'Charity and benevolence,' 'moral goodness,' 'patience,' 'fortitude,' 'meditation,' and 'knowledge.' Can any better injunctions or prohibitions be conceived?"

"I was told by the Llámas we met with at the foot of the Himálayas that some of the secondary injunctions and prohibitions also enjoin excellent lessons of humility, repentance, avoidance of luxury, and the like. Is it not a pity then that such a religion was wholly rooted out of the land?"

"It was not rooted out, my brother; it was not possible to root it out altogether. Its best portions were drafted into the Bráhman code by bits, the two faiths melting into each other to form the religion as it now exists."

"But were there not interchanges of persecutions and hostilities between them? I think it is so recorded in the accounts they both give of each other."

"Yes, there were quarrels and fightings between them; and these were continued for a good long period too. But they were finally concluded by concessions and adaptations; and it was only a small section of the Buddhas who, having resisted all efforts at conciliation to the last, were actually rooted out."

"What shape then did the conciliation you speak of, master, assume? In what representation of the deity is Buddha, or Ádi-Buddha, now to be traced?"

"In the character of Mahádeva. The name is that of a Bráhman deity, but under that disguise the god of the Buddhas takes precedence in the triune co-equality of Bráhmanism."

"How so? Is not Mahádeva generally represented as a free-liver, the associate of drunkards, and the celebrator of the Tántric orgies? What has he in common with Buddha?"

"Ah, my friend, the representation you refer to is that given of him by those who did not accept the idea of importing him into the Triad. But the more correct description given of him is that of an ascetic, as Buddha was, practising severe mortifications, and teaching them, as Buddha did."

"These different descriptions are very conflicting, Mohásoy. Like Mahádeva, his wife, Párvati, also has two distinct phases of character, one a very amiable one, which represents her as the type of beauty and gentleness, under the names of Umá and Gauri; the other a wild and fierce one, as exhibited in the characters of Doorgá, Káli, Bhairavi, and Chámoondi. I do not see what good end such contradictions were intended to secure."

"Reflect, and you will understand it, for it is by no means very difficult to understand. The world, as we find it, is not so full of amiability and goodness that it would have been content with the characters of Umá and Gauri only. There are stronger and wilder natures in it to break in, and to initiate these in religion is as needful as to initiate others. O, my brother, the stupendous whole which the Shástras represent is as perfect as human wisdom, based on divine teaching, could have made it. It was designed not only for this world, but for the worlds beyond it—alike for Bhu, Bhur, and Swar—the earth, intermediate space, and the heavens. How could it be of other character then than what it actually bears?"

"Then the real object in enjoining a divergent mythology, master, was, I understand you to assert, the bringing in of all sorts of recruits for religious enlistment, to leave them afterwards to grope out their way to truth in the best manner they might?"

"Exactly so, my brother. Mythology has a persuasiveness that renders it of essential help to all natures alike at the starting-point—that is, for the commencement of inquiry and action. After that we have reason and reflection to lead us to the goal."

"Which we could not possibly begin with?"

"No, certainly not. We see, hear, smell, taste, and feel long before we commence to think. Could we commence with thinking, to see, hear, and feel afterwards? The tranquillising effect of a panoramic system, like that of the Puráns, is indeed indispensably necessary for arousing the powers of reflection; and the way in which the Shástras have worked it out is not only faultless, but absolutely marvellous."

CHAPTER XXXI.

THE NEW ARRIVAL.

The religious discourses were continuous and many, though we may not refer to all of them here lest we should be getting behindhand with our story. They were always impressive and edifying; and the Sunyási began now for the first time to understand why he had not hitherto understood the drift of the Shástras aright. He yearned for more and more information, as doubt after doubt was removed from his mind, and there was no subject almost that did not come thus to be scrutinised and lectured upon.

"I fear, Mohásoy," observed the Sunyási one morning, "I fear I am wearying you with my objections and interrogations; but I want to learn, and you are able to teach, and that is my apology for troubling you."

The teacher smiled.

"Do I look as wearied, my friend, in answering you that you say you trouble me? Believe me that nothing gives me such hearty pleasure as to afford to others whatever instruction I may be able to impart. Should we not help each other with our knowledge? How else is knowledge to be acquired?"

"Well, master, I would beg of you then to explain to me the duties of a Bráhman, as enjoined by *Achár* and *Byabahár*, as distinct from the requirements of religion and philosophy. I am a Bráhman of the highest class by birth, but have led such a vagrant life from my youth that I have had little leisure to learn the duties required of me, and am really anxious now to make up for lost time."

"The duties of a Bráhman," replied the Paramhangsa, "are to bathe daily, offer oblations of water to the gods, holy sages, and departed ancestors, feed the sacred fire with fuel, and read the Veds, Puráns, and Itiháses. I suppose you have not been able to practise the last duty in particular very assiduously, but of course you know the *Gáyatri* and repeat it :—*Tat Sávitra varayam bhargo derasya dhimáhi, dhiyo yo váh prachodayat ?*"

"Yes, I repeat the prayer daily, both at sunrise and sunset, but beyond that my knowledge is very limited. I am certainly not well versed in the Veds, and I hardly know the Puráns better."

"If you know your Gáyatri well you know everything, for that is the cardinal doctrine alike of the Veds and the Puráns. But you should repeat the prayer at the three *Sandhyas* of sunrise, noon, and sunset, not at two only, as you say you do; for three, as I have explained before, is a mystic and sacred number, and imparts sacredness even to the Gáyatri. Many repeat the prayer with a *Japamálá,* ten, twenty-eight, or a hundred and eight times; but all have not time to do so, nor is it very imperatively required. Remember your Maker thrice daily and you do so thirty-three times and thirty-three million times, for three, thirty-three, and thirty-three millions are numbers reciprocally representable."

"Is there anything besides the repetition of the Gáyatri that is required of us with equal emphasis ?"

"Yes, abstinence—abstinence from pride, sensuality,

falsehood, and impurity of all kinds. But this is the requirement rather of philosophy and religion, than of Achár and Byábahár, and as such is more imperative even than the other duties I have alluded to."

"O, master! If abstinence be so essential a qualification of Bráhmanhood, who is a Bráhman in reality?"

"Who, indeed! We are Bráhmans by birth; we observe the purificatory rites of *Upanayána, Karnabedha*, and the rest; but the sacrifice of the heart, which is so particularly required of us, how few are able or assiduous to render? The Upanayána we accept by investiture with a sacred thread, and we display the thread over our shoulders and hang it out diagonally across our bodies. The Bráhman wears a cotton thread, the Kshetriya one made of hemp, the Vaisya one made of wool. But the thread is in every case but a token only of regeneration; the regeneration itself must be of the mind."

"But are there not sacrifices particularly enjoined whereby to make up for our shortcomings in this as in other respects?"

"Of course there are. But the real sacrifice required is still that of the heart, for which life is the only adequate substitute, on the principle that, having been unable to train the heart aright, we surrender to our Maker the existence that was given to us in trust."

"How so, Mohásoy? Are not sacrifices of animals expressly enjoined by the Shástras, and enumerated?"

"Yes, but only as partial substitutes at best. Originally life-sacrifices were human only, and the text says emphatically—'Since I cannot purify my heart, O God, suffer me to surrender my life to you.' The Veds explain in addition that the sacrifice of the horse was substituted for that of man, of the buffalo for that of the horse, of the sheep for that of the buffalo, and of the goat for that of the sheep—only because the personal sacrifice of the man himself would close the door of repentance and salvation."

"Then what is the virtue of a sacrifice as it is now made? To what extent does it benefit us?"

"The animal sacrificed is, by the force of the Mantras recited, identified with the sinner who offers him; and this self-sacrifice by proxy is held to be a sufficient expiation for the sins already committed by him. The prayer chanted over the sacrifice says expressly—'Whatever sins I have committed, sleeping, or waking, knowing or unknowing, thou art offered to expiate for it.' But it does not purify the heart, nor put a stop to the further commission of sins."

"It is a gain, however, so far as it goes, for it is desirable, of course, to be cleansed of the past—that is, if we are certified that we are really cleansed by the process."

"It is so stated in the Shástras, and must be so. But the course yet more positively enjoined is the sacrifice of the heart, for sanctification only can make the cure complete. He is a Bráhman who knows Bruhmu; and to know him it is not enough to get cleansed of the past, but to remain cleansed for ever."

"That is a state which must be especially hard to attain?"

"It has to be attained though, for there is no by-path in morals, as some authorities have taken so much pains to inculcate. The straight path is not merely the best but also the only path to go by."

"Where to, master? What is the object of the purity you so forcibly enjoin? If we must be thoroughly sanctified, wherefore must we be so?"

"That the highest and final end, the ultimate purpose for which we were created, might be accomplished. A clear conception of that end, and of the way to it, is possible only to the pure."

"Then what is that end or purpose, so far as the great master-minds of the world have yet been able to make out?"

"Ah, different thinkers have given very different names to it, my brother, just as different sages have given different names, even to the Deity. Some have called the purpose 'thought;' others, 'life,' 'real life;' others, 'happiness;' others, 'the knowledge of the unknowable;' others, 'absorption into the highest.' I would simply name it 'emancipation' with the Buddhas, and hold *emancipation* and *absorption* to be the same."

"And this emancipation you hold to be attainable by purity alone?"

"By purity and knowledge together, brother; it can have no other base."

"Ah, master, the doctrine you lay down is certainly beautiful, very beautiful indeed! But if purity be so essential to the attainment of the end, who will, who can be held worthy of it?"

"The whole human race, I hope," answered the Paramhangsa, with a smile of ineffable gratification. "If not in this life, in the next, or in the next after that, or later yet, and later still. The point to reach cannot be shortened to suit the convenience of anyone. We have to run up to it, and must do so. But I sincerely believe that as many opportunities will be given to us to try the race as we may possibly require, since the Greatest and Holiest could not possibly have made us in vain."

At this moment a third person glided softly and unexpectedly into the hut, and, approaching the speakers, stood motionless before them like a ghost.

"O, Monohur!" exclaimed the Sunyási, perceiving who the intruder was, "there is trouble in your eye, and your body has wasted down to a skeleton. Sad, very sad, must have been your reception at home to bring you down to this condition. But you need not speak of it to me. I did not very strongly dissuade you from going, for I had not the heart to do so; but I knew well all that you have learnt since. Sit down and listen to the instructions of this blessed man, and they will strengthen your heart and qualify it for its further struggles with life."

The answer of Monohur was a low heart-broken wail, and he sat down with an effort, as if in pain. The wildness and vivacity of his youth were gone, and his face was furrowed and wrinkled over with care.

"Is this any relation of yours?" asked the Paramhangsa of Bissonáth, turning his eyes towards Monohur.

"My pupil and my friend."

"He seems sadly distressed. What is it that weighs so heavily on him?"

"The loss of a most loving mother; and his grief is all the greater that he was not at her side when she died. He had fled away from her at my instigation, and was not able to see her afterwards."

"That is a great grief indeed," said the sage, "a grief for which there is no antidote but Gyán and Bhakti. You can see her again in the future, my son, if you deserve to do so."

"I have seen her in the present, father, though not in the flesh."

The Sunyási looked at his friend steadfastly as if he

doubted his sanity, while the Paramhangsa kindly asked him to open his mind freely to him, and to tell him what he had seen: "For it may be that I shall be able, under Providence, to apply the fitting solace to your wounds."

The kindness of the old man could not be resisted, and both he and the Sunyási heard with surprise the revelations that were made.

"Can such things be, or are they mere vagaries of a diseased brain?" asked the Sunyási, addressing the Paramhangsa.

"It is quite possible for such things to be, and I believe I understand the meaning of the sights which this youth has witnessed. As there was an epidemic prevailing in the land at the time of the lady's death, and as her son was not present on the spot, the funeral rites of the deceased were perhaps not very carefully performed, and the *preta*, or departed spirit, cannot obtain *gati*, or progress onwards, till those rites have been completed. The greatest service that you can now render to your deceased parent, therefore, my son, is to proceed straight to Gayá and perform the several rites there afresh, which will emancipate her spirit from the influence of this world, and speed it on to the intermediate stages of bliss, if not to ultimate redemption."

"O, Bábájee! my friend, my guardian!" exclaimed Monohur, the tears gathering in his eyes, "do you hear what the great teacher enjoins?"

"I do," said the Sunyási, "and am quite ready to accompany you."

And the very next day they left the *Tole* with the rising sun, and took the road to Gayá.

CHAPTER XXXII.

THE JÁL RÁJÁH OF BURDWÁN.

THE first place where our travellers halted, after leaving Sátgáon, was Ghol Ghát, the southern extremity of Hooghly, where the Portuguese established themselves after the decay of Sátgáon as a commercial port. The point indicates an eddy in the Hooghly river of much force and magnitude, close against which on the bank stood at one time a fortress built by Sampraya, the Portuguese General, the vestiges of which are still visible in the bed of the stream. It was here that Monohur and the Sunyási rested to decide on the route to be followed by them from that point.

"The floods have been heavy here, Monohur," remarked the Sunyási, "and a considerable portion of the Great Trunk Road has, I fear, been cut up. It will not be practicable, therefore, for us to follow up that line. We had better go hence to Burdwán, and from that place viâ Deogurh to Gayá."

"I have no wish in the matter, but yours, Bábájee; you understand these things so much better than I do."

They accordingly started again the following day, making straight up for Burdwán, the mind of Monohur depressed by a despondency which he could not shake off; and, though the Sunyási was untiring in his efforts to divert him, and even recapitulated for his edification many of the learned discourses and disputations he had listened to at Sátgáon, he was not very successful in re-animating him till the town of Burdwán was reached.

"You must not be angry with me, Monohur, but we are approaching a large and busy city, and you should not look so strange here as you do now, for people are sure to take note of it and misunderstand us."

"Ah, am I really looking very strange, Bábájee? How should I look then? Why don't you instruct me?"

"Resume as much of your former spirits, my son, as you can. We are bound on a pilgrimage; a sad one to be sure, but still we must bear up like other pilgrims, to avoid misconstruction."

There was no answer to this from Monohur but a sigh, and his pale face continued yet to bear its settled expression of deep melancholy and pain. The city of Burdwán was reached in this state, just at the time when it may be said to have been in a *furor*, on account of a celebrated Tichborne case which convulsed Bengal in 1838; and the Sunyási was now able to apply his hoisting-up lever more successfully than before.

"What is the excitement here for?" asked Monohur of his companion. "People appear everywhere to be divided into clamorous gatherings, eagerly discussing some important matter with violent gesticulations."

"O, a great trial is coming on here to-morrow or the day after, which we might wait to see decided without detriment to our particular business. It cannot detain us beyond a few short days, and I really think you would like to know all about it, for it is a matter of much importance to Zemindárs generally."

Monohur wished to resist the temptation thus adroitly thrown out to him, but was unable to do so; for though he was terribly out of sorts yet, the Sunyási had succeeded in exciting his curiosity.

"What is the case about, Bábájee?"

"Why, a certain person pretends that he is the veritable Rájáh of Burdwán, while another, who holds the estates at present, denies his pretension *in toto*. The whole story is so marvellous that it is worth staying here to ascertain how the contest may be authoritatively determined."

"I would have preferred to push on without stopping," said Monohur. "But, if it does not delay us much to hear out the case on the spot, I would certainly not think of opposing your wishes in the matter. What are the heads of the story, Bábájee? Can you tell?"

"O, the story is this: The Burdwán family, you know, is a very old one, much older than your own. It was founded by one Áboo Rái, who pretended to be a Kshetriyá by caste, though the people who knew him best preferred to recognise him as a Chuttree only. This man held a petty office in Burdwán, under the *fouzdár* of the day, some two hundred years ago, which enabled his son, Báboo Rái, to acquire three estates in the district, including Pergunnáh Burdwán. The times were unsettled, and a subsequent successor, whose character was nearly akin to that of a dacoit, was able to wrest from his neighbours, the Rájáhs of Chunderkoná and Gháttál, the estates which had belonged to them; and, the example being followed by other successors, several other estates, such as Tárkessur, Mundulghát, etc., were acquired, the final result being that the Burdwán *Ráj* became the largest zemindáry in Bengal. It became so unwieldy, in fact, that it began afterwards to be mismanaged, which led to portions of it being lost by sales, such, namely, as were acquired by the houses of Singore, Bhástárá, Jonái, and Telinipárá. To prevent further disruption, Rájáh Tej Chunder introduced the *putnee* system, by which the lands were subdivided and given away in perpetual leases, which secured to the original Zemindár a fixed profit without the risk of any loss at all."

"This is a wearisome account, Bábájee, and not by any means very instructive to me."

"Ah, I am coming very quickly, my son, to the strange portion of the story, which I am sure you will listen to with interest. The Rájáh Tej Chunder, that I was speaking of, who took so much pains to keep the zemindáry intact, had no son to succeed him. His only son, Pratápa Chunder, died in his life-time, upon which he adopted a son, named Máhátáb Chánd, the son of one Parán Báboo, a relative. Accordingly, on Tej Chunder's death, the zemindáry was assumed by Máhátáb Chánd as legal heir of the deceased, and he has continued in possession of it to the present time. The pretence of the claimant, who has now come forward, is that he is the identical Pratápa Chunder, the son of Tej Chunder, who was reported to have died."

"How is that possible, Bábájee? I mean how could there be any doubt in the matter of Pratápa Chunder's death? Surely the death of the heir of such an estate could not but have been known to all Burdwán at the time it occurred."

"And so it was; but the story now urged by the claimant is most curious on that very point, and not very improbable either, all things considered. He asserts that, as Parán Báboo possessed the ear of his father, the machinations of the former so prejudiced the latter against him that his life was made very unpleasant to him, and that some attempts having also been made by Parán Báboo to carry him off by poison, he was compelled to keep as much aloof from Burdwán as he could. He accordingly passed much of his time in Calcuttá, and at Chinsuráh, where, falling into bad company, he led a life of riot and dissipation, abandoning religion and the austerities of caste, and finally crowned the catalogue of his iniquities by the commission of a particularly heinous crime."

"Well?"

"Subsequently the young man repented, and so sincerely that society had no charms for him, and he lived almost alone by himself, brooding over his follies and crimes. At this stage it was suggested to him that he might expiate his wickedness by atoning for it in such manner as the Shástras prescribe; and, on consulting the oracles of Hinduism, an *incognito* pilgrimage for fourteen years was recommended to him, which he decided on performing.

"'You must be mad to think of adopting such a suggestion,' observed several of his former companions, with a view to dissuade him from leaving them.

"'I would be mad indeed,' was his reply, 'if I did not adopt it. There is nothing on the earth that I care to live for now if I may not get cleansed of my crimes.'

"He was afraid, however, lest his father should not assent to such a prolonged absence from home as the pilgrimage involved, and also that Parán Báboo might attempt to take his life if able to follow him in his flight; and he resolved therefore to carry out his intent without taking anyone into his confidence, in such manner as would avert suspicion, and, at the same time, shield him from the antipathy of his enemy. To this end he feigned a mortal sickness, was conveyed to Ambiká Culná, the family burning-ghát, and, affecting to be dying, had himself placed on the verge of the Hooghly, when he conjured the people about him to withdraw, that he might offer up his soul to his Maker by unreservedly confessing all his iniquities. He had two friends, he says, to help him at this strait, one of whom got a boat for him, which was kept waiting in the middle of the stream, while the other gave him notice of the arrangement. He then threw himself into the river, and, being a bold swimmer, dived across to the boat, which instantly set out for Dáccá."

"Ah, he must have been a daring youth indeed if he was really able to make such an escape as that. Well, what followed?"

"From Dáccá Pratápa Chunder went to wash himself at Bárni, the confluence of the Gungá and the Brahmapootra where we have bathed; and, having ascertained that there was no pursuit after him, he continued his pilgrimage to many distant shrines in different directions, visiting even the Punjáb and Cáshmere."

"Well?"

"Having finally completed the course of travelling dictated by his remorse, Pratápa Chunder returned to Burdwán after the lapse of some twenty years, but only to find that his father was dead, and that the *Ráj* had been assumed by the son of Parán Báboo; and he is fighting out stoutly now to recover his own."

"His story is a very circumstantial one, and ought to be supported by very circumstantial evidence. If he escaped from Culná by diving into the river, how came it to be believed at the time that he had died?"

"He explains it by stating that, as soon as Parán

Báboo came to know of his escape, he procured a dead body and had it burnt on the river-side with great ceremony as that of the Rájáh's son, which deceived Tej Chunder and all others, and cut off the ground under Pratápa."

"There must have been many witnesses of the cremation, and all of them could not have been Parán Báboo's people. Did nobody get an inkling of the deception practised by Parán?"

"There was a crowd of witnesses of course, but they either had no means of knowing that it was another body that was being burnt, or were persons interested in upholding the deception that was practised."

"Do you believe the claimant's story yourself, Bábájee?"

"I am rather disposed to do so, but should like to hear all that they may have to urge in Court on either side. The best part of the evidence ought to be forthcoming at the trial."

They were both present at the trial, but were rather disappointed at the proofs which were offered, which consisted simply of deliberate swearing on one side, opposed by equally deliberate swearing on the other. On this evidence the Court held that the claim was not substantiated, and the claimant was punished for false personation.

"How *false*, when no attempt has been made to establish that he is other than what he professes to be?" observed the Sunyási, turning towards Monohur, in a dissatisfied tone. "His identity with one Kristo Láll Brahmacháree was repeatedly asserted. Why was it not proved by the testimony of such people as may happen to know the Brahmacháree best?"

"Because no one was willing perhaps to come and peach upon a poor fellow already pushed to the verge of the precipice on which he stood."

"No, no; it is not that at all," said the Sunyási, looking very wise. "There has been a great failure of justice here, my son, and I am afraid it is the long purse of the occupant Rájáh that has given him the victory."

This set Monohur a thinking on the subject again, the result of which was the germination of new fears.

"I am afraid, Bábájee, that there is in this case an unfortunate resemblance to mine," said he at last. "Here have I been wandering hither and thither unknown to the world, like Pratápa, and who knows but that somebody else may not have meanwhile appropriated my estates to himself?"

"Ah, that is not possible as regards yourself, my son. Your estates are in very safe keeping—namely, in that of my brother, the priest of Nággesur Mahádeva, at Boná Ghát."

CHAPTER XXXIII.

BYJANÁTH, OR DEOGURH.

"Let us proceed quickly now to Gayá," said Monohur; "we have lost much time, somewhat unprofitably I think, at this place."

The Sunyási did not contradict his companion, nor look offended.

"I have just received intelligence," said he, "that the road through Deogurh is now practicable, and we need stop nowhere on it till we come to that place, which is about half-way from this to Gayá."

"Will it be necessary to stay for any time at Deogurh itself?"

"No, certainly not. The spot is a pretty one, one of the prettiest in all Bengal; but there is nothing in it that need detain us beyond a single night."

Deogurh, or Byjanáth, is situated in the extreme north-west corner of the district of Beerbhoom, and is mainly remarkable for a group of handsome temples and a small pellucid lake, which are visited by Hindu pilgrims from all parts of India, and especially from Rájpootáná and the countries adjacent to it. The resort of pilgrims to it from Lower Bengal is also great, chiefly because the site lies almost on the direct road from Calcuttá to Benáres; but this road was at times so infested with robbers, and the annoyance caused to the pilgrims thereby was so

BYJANÁTH, OR DEOGURH.

great, that the Government had to interfere to make it passable. This led to the appointment of *Ghátwáls,* or guardians of the passes, who were no other than the robbers themselves, made merry on finding that, instead of being punished for their misbehaviour, they were endowed with gifts of rent-free land, for the performance of a duty which only meant the compounding of violence by the levy of a fixed black-mail. The exaction, however, was never complained of by the pilgrims, who were delighted with the safety it ensured; and Monohur and the Sunyási proceeded on their journey without experiencing any trouble or inconvenience, and more easily, in fact, than the latter had expected.

"The road is very solitary, Bábájee, but the rocky scenery around us is quite charming to look at."

"Yes, it is an easy and agreeable enough road now," said the Sunyási; "but I know of times when it was otherwise, when travellers shivered at the sight of those very rocks which appear to be so pleasing to you."

"Ah, I have heard that these barren passes used to be guarded by monsters in the past, though there is nothing here to frighten us at present, except yon crouching toll-gatherer, who is waiting there, I suppose, for the fee."

The Sunyási looked towards the figure to which his attention was drawn.

"That is the Ghátwál's man to be sure," said he, "and, if you remove the covering from his head, you will find in him the identical monster who illustrated the stories of old. But the fiends have no longer as much liberty as they had before, and, this pittance paid, we have nothing more to fear from them, though there is no doubt that they would have crushed us against yon jagged stones before allowing us to pass by them so easily, if they could have had their own way yet."

As he spoke these words he dropped the usual pass-rate into the hands of the Páháriáh, who scarcely moved from his post to receive the money. Monohur had a good steadfast look at the man, and was not indisposed to admire his well-knit frame, but his attention was sharply drawn away from him in another direction.

"We see something before us now at a distance, Bábájee, don't we? Something like buildings with spiry summits mingling with the skies?"

"Your eyes are younger, my son, and see further than mine. But I think I perceive now what you refer to. They are the cluster of temples which have made their site so famous."

"Yes, the temples indeed!" exclaimed Monohur; "and they could not look finer than they do now. I quite enjoy the sight from this distance, Bábájee. They all seem to be very handsome edifices, but the great temple in the middle looks by far the best."

The temples at Deogurh are twenty-two in number, all surrounded by a wall inclosing an extensive court-yard paved with reddish stones. The great temple, which had particularly arrested Monohur's attention, has the reputation of having been built by one Poorun Mul, a Rájáh of Gidbaur, who also established a *melá*, yet held at the place at the time of the Holi festival, which lasts for eight days.

"I thought you had got tired with everything, Monohur," observed the Sunyási, who had scarcely yet forgotten his companion's condemnation of their short stay at Burdwán, "and am glad indeed to find that you are pleased with the sight now before you."

"O, father, I am still very anxious to push on to Gayá quickly, but cannot help regarding our arrival here at this moment as somewhat of a coincidence. The place is a peculiarly sweet one, and very well adapted, I think, for the rest we absolutely require to recover from our weariness. To look at yon buildings illuminated by the afternoon sunlight is in itself a reviving sight to me."

"Yes, a night's rest here, Monohur, is certainly necessary for us; nor will it delay our journey in the least. But we must leave the place to-morrow at dawn, so you had better make the best of the daylight yet remaining by inspecting everything that has to be seen."

Baidanáth is a name of Mahádeva, and the place is so called after him; but the local tradition in regard to the name which Monohur learnt was different. He had scarcely entered the stone porch, which leads to the temple-yard, when he was met by a priest with silver locks, who, pleased with his frank, wondering countenance, offered to show him over the place.

"Whence come you, my son? And whither are you going?"

"O, father, we come from Sátgáon, viá Burdwán, and are going to Gayá."

"Your stay here then must be of the briefest, I fancy, for people bound to Gayá have mostly a painful duty to discharge, and can scarcely wish to rest anywhere on the journey."

"That is exactly our case, Mohásoy, and we leave this place early to-morrow."

"Then come along with me now, my son. There is enough of the day yet to walk over the sacred precincts.

I divined your errand here at once, and have come forward to help you."

The face of Monohur was lighted with a transient gleam of joy, and, accepting the offer of the old man with thankfulness, he followed his footsteps with alacrity, carefully criticising the beauty of each edifice to which his attention was drawn.

All the temples were found to be more or less old, but they were very massively built, and had quite a holy look; and several of them had large stone figures cut on them, which were particularly striking. The terrace on which the temples stood was surrounded by ponderous moss-grown balustrades on three sides, and at each angle of it was a broad flight of steps leading down to a second terrace with sloping green banks that melted into the turf on the lawn. Something more than an hour was spent in walking over the entire area, and, though every temple was visited and minutely looked into, Monohur was yet sorry when it grew dark.

"Is there no story, father, connected with the erection of these edifices, or the establishment of the shrine?" asked he now of the priest. "By whom was the site chosen? By whom built upon?"

"Ah, the story! Every pilgrim takes the greatest interest in that, and is eager to hear it retold, though it is nothing but a mere story after all. I cannot vouch for the truth of it, my son; nay, I may say that I take it for a tale only. But I shall tell it to you willingly since you so earnestly wish to hear it."

"Yes, father, I do; and I shall listen to your narrative with great interest."

"It is this then, my son—

"They say that there was once a rich Goáláh in this

place, named Byjoo, who had a supreme contempt for the Bráhman character, which, he held, was a mere compound of idleness, profligacy, and falsehood. He made a point therefore to insult and maltreat the class.

"'Art thou mad, Byjoo, that thou darest to rise up against us?' remonstrated the men who were thus persecuted by him. 'Knowest thou not that he that ill-uses a Bráhman is no better than an infidel?'

"'I know more than that, surely,' replied Byjoo. 'I know that ye are Bráhmans in nothing but in name; that ye are bloodthirsty robbers and thieves, the seducers of youth and innocence, impostors and hypocrites; and shall I not do the duty I owe to my Maker by driving ye out of this place?'

"'O monster of ingratitude, what impiety art thou speaking? Are we not God's vicegerents on the earth, and shall a low-born Goáláh abuse us with impunity?'

"'What, ye foul-mouthed villains! dare ye speak of yourselves and the Deity in the same breath, and shall I not sweep ye out of the country with the besom and the broom?'

"And he actually did so persecute them that they had no safety except in flight. They did not retire, however, without attempting to raise the people against him.

"'Will ye acknowledge such an infidel as your chief?' asked they of the Goáláhs.

"But their appeal elicited no such response as they had wished to evoke.

"'Yes,' answered the Goáláhs. 'He is as worthy a chief as any we could wish for. It is not for us to judge between you and him.'

"A short time after, a number of Byjoo's cows having strayed into the jungle, Byjoo was obliged to go out in search of them. It was a sultry, drowsy evening, and he went with a rod upon his shoulder to drive the cows home. He had scarcely entered the outskirts of the jungle, however, when he was startled to see a stranger approaching him—a white-coloured being, dressed exactly as Mahádeva is exhibited, and having all the emblems of that deity about him.

"'Whither bound, Byjoo?' asked this individual of the Goáláh.

"'To search for my cows.'

"'O, I shall help you to find them. Stay here with me, and they will come to you;' and the words had scarcely passed forth than the cows began to come in from every direction.

"'Who are you, lord?' asked the Goáláh of the appearance in dismay.

"'Don't you recognise me by my habit, Byjoo? I am Mahádeva, whom the Bráhmans you despise affect to adore.'

"'Ah, have I done wrong then in persecuting and punishing them? O, give me time, lord, to repent if I have sinned against you!'

"'No, Byjoo, no; thou hast not sinned against me. Be not afeard, for I am neither rigorous nor revengeful, except towards those who practise iniquity. Far from being offended, I have been much pleased with thy treatment of my Sabáits, for they are really as despicable in character as you take them to be, and they bring discredit on my name. Thrash them out of the country therefore, Byjoo, and get me a new set, and I shall exalt thy name higher than all thy wealth may.'

"Byjoo did as he was told. The Sabáits of the god were ignominiously expelled from the country and a new set brought in; and from that day Byjoo had the august addition of 'Náth' or 'Lord' attached to his name."

"I suppose the place rose into note under the *régime* thus introduced?"

"Yes, the fame of the story went forth far and wide, and merchants, and rájáhs, and priests vied with each other in establishing the sanctity of a site where Mahádeva had personally appeared, and in beautifying it with the temples you have seen."

"Are they all dedicated to the worship of Mahádeva then?"

"All, with the exception of the last three we went to, which are dedicated to Tripoorá Soondari, the wife of the deity."

Monohur had a good sound sleep that night at Byjanáth, but it was nevertheless full of dreams. He saw the shade of Byjoo again and again; he saw his cows also; but the all-engrossing vision of the night was that of Mahádeva, who appeared to be smiling as propitiously on the sleeper as he had done on Byjoo in the tale. It was with great alacrity therefore that Monohur got up next morning on being summoned by the Sunyási to resume their journey.

CHAPTER XXXIV.

AT GAYÁ.

A PILGRIM to Gayá sets out for the purpose of freeing his ancestors from purgatory, and for procuring their admission into heaven, and before starting from home has to shave his head and face and make presents to the Bráhmans. This Monohur had not done, for the idea of starting for Gayá did not originate at Boná Ghát but at Sátgáon, which was not his native village; but, as Byjanáth was a sacred place, the Sunyási and the temple priests were quite in accord in recommending the omission being now rectified.

"What am I to do then? What is the course to pursue?"

"Shave yourself within the sacred inclosure here, my son, give what presents you choose to the Bráhmans and the poor, and call upon the souls of your ancestors, and especially on the soul of your mother, to accompany you on your journey."

Monohur did as he was directed, the last act with streaming eyes; and he was fervently blessed by the silver-headed priest who had conducted him over the temple grounds, and was assured that the preliminaries had all been carefully gone through.

"You have sad memories to disturb you, my son," said the old man with much tenderness, after having observed his grief; "but the sense of pain that weighs you down so heavily at present will, I am sure, be much allayed when your mission at Gayá is over. Do you know anyone there to go to? If not, I shall give you a note to an old *Tole* mate of mine, named Lakshmi Náráyan Pundit, who will be glad to see that you are not inconvenienced there in any way, nor imposed upon."

This was a desirable arrangement, for the Gayáwál Bráhmans have at all times retained a name for unfairness and deceit; and Monohur thankfully received the billet that was given to him.

"Is there anything more to do here or on the road, Mohásoy?"

"No, my son. You have only to transport yourself now, as quickly as you may, to the abode of my friend."

The city of Gayá stands on the Phálgoo, some sixty miles to the south-west of Pátná. The site is picturesque and hilly, but was not easily accessible till the recent opening of the railway to it. Our pilgrims had a hard time of it in their day; but they were accustomed to all sorts of privations, and it boots not to describe how the place was eventually reached by them. The name of Pundit Lakshmi Náráyan was one of great celebrity there, and no difficulty was experienced in finding him out. He was an old man himself, but still very attentive to strangers; and he received Monohur and the Sunyási with great pleasure and cordiality, and made all the arrangements necessary for accommodating them comfortably, and for carrying them through their course of devotions.

"There is one thing that troubles me," said he, "namely this, that I am too imbecile to help you through your work personally. But I shall find a good Gayáwál to attend on you, and you may depend on his directions as safely as on mine."

The Gayáwál selected came shortly after, and he certainly seemed to be an honest man—as honest as a Gayáwál Bráhman can well be.

"I am at your service, my son," said he to Monohur. "But you have first to decide how many Tirthas you will visit; for some visit one only, others two, others thirty-eight, and others again all the forty-five that exist."

"Well, since I am here I shall visit the whole of them," said Monohur; "but I would first of all perform my mother's *shrád* wherever it has to be made."

"You must do that on the banks of the Phálgoo," replied the Gayáwál, "and then go on visiting the several Tirthas in regular succession, depositing at each of them a *pinda*, or ball of rice, for the acceptance of your parent, while I shall recite the usual prayers over the offerings on your behalf."

"Should I not repeat the words after you?"

"Yes, if you can do so with celerity; otherwise it will be enough for you to repeat the leading words while I get on with the rest; and this is the course that is most usually followed."

They began their devotions by repairing to the banks of the Phálgoo, which are held to be particularly holy for a distance of about half a mile, within which the *pinda* for redemption has to be offered. The *shrád* is performed on a piece of ground especially set apart for the purpose, in which a small *bedi*, or altar, is marked out. On the *bedi* are laid thin stalks of *kusa* grass, while hard by are arranged small vessels, or *khooris*, of rice or barley, *til*, honey, and *chandan*. The *pinda* is a ball of rice or barley, and the person offering it has to place it on the *bedi* in the manner indicated to him by the priest, and then to scatter over it whatever else (gold, clothing, betel-leaf, areca-nut, etc.) which he may wish to offer. Water is then either gently poured over, or sprinkled on it, and with joined hands the performer of the rite beseeches the spirit of the ancestor to whom the offering is made to come and accept of it.

The *pindas* offered by Monohur were formed of rice and milk, and were many in number—namely, one for each of his parents, two for his two grandfathers, two for his two grandmothers, with others for uncles, aunts, and other near relatives. They were offered one after another, the *bedi* being previously sprinkled over with Tulsi leaves and the *kusa* grass, while *kusa* grass knots were twisted round a finger of each hand to purify the hands for the performance of the ceremony.

"It was here that Rám Chandra performed the *shrád* of his father Dasaratha, by offering to him a *pinda* of sand," said the Gayáwál to Monohur, "and with a heart equally devoted do thou offer, O my son! the first *pinda* to your mother."

Monohur did as he was told, almost trembling with emotion, but without omitting any of the forms required to be observed.

"Now invoke the spirit of your mother and beseech her to accept of your offering."

He did so with a heart bursting with love and devotion, and looking upwards towards the sky saw, through the tears that dimmed his eyesight, the shade of his mother looking exceedingly beautiful and compassionate, but habited in such shining white as almost bewildered his brain.

Monohur uttered a cry of anguish.

"O, mother, dearest mother! take me with you now and for ever, and I shall never leave your side again!"

"Good son of a good mother," said the priest, "you must not distress yourself in that manner now, for you have plenty of work yet to get through. Your mother cannot take you with her, for she is a spirit come hither from the spirit-land, whither you may not follow her at present. But she will watch over you ever, since you have performed her *gati* and opened the door of salvation to her."

The other *pindas* were now successively laid on the *bedi*, and the same formula was gone through over each, though more hurriedly than in the first case, owing to Monohur's mind being yet much agitated and disturbed.

"We may stop here now, I think?" asked the Sunyási in a suggestive way, as soon as the last rice-ball had been thus disposed of.

"Yes, we may. Your young companion is too much affected already to be able to do aught more to-day."

The observances were renewed next morning by the party proceeding to *Pretsilá*, or the Ghost Hill, at a distance of about seven miles from the city, where a temple stands on the hill, which is reached by four hundred rocky steps.

"Have we to get up by these slippery ascents?"

"Yes, to offer the *pinda* at the temple itself, and then you get down again and bathe in the Brahmákoond yonder, and perform your devotions at the shrine of Párvati."

It was with some difficulty that Monohur was able to comply; but this was only the first of his troubles, and there were a multitude of them yet to go through. After coming down from one hill he had to ascend another, named *Rámsilá*, which, though not as high as *Pretsilá*, was found to be more tedious to mount owing to the steps being wider; and at the foot of this hill also there is a tank named Rámkoond, where an offering had to be made. The next thing after that was to deposit an offering at the foot of a *Burr* tree, which closed the devotions of the day.

The course for the third day was confined to visiting five sacred places within the city; and Monohur was already congratulating himself that the most wearisome part of the work was over, when he was called upon, on the fourth day, to go out beyond the city on a round o Tirthas that knocked him up completely before half the day was over.

"I am feeling very weary. Can we not stop here for the day, father?"

"Not at this stage surely," said the Gayáwál. "The *bedis* have to be visited in proper order, and on particular days, and a good part of to-day's work remains yet to be gone through."

"What you say is the letter of the rules perhaps," answered Monohur, somewhat pettishly. "May we not read their spirit more favourably?"

"Ah, yes, the spirit is doubtless the real thing, my son; but the letter must also be observed, and you surely cannot close for this day without visiting the fig-tree at Buddha Gayá, under which Sákya Muni sat in meditative abstraction for five years."

"The tree under which Sákya Muni performed his devotions? Do I hear you aright, father?"

"Yes, my son, you do."

"Why, Sákya Muni has been dead now some two

thousand and five hundred years or so. Can the tree be as old as that?"

"Even so; for that tree can never die."

"It is very hard to believe that, surely; but, at any rate, you have dispelled my weariness, father, by exciting my curiosity, and I would go to it at once by all means."

They did go to the tree accordingly, and devoutly was the *pinda* offered at its foot. But the appearance of the tree did not quite establish the marvellous age assigned to it, and Monohur was unable to grant the implicit conviction demanded of him on that point. The trunk of the tree was much decayed indeed, and most of its branches were barkless and rotten; but the stem and branches on one side were yet green, and it seemed as if this result had been attained by planting a new tree inside the decaying stem of an older one.

"It is a high tree," said Monohur, "and decidedly old, but certainly not older than a hundred or a hundred and fifty years, I think. Two thousand and five hundred years is apparently a most preposterous age to claim for it."

"You are talking foolishly, my son, of things you do not comprehend. Look at the tree with the eye of faith and you will think very differently of it than you do now. It was blessed by him to whom it gave shade to eat his rice and milk, and also by the Devatás who crowded around the sage to listen to his instructions. Can such a tree ever shrivel up or die?"

Monohur received the reply dubiously, with the air of a person who had little sympathy with such monkish beliefs; but no further discussion on the point was called for, and he was wise enough to keep silent where discussion could only lead to misconstruction.

The devotions of the fifth day were commenced by a visit to the famous temple of Vishnupad, which bears the mark of Vishnu's foot, which was most devoutly worshipped by the Sunyási. The number of *bedis* here was so great that it took the pilgrims five days to perform all the *poojáhs* that had to be gone through, after which they crossed the Phálgoo to visit Rám Gayá, a small wooded hill opposite to the city.

"I am quite sick of this wearisome round of services, Bábájee," complained Monohur to his confidant and friend.

"So am I," replied the Sunyási; "but we have begun and must finish them properly, and a day or two more at most will give us the wished for relief."

The relief came at last, the devotions at all the forty-five Tirthas being finished in fifteen days.

"I congratulate you heartily on the completion of your errand here, my son," said the priest now to Monohur. "Are you well satisfied with the manner in which I have performed my duty to you?"

"Certainly," said Monohur, "and we are very much beholden to you for it."

"You do not seem to be half as grateful for it though as you ought, young man," replied the Gayáwál, more severely than he had ever spoken to Monohur before. "Do you know what service I have rendered to you by my ministration? I have not only opened the road out of purgatory for all your ancestors, but have secured their and your salvation also."

"O, father, I fully appreciate your labours," responded Monohur, "and am really very grateful for them;" and the Gayáwál was not unwilling to believe that it was so when a few bright silver pieces were slipped into his hands.

s

CHAPTER XXXV.

SÁKYA, AND SOME STORIES ABOUT HIM.

PUNDIT LAKSHMI NÁRÁYAN was a very amiable old man, habitually distinguished by an undefinable expression of good-nature in his face, which was a faithful index of the gentleness of his heart. He was a strict Hindu, and, despite his scholarship, believed sincerely with the Gayá-wál that the Buddha fig-tree was two thousand and five hundred years old. There were several other orthodox stories of similar character to which he clung with equal tenacity; and it gave him great pleasure to dilate upon these for the edification of those who came within the range of his beneficence or instruction.

"You believe, sir, that the tree is two thousand and five hundred years old?" asked Monohur of the scholar somewhat anxiously.

"I can have no doubt on the point, my son," was the reply. "Sákya Muni was a great saint, and it was nothing for him to confer freshness and immortality on a tree."

Monohur looked doubtful and unsatisfied, upon which the Pundit uttered something like a sigh.

"I cannot blame your incredulity, my son," said he; "but the people of Gayá knew Sákya personally in the past, and were witnesses of all he did among them; and we, their descendants, are bound to accept their convictions as they have come down to us."

"The argument is hardly logical, Mohásoy," said Monohur. "The contemporaries of Sákya at Gayá may have heard him bless a tree, but they were not witnesses of its long life, and it is that marvel only that I hesitate to accept."

"I understand your difficulty, my son. The science of the age regards the utterances of orthodoxy as ignorant mistakes, while orthodoxy regards the objections of science as dogmatic nonsense. With so much difference to start with an agreement in belief between the two is of course not to be expected. But the lives of our Rishis were all more or less marvellous, and of none more so than of Sákya, and it does appear to us of the old school that the time for wondering at such relations has long gone by."

The Pundit spoke with some feeling, and Monohur hardly knew what reply to make to him.

"For my own part, Mohásoy," said he at last, "I do not exactly disbelieve all that is said of the sayings and doings of our older sages; and of Sákya in particular I would be loath indeed to speak except with veneration and love. But the tree—"

"O, let us abandon the tree then, if it be the only stumbling block between you and me," replied the Pundit, smilingly, "or rather let us throw it down as a bridge to get over the disagreement that momentarily separates us. What is your opinion of the other marvels related of Sákya?"

"I can hardly have any opinion, sir, of what I do not know. I am very ignorant of the history of his life, and would like exceedingly if you would recite some of the more remarkable passages of it for my instruction."

"Most willingly will I do that," said the Pundit; and

he began the narration in a very sweet manner peculiar to himself.

"Sákya was the son of a Rájáh of Kapilávastyá, named Suddhodana, by his wife Máyá. At the conception of Máyá the worlds were filled with light, the deaf heard, the dumb spake, the lame walked, the crooked were straightened, and all beings in heaven and earth were filled with joy."

"This I can well believe in with you, Mohásoy, for it was only an especial way elected by the Most High to signify to the world that He had sent an especial agent for its instruction."

"Yes, and it was particularly announced at the time by far-seeing prophets and seers that if the child in Máyá's womb reigned on his father's throne he would be a *Chakravati*, or universal sovereign, while if he became a recluse he would be a Buddha, and the greatest of the Buddhas, who would make all the worlds glad with the ambrosia of *Nirván*."

"And what did he choose, sir, to begin with?"

"He was brought up by his parents in accordance with his birth; and it was not till he had grown up and had become a father that his mind was otherwise turned. It was the sight of a corse lying on the road-side that effected the change.

"'I am a prince, young and vigorous,' said he mournfully, as he looked at the dead, 'but, like that body, I too must die. Nothing on earth is stable, nothing real. Why should I not endeavour to find out what reality is?'

"He determined to be a recluse to this end, and, deserting wife, child, and parents, he went out of his father's house to beg his living in the streets. A peasant's wife having, in responding to one of these calls, come out, leading her child by the hand, the thoughts of home, wife, and child were recalled to his mind, and overwhelmed him with agony. But he arose purified, murmuring that his mission was, not to care for the welfare of any particular family, however dear it might be to him, but to free the world from the thraldom of death."

"What a brave, noble idea that was indeed!" exclaimed Monohur, with unfeigned applause and the moisture of admiration in his eyes; while the Pundit went on rehearsing his story, pleased to find that he was listened to with attention.

"One day a mother, having lost her only child, came to Sákya, asking him to restore his life, 'For surely,' said she, 'thou canst do it if thou wilt.'

"'Get me a handful of *dhán* then,' said the sage, 'from a house in which no person has ever died, to enable me to accomplish what you desire;' and the woman went forth readily to get the article required.

"But there was no such house to be found anywhere, for in every place they complained of having lost husband or wife, brother or sister, son or daughter; and the truth thus gently taught was learnt, and the woman, coming back to the sage, simply laid herself at his feet.

"'You thought that you alone had lost a son,' said Sákya to her kindly. 'The law of death is for us all. Follow me if you want to know what the law of life is.'"

"This was a very superior lesson indeed, and most naively imparted," said Monohur; "and you see, Muhásoy, how Sákya avoided attempting a miracle when he was sorely tempted to commit himself."

"Ah, but I have not exhausted the history about him, my son. He did work miracles, or wonders at all events, of even greater import than conferring immortality on a tree; and of such a character was his performance at Rájowlee, which he passed on his way to Gayá.

"Rájowlee, as you have seen it, is a goodly town to this day; but at the time of Sákya it was of much larger dimensions, and the residence of a king. The Rájáh was great in every respect, but extremely unhappy, for a terrible Rákshasi went about the city, from house to house, at night, and eat up every man and woman who was unable to escape her. No traces of the demon were found in the day, and no one had the slightest idea as to where she lived, or whence she came.

"The king ordered several precautions to be taken against her depredations; but they were of no avail. His soldiers could not keep her out of the city at night, nor were his police able to find out where she burrowed in the day.

"It was at this juncture that Sákya entered the town, clothed in the habit of a *Bhikshu*, and carrying with him a *Námmálá* and a few *Poonthees*.[1] He arrived late in the evening, and applied to a woodman for quarters for the night.

"'You are very welcome surely,' said the woodman's wife. 'Our house has little accommodation in it, and our means are slender; but everything that we have is freely at your disposal, since you have not despised to honour us.'

"'O, good dame,' said the sage, 'my wants are even less than your means, and I shall surely remain better here than under richer roofs.'

"'Make yourself comfortable then, in your own way,' said the woman, 'and mind this, only that you keep the

[1] Sacred books.

door of your apartment fast at night, and take not a wink of sleep. We sleep in this city at day-time, and watch in the night.'

"'Ha! That is a rather unusual practice. May I know the cause of it?'

"'Yes,' said the woodman's wife; and she related the story of the Rákshasi as you have heard it.

"'Very good, dame,' said Sákya. 'Now make me a fire before the door of your house and I shall sit up there the whole night and protect all of you here, and, may be, I shall also be able to discover the Rákshasi.'

"'Don't be so rash as that,' remonstrated the woman. 'It will go hard with us if a Bhikshu is killed in our house; and for your own sake also we dissuade you from undertaking such a risk.'

"'But there is no risk at all to me, dame,' answered Sákya. 'The Poonthees I hold in my hand are feared even by the Devas in heaven, and the Daityas in *pátál*, and no Rákshasi will ever be able to harm me while I am so armed, for they are far more powerful than *khargas* and *parásus*.' Saying this the sage drew out a small Poonthee, and sat by the fire lighted for him to read.

"At night the yell of the Rákshasi was heard as usual, mingled with screams of fear from the people, and the terrible visitant was seen passing from house to house, doing as much mischief as usual.

"'Where is she?' asked some in deadly fright.

"'There, doubling yonder corner,' stammered others indistinctly in reply; and all eyes were involuntarily turned to the corner indicated, where stood the woodman's house, with Sákya on the watch.

"The Rákshasi saw the Bhikshu, and stretched out her arms to seize him; but she started back the moment the Poonthee was raised against her, and the sage having at the same time thrown a handful of dry beans into the fire, one of these refracted back hot and burning, and struck the fiend in the eye. With a fearful howl the Rákshasi fled, and everything was quiet in the city for the rest of the night.

"The door of the woodman's house was besieged by a large number of visitors early on the following morning, all anxious to greet the Bhikshu with thanks for having so successfully repelled the demon during the night, which had never before been achieved.

"'But surely she will come again? Can you not destroy her for good?'

"'It is for the king to do so. I can find out the Rákshasi for him if he wishes it.'

"The king heard with delight the account of the Bhikshu's adventure as it was related to him; and, when it was further reported that the young mendicant had offered to point out the Rákshasi to him, he deputed his officers of state to beseech him to come to the palace to advise and direct him.

"'Will you find out the Rákshasi for us, O youth; her who has depopulated my capital for so many years?'

"'Yes, sire, if you will allow me to search for her in every place.'

"'You can do that assuredly, and no one will care to hinder you;' and Sákya went from house to house, but could not find the wicked being anywhere.

"'Well, you have not been successful in your search yet, Bhikshu. Do you despair of it?'

"'Certainly not,' said Sákya, 'for your own palace still remains unsearched.'

"'My palace! Surely the Rákshasi cannot be here?'

"'I am unable to answer you till I have looked for her in it.'

"'Be it so then,' said the king, 'and I myself will show you over it;' and there was silence all through the building as the Bhikshu, accompanied by the king, went from room to room, looking fixedly at the face of every inmate, till he came to the apartments of the king's most favourite wife.

"'You cannot enter here,' said one of the female servants of the queen.

"'Why so?' asked the king, in a rather unpleasant and peremptory tone.

"'Because the queen is unwell, my lord, and keeps her bed.'

"'Unwell? I did not hear of it. Unwell since when, and what is she ailing of?'

"'She fell sick last night, and an eye of hers is distempered. She cries out and says that it is burning; and she will not see anyone.'

"'That is the Rákshasi, O king!' said Sákya; and he related the whole story of what had taken place in the night.

"'Ah! it is just what my mind had foreboded, and yet refused to believe. Great is your penetration and knowledge, O sage, and you must suffer me to be a Bhikshu with you that I may gather wisdom from your lips.'

"The Rákshasi was buried alive by order of the king, who became a Bhikshu; and he accompanied Sákya in all his wanderings."

"The tale is a pleasing one," said Monohur, "but you must really excuse me, Mohásoy, if I cannot force my mind to believe in Rákshases and Rákshasis; nor would

Sákya perhaps have much liked the connection of such a story with his name."

"Why not? It says nothing but what bears the most honourable testimony of him."

"Ah, that of course. But what I have heard of Sákya, represents him as the very symbol of truth, while those accounts of Rákshases and other similar beings, though they are extremely popular, are, it appears to me, all more or less untrue."

"Do you say that, Monohur," exclaimed the Sunyási, "after what you saw yourself at Boná Ghát on your return home?"

Monohur was almost struck dumb by the argument *ad hominem* advanced against him, but still endeavoured to make a distinction between a belief in spirits and one in Rákshases and monsters.

"That is a distinction without a difference, my son," said Pundit Lakshmi Náráyan. "You, who have had a personal illustration of the supernatural, ought to be the last person to doubt the accuracy of such a long and well received story as that I have narrated to you. There are really more things in heaven and earth than we do or can possibly know of."

CHAPTER XXXVI.

AT BENÁRES.

THE seven pre-eminently holy places in India are: Káshi, Kánchi, Hurdwár, Ayodhya, Prayága, Jagganáth, and Mathoorá, and of these Káshi is held to be the most important—that is, the most sacred seat of Hinduism. It has, in fact, the credit of being a portion of heaven let down upon the earth for the salvation of mankind, and forms the chief stronghold of Saivaism, as it was of Buddhism in the past.

"Where do we go now? Which is the next Tirthasthán for us to visit?" asked Monohur of the Sunyási, in a consulting tone.

"Siva Dhaniya Káshi![1] Siva Dhaniya Káshi!" burst forth the latter in an exulting strain, starting from his seat. "We are now nearest to it, my son, and should see it before any other place."

The enthusiasm of the Sunyási was quickly caught by Monohur.

"I too am very anxious, father, to see that ancient seat of learning and holiness, to hear the very name of which both delights the ear and purifies the heart."

"You are right, my son, you are right; for such in truth are the virtues of that name. There is no holier

---

[1] *I.e.* Káshi exalted of Siva.

place than Káshi on the earth, for it is the residence of all our thirty-three millions of deities; and its purity is so great that to the Hindu death in it secures immediate salvation, while even to the Mlech'ha (impure), though he may not obtain emancipation thereby, his sins are forgiven him."

"Should we not make it our home for good then, Bábájee, seeing that we have no other place to retire to?"

"No, my son. You are young, and I am too worldly-minded yet to advise you to withdraw yourself from your kind in the prime of life, even for a residence in Káshi itself. Káshi is the final home of all orthodox Hindus, but only after the decline of life has been reached. It would suit me well as a place of rest, if I chose to remain in it and could do so; but you have other duties in the world to perform, and must not fly from them."

"I do not feel so, Bábájee. Since my mother's death I have known no such thrilling delight in life as I might not easily give up."

"One chain, and perhaps the most pleasing chain of all, that bound you to the world has indeed been very abruptly broken; but we shall forge others for you, my son, which you must bear, and which you will bear willingly when you get accustomed to them. Life has many duties, and you must be true to them all."

Monohur gave no answer, and was perhaps unequal to do so; nor did the Sunyási care to pursue the subject further. There was much to do in connection with their forward journey, and he was soon very busy with their details.

The road from Gayá to Benáres passes through a most beautiful country, though in some places it is excessively lonely, nay, almost alarmingly desolate. As a rule, however, pilgrims encounter no disagreeable stoppages on it, beyond perhaps the challenge of an exacting chowkeydár, or the clamorous expostulations of the ferryman on the Soane, and these were the only two impediments that our travellers met with.

"We have reached the sacred city at last," exclaimed the Sunyási, as they arrived on the banks of the Ganges. "Yonder is Rájghát before us, and we have only to cross the river."

"Ah! is that the front of the city then that we see on the other side of the stream? What a beautiful panorama it presents indeed! Such a place must surely be worthy of the gods!"

Benáres is built on a bend of the Ganges, and extends, or extended at one time, from the Barna Nuddee on one side, to the Asi Nulláh on the other, which accounts for its name of Barna-Asi, or Báránasi. Its outward appearance is that of a high semi-circular amphitheatre of about four miles in length, overgrown with temples from one end to the other, and having a frontage of bathing *ghâts* of superb design. The river before it is crowded with boats, and the *ghâts* and river-banks are at all times full of pilgrims and bathers. The bank opposite to the city, where Monohur and the Sunyási now stood, is called Vyasa-Káshi, as having been set up by the great compiler of the Veds in rivalry to the gods; and, in derision of his effort, it has ever since been held that a Hindu dying at this place becomes an ass at his next birth.

"Let us quit this spot quickly, my son," said the Sunyási; and he began to hail out lustily for a boat.

"Why in such a hurry, Bábájee? Why not enjoy for a while the wonderful sight before us? Have you got wearied of it so soon?"

"Wearied of it? Of course I am. The ground we stand upon is accursed, and no Hindu should willingly tarry on it longer than he must."

A boat being now got Monohur and the Sunyási were ferried over the river with celerity, after which they entered the narrow streets of the sacred city, which they found crowded with hosts of pilgrims. The devotees were of all classes, and bore every variety of feature and appearance; but by far the most remarkable among them were the Byrágis, Sunyásis, and Fakirs, who were congregated in great numbers, and were very much honoured.

"There are many men of your cloth here, Bábájee," said Monohur; "but they do not, generally, seem to be much accustomed to abstinence and the mortifications of the flesh, which the Shástras require of them."

"Ah, my son, what you say is indeed true to a great extent, the Mohunts and Fakirs being for the most part drawn from the dregs of society by the desire of gain. But there are, nevertheless, those among them, Monohur, who are of a very superior character in all respects—well-read Pundits, thoroughly acquainted with the Veds and the Puráns, and very rigorous and strict in their discipline."

"Even more remarkable than the Mohunts and Fakirs, Bábájee, are the bulls which are passing so listlessly through the crowd; and I see that they are receiving offerings of flowers and food-grains from several people."

"They have a right to them, my son, for they are sacred to Mahádeva, to whom the city belongs."

"And the apes and monkeys seated upon the temples and surrounding walls, are they also sacred to the god, and entitled to be fed and worshipped?"

"Yes; and don't you observe how patiently they are waiting for the largesses to which they are accustomed?"

"Then let us do as the others are doing," said Monohur joyfully; and they fed and decorated the bulls, and threw out plantains and nuts among the apes as they passed on.

In the immediate vicinity of the temples several pilgrims were seen measuring the road with their bodies by continuous prostrations, a form of reaching a holy place which is held to be particularly efficacious. Monohur, who knew of the practice, was preparing to follow it when he was held back by the Sunyási.

"It will be enough, my son," said the latter, "if I do that for both of us, as I am used to it;" and he at once began his prostrations the moment the *pataká*, or ensign, of Visheswara's temple was visible to him.

Visheswara, as the sovereign deity of Benáres, is always the first to be visited by pilgrims. The temple dedicated to him is small, and stands in the midst of a roof-covered quadrangle, surmounted by a gilded tower.

"Siva Dhaniya Káshi! Siva Dhaniya Káshi!" were the words repeated here by every mouth with thundering acclaim, and by none more loudly than by Monohur, who caught the infection easily from those around him.

"What is the offering to make here, Bábájee?" asked he of his companion.

"We have only to pour water on the Lingam," said the Sunyási. "Mahádeva delights in nothing so much as in the water of the Ganges and the leaf of the *Bel* tree;" and the god they saw was soaking in water.

"Anything else to perform?"

"No, pass on; there are many shrines to visit, and me is very precious."

But here the *Gungápootra*, or priest of the temple, who was quite alive to his own interests, interposed.

"You are mistaken, friend, in believing that you can pass on without paying the officiating priest. Your worship goes for nothing if the priest be unpaid."

"O, I forgot, brother. Don't be angry with us for a mistake. Here is a *dumree* for you;" and the *dumree* (a copper coin) was cheerfully accepted, for nothing, however trivial, comes amiss to a Gungápootra.

The next place visited was the *Gyánkoop*, or Well of Knowledge, the place where Visheswara lay hid during one of the Mahomedan invasions of the city, and where, it is said, he has resided by choice ever since.

"It is very dark below, and I can see nothing there," observed Monohur.

"O, my son," said the Gungápootra who acted as showman at this place, "wisdom is darkness unto the uninitiated, but is the only road to light. Primeval darkness sits within the well. Thou canst see light only after having fathomed the depth of that darkness."

Monohur did not understand the jargon, nor had he time to waste in attempting to do so. They were hurried forward, as all at Benáres are, and stood next before the temple of Annapoorna, or the feeding-mother, the goddess of greatest repute in the city, who has a separate quadrangle to herself, and is exhibited dressed in jewellery.

Monohur stood exactly opposite to the goddess, face to face, and seemed to be rather astounded, if not frightened, at seeing the representation. But the other pilgrims evidently beheld it with different eyes.

"Is she not charmingly beautiful?" asked one of another, in the ardour of his devotion.

"Could she have otherwise ravished the heart of

Gauri Shunkur, and retained it ever so long?" was the significant reply.

The third deity visited was Bhaironáth, the Kotwál-god of Benáres, who keeps the city from evil spirits, and is armed with a *dunda*, or cudgel, which it is reported is freely used in the discharge of his duty.

"Ah, this is a god to my liking surely," said Monohur. "His club ought to be a terror to the evil-minded."

"And so it is," responded the Sunyási; "it effectually keeps the city clear of all knaves, mischief-makers, and evil-doers. But the god holds, nevertheless, a subordinate position, for he is only Mahádeva's chief officer of the peace."

Speaking in this vein, they proceeded to the Manikarnika Ghát, which stands in the middle of the river-bank of Benáres, and is held sacred to Vishnu, though it derives its name from an ear-ring of Mahádeva, or of his wife, having fallen into the sacred well, which more especially consecrates it. The well is square, and is encased in a series of stone steps which lead down to the water, which, though very dirty itself, has the reputation of washing away all sins, past, present, and to come.

"Just mark, Monohur, how the lower steps of the well are without any joinings at all. The original well, which was made by divine hands, is inclosed by those steps. The ground having risen afterwards it was found necessary to construct additional steps for the convenience of pilgrims. But human hands could not do without joinings, and the sacred division of the well is exhibited to this day in broad relief. Could there possibly be a better proof of the holiness of the place?"

Saying this the Sunyási descended into the well and bathed in it devoutly, along with some other pilgrims

T

who were equally particular; but Monohur, in common with the greater number, was content to sprinkle a few drops of the dirty water on his head, which is held to be quite as efficacious as complete immersion.

"Let us proceed now to visit the temple of Briddha-kál, or 'Old Age,' which, the Gungápootra will explain to you, has the reputation of healing all diseases and of prolonging life."

"How so?" asked Monohur, turning round to the Gungápootra for the information which he was expected to furnish.

"O, the tradition is," said the priest, "that in the Satya Yug an old and imbecile Rájáh, who took up his quarters here, having found favour with Mahádeva for his devotions and virtue, was completely healed of his illness and made young again. The temple was erected by him in grateful acknowledgment of the favour he had received, and, on his beseeching the god that the miracle performed on him might continue to be performed on the spot, his prayer was acceded to."

"Do old men then actually get young at the place to this day?" asked Monohur, with surprise.

"Not in the flesh, my son," replied the Gungápootra, "but in the spirit. The mind gets the innocence of childhood restored to it by worshipping at the shrine."

The number of shrines visited and of ceremonies performed were more numerous at Benáres even than at Gayá, and our travellers were necessarily compelled to remain in that city for nearly a month. Among the sacred places seen by them, other than those we have already named, were: the temples of Kedáreshwar, Doorgá, and Gauri; the Dasasamedh Ghát; and the Barna-Sangam and the Asi-Sangam, or the confluences of the Barna and the Asi respectively with the Ganges. At all the places visited there were some act or acts of devotion to perform; but, fortunately, the pilgrims were not required to perform every one of them personally, as the Gungápootras are indulgent guides, and are at all times eager to relieve the devotees of several observances, which they take upon themselves to go through for a consideration. The result being the same so far as the religious welfare of the pilgrims is concerned, even the Sunyási was glad to avail himself of such relief freely, and Monohur of course followed the example of his friend.

"Well, have we anything more to do here?" asked the Sunyási of the Gungápootra, when he found that the entire orthodox course of devotions was exhausted. "Have we not come to the end of the Tirthas now?"

"No, not yet," observed the priest, "for you have still to perform the pilgrimage of the Pánchkosi, which is an act of the greatest merit, and must on no account be omitted."

"How traverse the entire circuit of the road?" asked Monohur in alarm.

"On foot, and fasting all day," was the prompt reply; "and the worst of it is that this duty cannot be performed by proxy."

"But the distance is immense. It will take some days to walk over it. How then can that be done fasting?"

"O, very easily; for you fast only during the day. You set out early in the morning after bathing, and then stop at sunset at whatever place you may have arrived. you eat and rest there for the night, and then start afresh on the morrow, getting on just as on the previous day."

"Is there any particular point to start from?"

"Yes, Manikarnika Ghát is both the starting and the terminating point, for it is the *Mookti-Kshetra,* or place of final emancipation."

It took them just five days to perform this pilgrimage.

CHAPTER XXXVII.

STORIES ABOUT THE *DAKSHYA JAGYA*, AND THE *PISÁCH MOCHAN*.

MONOHUR was delighted with everything he saw at Benáres, and exhibited no small amount of intelligence in the comments he made.

"Now this is a place I like, Bábájee, even though it be really no better than a mart. It is large, stony, and crowded, which I, of course, abominate; but most of its *Mahalás* are snug and cozy notwithstanding, and what I like above all in it is that it is old, so very old."

"Why, what has its age to do with your liking, Monohur? Are not the terms 'old' and 'nasty' held to be nearly synonymous?"

"Not by all, surely?" answered the youth. "I regard the antiquities here to be worth looking at continuously, and it cannot be less pleasant to listen to the old, old-world stories about them."

"I don't know, my son, but that you would tire both of the tales and the antiquities before a week or two were over if you had nothing else to attend to; and you may commence the experiment even now by sending for some of the Gungápootras, who are the natural exponents of both."

"The Gungápootras? O, they would tire me to death in no time, I know. I should send for them only if I wanted to be bored. But if you could tell me any stories of the place yourself, Bábájee, would I not listen to them with avidity?"

"I know no such stories, my son, or I would willingly tell them to please you. All I could relate to you in respect to the place are at best some old Pouránic legends, which I may have heard in former times, should you care to know of them."

"Ah, anything from you, Bábájee, would, you may be sure, be very acceptable to me; and the older the account the greater should be my happiness in listening to it."

"Here is one then," said the Sunyási, "to begin with. I will give you an account of the *Dakshya Jagya*, Benáres having been the theatre of it, or at all events the capital of the king who performed the sacrifice— perhaps elsewhere, as others relate.

"Dakshya lived in a very remote age, you know, and gave his daughter, Sati, in marriage to Mahádeva. He was a rather queer-tempered old man, though for a long time he agreed well enough with his son-in-law, from being much attached to his daughter. But Mahádeva was always a careless chap, and on one occasion happened to be particularly inattentive to his father-in-law in an assembly of the gods where both of them were present.

"'Ah, he is disrespectful already,' said Dakshya to himself, 'and if I do not repay the slight in kind, he will doubtless become more and more impertinent hereafter;' and he began to make preparations for holding a religious festival, at which all the gods, demi-gods, and sages were invited.

"'We have received no invite from the king,' said Mahádeva to his wife.

"'O, papa has become old,' said Sati, 'and must have omitted us by mistake.'

"'It looks more like a defect of the heart,' said the god, 'than of the memory. I think the old gentleman intends to insult us.'

"'Impossible! He cannot mean that. Allow me to go over to him, and I shall set the matter right at once.'

"Mahádeva did not like the idea of his wife going even to her father's house uninvited, but eventually yielded to her importunity, and she went. But she was carelessly welcomed, and when the feast was served out there was no portion for her husband, which she was entitled to receive in his absence in addition to her own.

"Sati's eyes wandered sadly to her father's face, as if in the bitterness of her heart she wanted to understand whether any real offence were intended.

"'O, Sati, why are you looking in that way at me?'

"'I want to know why you have become such an unkind father to me so suddenly.'

"'Why? How? In what way?'

"'By omitting those little attentions which I and my husband are entitled to in this house, and were accustomed to receive.'

"'Speak of yourself, Sati—speak of yourself. A female always makes herself ridiculous when she speaks of her husband; and of your husband in particular the less you say in such an assembly the better:' and he went on descanting derisively on the personal appearance of his son-in-law. Sati remonstrated, and then spoke angrily, defending her husband; and, on her vehemence being laughed at and slighted, she beat her head on the ground in fury, and a shower of blood fell on the place from heaven.

"'You are creating a disturbance here, Sati, and had better go home to your husband,' said Dakshya, seeing that many of his guests were leaving the Jagya dissatisfied.

"'You have traduced my husband before your guests, and I shall not go back till I have avenged his honour;' and, becoming more and more excited, she threw herself into the fire in which the *homa*, or sacrifice, was being consumed, and was burnt to death.

"'I seek an urgent interview with you,' said Nárada to Mahádeva, running up to him and disturbing his meditations.

"'Why, what is the matter?'

"'Your wife, Sati, has killed herself on the *homa* fire in your father-in-law's house, for his having spoken unkind words of you before the other gods.'

"'Killed herself!'

"'Yes.'

"A frown like the thunder-cloud gathered on Mahádeva's brow, and the lightnings flashed from his eyes. The frown and the lightnings resolved themselves then into an army of demons, and Mahádeva called forth a giant named Birbhadra, and placed him at their head.

"'My father-in-law, Dakshya, is celebrating a religious festival in his house. Go there and get up a fight, and break up the assembly and the sacrifice.'

"The demons were only too glad to obey, and there was a terrific fight between the assailants and the assailed. The latter had the worst of it in the end, and many of them were killed, the head of Dakshya being cut off by Birbhadra.

"'This is a very serious affair,' said Bruhmá, 'and yet I do not see how I can interfere in it at all.'

"'You had better talk over the matter with Mahádeva,' suggested his better-half, the goddess of wisdom, 'and prevail on him to mollify his wrath.'

"'He will hardly like to be reasoned with at present, I fear,' answered Bruhmá; 'but I shall try my best to do as you propose:' and he went over to Mahádeva with that intent.

"'You have not acted well in this matter, brother,' said Bruhmá, addressing the Destroyer, 'though I admit that you were much wronged at the outset.'

"'Why, what have I done?'

"'Oh, nothing personally; but come with me and see what Birbhadra and his imps have been doing on your behalf.'

"Mahádeva did go with Bruhmá, and his heart was touched at the sight of the bleeding gods and slaughtered demi-gods and kings pointed out to him.

"'Yes, brother, I have done wrong, as you say. My wrath was excited, and the vengeance taken by my demons has been unduly severe. But behold the half-burnt body of Sati near the fire! Seeing it how can I repent me of what has happened?'

"'Ah, brother, Sati is not dead; your wife can never die. She has only passed out of one form to assume another, and you will find her again as Párvati, the daughter of Himávan; but where, where shall we find the kings and demi-gods who have been destroyed?'

"'I shall restore all of them to life, brother, if only to please you,' said Mahádeva; and he directed the mutilated parts of the different bodies to be collected and put together, and then breathed the breath of life into them again. The head of Dakshya only could not be found, upon which that of a goat was substituted, and he came back to life half goat and half demi-god, as he is represented to this day."

"And Sati, the martyr-wife?"

"Her half-burnt body was taken up by her husband, and he raved and groaned over it like a madman, till, on the identity of Párvati with the deceased being established, he married her."

"O, Bábájee, did not the Parumhangsa of Sátgáon tell you that the religion of Buddha was not extirpated but fused into Bráhmanism? I think this story explains how that happened."

"Indeed! In that way, pray?"

"Why, let us understand first that Mahádeva, or Buddha, waged a bloody war with the king of Káshi, which was then, as it is at present, the stronghold of the gods. The first result of the contest was that Bráhmanism was all but destroyed, upon which the most prominent of the Bráhman leaders, Bruhmá, made overtures of peace and amalgamation, which were eventually effected by all the gods and demi-gods being restored, though the amalgamation was so incongruous that such discordant elements as a goat's head and a human body had to be united together."

"Ah, that is capital, Monohur! You are becoming a philosopher in earnest. I don't think that your explanation of the story will bear examination; but it is not unworthy of the schools. I can tell you another story which may be interpreted in the same vein by any amateur philosopher or theologist."

"Let us have the story first, Bábájee. The interpretation of it you may safely leave to me, and it will go hard with your unprofessional pupil if he be not able to make something out of it."

The Sunyási smiled.

"We have bathed together in the Pisách Mochan tank on the outskirts of the city, Monohur. Do you know how the origin and sanctity of the cistern is accounted for?"

"No, nor have I the slightest idea on the subject."

"Well, Benáres, you must remember, was the place where the gods held their earthly assemblies in the days of old. A powerful demon, or Pisách, said to himself— 'Why should I not have admittance among the gods, seeing that I am stronger than most of them?' He accordingly decided on forcing his way into their assembly, and, approaching Káshi, endeavoured to cross the Pánchkosi road. When he had all but done so he was stopped by the gods.

"'Get back at once or take the consequences of your temerity,' cried they.

"'I shall not go back after having come so far,' said the Pisách decisively; and he fought bravely with the gods though alone, and, proving stronger than them, penetrated the sacred inclosure yet further, and almost entered the city, when Bhaironáth appeared on the scene with the tremendous club you have seen in his hand.

"'I have never missed my aim, Pisách,' said Bhaironáth, 'and will surely smash your head for you if you do not go back at once;' and, as the Pisách would not do so, his head was smashed as sorrowfully as Bhaironáth had threatened. But though thus severely handled the Pisách was not dead; and, being unable to fight further, he changed his attitude now into humbleness and prayer.

"'O, Mahádeva!' cried he, 'since I have entered your

holy city, allow me a place in it, I beseech you, and to be counted with the gods.'

" Mahádeva, ever merciful, was pleased to agree, and the Pisách was deified, and is worshipped after the manner we have ourselves observed, on the very spot where he was made headless by Bhaironáth."

" Ah, Bábájee, the meaning of this story also is palpably the same as of the other. It too refers to a religious war between the Bráhmans and the Buddhas, and explains conclusively how the contest was settled. The Paramhangsa's reading of the Shástras is fully vindicated—namely, that Buddhism was not rooted out of the country, but was compounded with the Bráhman code."

CHAPTER XXXVIII.

THE NAWÁB'S RULE.

WHEN the round of enjoyments at Benáres was finally gone through the grave question came up for decision as to whether the next move should be towards Ayodhyá or Prayága.

"Which should it be, Bábájee? Which is likely to be the more interesting place to us?" asked Monohur.

"O, I have seen both of them before, and have no reason to prefer one to the other," said the Sunyási. "Your wish, in whichever way you may decide, is mine."

"Let us go to Ayodhyá then," said Monohur, "for Prayága is only a bathing-place, while at Ayodhyá we shall see the remains of the glories of Rámá and Dasarath in the past."

"Ah, you will be sadly disappointed in that, my son," replied the Sunyási, "for you will see nothing there but some crumbling mounds of brick, as no better remains survive; while at Prayága you would see a flourishing city, something akin to, though not exactly like Benáres."

"The mounds are the very things I would wish to see then," observed Monohur, "and the more ruinous they are the more would they be to my liking. I have had enough of a large and flourishing city here to be sure."

"Though you liked it so greatly only the other day for being so old and cozy?"

"Yes, and I like it very well even now. But to those who are for seeing different sites variety should always be more welcome."

"Your reply is rather self-contradictory, Monohur; but since you are for variety now let us get off from this place at once;" and, leaving the Grand Trunk Road, they took the direction of Ázimgurh and Oude, their way lying through a very pastoral country, splendidly timbered and abounding in game.

"Ah, Bábájee, is not this sudden transition from a bustling and noisy city to such a wild and secluded route delightful to the senses?"

"Delightful indeed, but still not quite so cozy and snug as hiding one's self in an old noisy city," answered the Sunyási in a bantering tone, "since we have neither antique relics here to pore over, nor tales about them to listen to."

Monohur did not take offence at, nor indeed hear, what was said to him. He was absorbed in his own thoughts, and went on speaking as if he had not been interrupted by any reply.

"When I see the wild deer gamboling before us as now, and flocks of pretty coloured birds sweeping overhead in the sky, I feel almost as if a new phase of life had suddenly come upon me."

"That is only on account of the novelty of the thing, my son. Further and continuous acquaintance with the deer and the birds will in a short time make the new phase quite as tiresome as the oldest antiquities and their tales, for in point of fact there is not much of poetry in life, whether it be in a busy ancient city like Benáres, or in a woody, lonesome glade like this."

The creed thus laid down found no response in Monohur's heart. The Sunyási was essentially a man of the world, and did not appreciate pastoral beauty except perhaps in print. He had a keen brain which was always at work, and had no care for such pleasure or enjoyment as comes through the eyes and the ears. Monohur, on the contrary, being young, wild, and unbroken, had his eyes and ears always open to the beauties around him; and, keeping to the quietest by-paths of the wood, he went on and on without feeling any weariness of either mind or limbs. The deer looked at him wistfully before bounding away from his path; the squirrel gave him a twinkle from its roguish eye; and the pheasant-cock wheeled over him with a hoarse cry that was not unpleasing to him.

"Is it a jungle that we have entered, Bábájee? The sun is going down rapidly, and I don't see any habitation of man in our neighbourhood."

"O, never fear for that, Monohur. I know the road well. We shall soon be out of the wood, and long before sunset surely."

They were out of the wood already, and Monohur was just getting dissatisfied with the dull, prosaic country into which it had brought them, when they fell in with the cowherds of the border villages driving their cattle home. A dispute was running high among these men, and very uncomplimentary words were being exchanged, which threatened to bring on a fight between them.

"What is it that you are quarrelling about, friends?" interposed the Sunyási, in virtue of his cloth, in the hope that his interference might in some way be of advantage to himself and his companion. "What is the point at issue between you that you are getting so warm over?"

"Ah, you shall decide between us, Sunyási. We are

two parties here, one from Doorgápore and the other from Sundegáon. Now these fellows from Doorgápore have been grazing their cattle within boundaries belonging to our village, and should we not break their heads for that?"

"No, no; I say 'Nay' to that. It is scarcely fair, friends, to break heads for a few mouthfuls of grass eaten by our sacred goddesses, the cows. Why not arrange it in this way: Feed your cattle for the same number of hours within the borders of Doorgápore, that the Doorgápore cattle have fed within yours?"

"There is no reason why we should not agree to that," said the men of Doorgápore joyfully, for they were in the minority as to numbers at the spot, and disliked the idea of a row. "We were not aware that our cattle had trespassed till it was too late to prevent it."

The Sundegáon cowherds were, however, averse to accept the decision. "It would be mean," they said, "to settle an affair of this sort in the way proposed. What objection was there to have an open fight?"

"Why, are you not afraid of the police?"

"The police! What police? Our villages are within the Nawáb's territory, and no police interferes with us in Oude."

This our pilgrims soon found was the actual truth. They were just passing out of the English frontier and entering the dominions of the Nawáb of Oude, and throughout the entire country there was no law but that of force, no right but what was self-assumed.

"Well, if you do not fight with them now won't the Doorgápore people reciprocate your friendliness at a future time? And is it not better to have a good understanding among neighbours, than an enmity which must work as a seesaw, sometimes in your favour, and perhaps as often against you?"

"Yes, but we do not care for that. It is all lawlessness here. Why should we hesitate then to be as lawless as the rest?"

"Why not rather be lawful yourselves, and make the rest equally lawful by your example?"

"Make the fellows of Doorgápore lawful? O, you don't know them, Sunyási. They are a wicked set altogether, and will never make true friends."

"I will be bound that they will," said the Sunyási, and the cowherds of Doorgápore swore on their faith that they would; whereupon, after some further palaver, the misunderstanding between the two parties was patched up and sealed with the seal of forgiveness.

"It was very good of your friend to get us out of trouble in the way he did it," said a cowherd of Doorgápore speaking to Monohur, on the affair being finally settled. "Can we be of any use to you in any way?"

"Yes, certainly. We are pilgrims bound for Ayodhyá, and if you will only house us for the night we shall be amply repaid for any service that we may have done to you."

"Gladly shall we do that," exclaimed several voices; and the Sunyási and Monohur were safely accommodated for the night in the village of Doorgápore—safely, but not quietly, owing to the constant self-assertions of authority throughout the Nawáb's dominions.

"We are comfortably lodged after all; are we not, Bábájee?"

"I am afraid not, Monohur. I do not like the look of these people here, and I don't think we shall have much rest among them."

"You are endeavouring to frighten me; are you not?"

"No, my son; and there is nothing to be really afraid of. I am only preparing you for the discomforts I apprehend."

And they came as quickly as the Sunyásí had foretold.

A short time after nightfall there was one perpetual howl from a neighbouring hut which prevented the pilgrims from sitting down to the repast they had prepared for themselves.

"What does that cry mean?" asked Monohur of the person they had lodged with.

"O, nothing; our neighbour, Kefátooláh, does not agree with his wife, and it is only a repetition of their usual matrimonial love-passages."

"But the howl is expressive of great pain, and seems to require some personal interference; does it not?"

"No, no: there must be no interference of any sort, my friend. Even our police does not interfere with us, except it be to carry out the Nawáb's *hookum;* and wherefore should we among ourselves?"

"I would rather not stay with you then than not interfere," said Monohur; and he rushed out to ascertain what the matter was. It was simply this: The man Kefátooláh, returning home from his day's work, and feeling tired and hungry, had asked his wife to get some food ready for him.

"You shan't have any," said the sweet-tempered woman, "till you have settled the remaining unadjusted money-claims between us."

"Dare you give me such an answer as that, you bitch? I shall settle all accounts with you then in a trice;" and, saying this, he got hold of her, and, throwing her on the ground, tied her neck and heels together, and, leaving her in that position, went out of the house. If Monohur had not come to the rescue of the woman it would probably have gone very ill with her, for the howls she began with were getting fainter and fainter, and the effects of suffocation were becoming visible on her.

"I hope we may pass the rest of the night more quietly," observed Monohur. "I am much knocked up, and should so like to have a little sound sleep now."

"You won't have that here, my son. Take your meal quickly, and then snatch such slumber as you may. I am afraid these people will not keep quiet for any length of time."

"Don't we hear something already?"

"Yes, indeed, we do. But you need not have such quick ears here. This is the region of misrule and anarchy, and they live here at boiling point at all hours."

The noise this time also was a howl, proceeding, as before, from a female, in proof of her husband's love. The name of the husband was Házári Beg; that of the wife Onruput. The latter was barely thirteen, and had been suffering from fever for some days, and, as in the other case, the husband's evening meal had not been prepared.

"Get up, you lazy slut, and prepare my food, since there is no one else in the house to-day to do it."

"I cannot. Why don't you prepare it yourself?"

"I prepare my own food that you may lie at your ease, you vixen? Is that the housewifery you have learnt at your father's house? Get up this instant, or I shall take the flesh off your bones for you."

But she could not get up, and Házári Beg, unable to control himself, heated a *kulki* and branded her with it on the right side of her face, the left shoulder, and the abdomen.

Both Monohur and the Sunyási went over quickly to the assistance of the poor child, and the art of the latter, or rather his magic, as he pretended, gave her some relief. Monohur was for giving a tremendous thrashing to her husband.

"If there be no police here why may not every man who can, take upon himself the avenger's office?"

But the husband had bolted.

There was a third disturbance again towards the end of the night, which dispelled the sleep in which Monohur had finally fallen; and he got out of bed with a curse at the Nawáb and his people, great and small.

"O, Bábájee, if I had known of the state of the country here, I should certainly have preferred to proceed to Prayága instead of Ayodhyá. What is the upshot now?"

The upshot was this—

A fruit-seller named Torul, with his uncle, Gujráj, had been watching the fruits in their orchard from a *máchán*. At about three o'clock in the morning a party of twelve persons broke into the orchard to steal the fruits. Torul remonstrated, but they would not listen to him, and went on plundering till the uncle and nephew, by dint of their howling, brought out the whole village to their aid.

"What do you want with us?" demanded one of the robbers of Monohur, who was among the first to appear against them.

"Immediate restitution of the fruits, knave."

"Ah, that is not the rule of the country, my friend. You must be some stranger here from foreign parts to insist on restitution before having captured your pillagers;" and they effected their escape nimbly, flinging clods of earth at their pursuers to keep them at a distance.

"Are these crimes peculiar to the place, Bábájee?"

"No, by no means. They occur everywhere to a considerable extent. But they are constant at this place, because there is neither law, rule, nor authority here to check them."

"O, father, the English government, that we have been trying so strenuously to upset, is bad enough to be sure. But is not the Mahomedan government, which we wished to re-establish instead of it, much worse?"

CHAPTER XXXIX.

THE RÁMÁYANA, AND A MISSING CHAPTER OF HISTORY RECOVERED.

MONOHUR sang a psalm of thanksgiving when, after much toilsome marching, the banks of the Gográ were reached and both he and the Sunyási stood together on the veritable site of Ayodhyá a short while after.

"Well, what do you see before you, Monohur? Is not the sight really grand and startling?"

"What sight? I see nothing here but some dull mounds of broken brick."

"And not the city of Dasarath, which you have so longed to look at?"

"What do you mean—what can you mean, Bábájee? Are these the ruins of Ayodhyá?"

"Yes, my son; these shapeless heaps of rubbish are all that are now to be seen of it. Is not the sight marvellously disappointing?"

Monohur was perplexed and grieved, advanced and receded, and knew not whether to laugh or cry. To say that he was greatly disappointed would scarcely express what he felt.

"Is this indeed the city of Dasarath which was twelve *yojanas* in extent?"

"Yes, all that remains of it above ground now," answered the Sunyási.

"And underground? Do you mean to say that any portion of the city, or anything belonging to it, is to be found underground now?"

"I know not, my son; but I have heard several pilgrims say that they have dug out gold and precious stones from under these piles, and, if they did so, there must be more of the city below the surface than what we see above it at present."

"Is the story likely, do you think?"

"Not at all unlikely, Monohur; though I myself have never had even a glimpse of the hidden remains they speak of."

Monohur moved forward towards the mounds without further speech, and, in common with other pilgrims, both he and the Sunyási went through the usual *pradakshinás* round the sites of imaginary temples, bathed in the holy pools, and performed the customary ceremonies as at other shrines. When a superstition is once impressed strongly on the mind the force of imagination alone is capable of conjuring up all that it wishes to believe; and there is no doubt that our devotees saw at this moment the ancient splendours of Ayodhyá in their distinctness in their minds, even though no traces of them were to be found outwardly on the ground.

"O, Bábájee, you have read the Rámáyana. Relate some of the leading incidents of it now, since to listen to such recitals here is held to be very efficacious, and is the more necessary that no marks of Ráma's glory are any longer to be met with on the site."

"I have not *read* the Rámáyana, Monohur, for the work is very bulky, and my opportunities of reading and writing have been but small. But I have frequently *heard* the story recited by the Kattaks, and could have gone over a great part of it word for word if we had the time. You also must have heard the story, at least in parts. Why not recall the main incidents of it then to your memory, which will sufficiently answer the purposes of salvation?"

"Ah, yes, but I want your assistance to connect the links I remember, my knowledge of the story being very disjointed and incomplete. Let us sit down on this mound, Bábájee, and, while you sketch out the principal divisions of the story, I shall compare the facts I know with your recapitulation of them."

"You think too highly of my power, Monohur, if you suppose that I can give you aught but a bare skeleton of the story in such an off-hand way. I could repeat the sing-song accounts given by the Kattaks well enough of course; but it requires more careful study to epitomise them than I am capable of."

"Then give us any account of the work you can, Bábájee, and you may depend upon it that I will not attempt to analyse your narrative too carefully."

"On that understanding I will do my best to comply," said the Sunyási; and he began his account the moment they were seated on the mound.

"The main divisions of the Rámáyana are seven," said he, "the first being called the *Balya Kánda*, which refers to the boyhood of Ráma and the antecedent history of the family."

"I have heard a great part of that section, Bábájee, from my mother," said Monohur. "Her heart's wish always was that I should imitate the doings of the youthful hero and get a wife like Sitá, though she ever added that it was not possible for any man or woman to be like either one or the other."

"The second book," continued the Sunyási, "is called the *Ayodhyá Kánda*, and describes the transactions which led to the banishment of Ráma, and the manner in which he submitted to the parental command."

"But I have never been able to understand, Bábájee, why Dasarath should have complied so easily with the requests of Kaikeyi when he felt so strongly that they were ungenerous and unjust. A little firmness on his part might have broken up all her machinations, I think."

"O, my son, the king had previously promised to grant her any favour she might ask. How could the royal word be broken? He died of grief for the absence of Ráma; but the credit remains that his engagement was literally fulfilled."

"Ráma was accompanied to the forest by his wife, which was very natural; but why by his half-brother, Lakshman, also? What business had the latter to desert the old king at such a time for his brother's society, or for that of his brother's wife? Did he love the brother and his wife more than his aged parent?"

"No; he was the best of brothers indeed, but not an undutiful son. Dasarath was a king, living in his own capital, surrounded by every comfort that he could wish for. The position in which Ráma was placed was different. He might require assistance in the forest against unknown enemies; and Lakshman, anticipating such need, went out to afford what help he could, and since the world began there never was a brother better fitted for the task. I cannot conceive a better character than that of Lakshman, Monohur. View him in any light you please, he always stands forth as the knight without reproach or shame."

"Well, and the story after the banishment?"

"The details of it are given in the *Aranya Kánda*, which describes how they lived as hermits, wandering among different settlements, and affording protection to the sages against the Rákshases who ill-treated them, till the rape of Sitá by Rávana changed the whole character of their lives."

"And brought on the war?"

"Yes; Ráma, after the abduction of his wife, had to find allies to assist him in her recovery, and the *Kishkindya Kánda* narrates the occurrences at Kishkindya, the capital of Sugriva, the monkey-king, who was his chief ally. The bears of the forest also assisted him; and with a powerful army thus organised he marched for the conquest of Ceylon."

"But were they actually bears and monkeys that swelled his ranks? What is your personal idea on the subject?"

"The chiefs who led them were demi-gods, my son; their followers were probably mountaineers and foresters, whom the poet, for their rough and uncivilised manners, was content to immortalise as bears and monkeys."

"They were great warriors, all of them, and I would have venerated them for that only, even if they had been ten times more uncivilised than bears and monkeys. Don't we come to the war now in the story, Bábájee?"

"The fifth is the *Sundara*, or the beautiful, *Kánda*, which describes the passage of the straits by the allied army and its approach towards Lanká, and also gives an account of the exploits of Hanumán, who was sent to the enemy's capital in the double character of envoy and spy, and managed to have an interview with Sitá."

"And the war?"

"It is described in the sixth, or the *Yudha Kánda*, which records every individual achievement and its result with a spirit-stirring eloquence which it is not possible to reproduce, and I shall not even attempt therefore to do so."

"Who were the best fighters in the war, think you?"

"Indrajit, Ráma, and Lakshman, and of them, though it may be heresy to say so, Indrajit appears to me to have been by far the best."

"But he was defeated?"

"Yes, defeated and killed by Lakshman, as Rávana was by Ráma, the final result of the victory being the recovery of Sitá, with whom the conqueror came back to, and was crowned king at, this spot."

"Where no traces of him or his, alas! are now to be traced? Is it not so, Bábájee?"

"It is indeed! and that tribute, Ráma, like the meanest of us, had to pay to his human birth. Humanity is nothing, and we see before us that even Ráma's humanity has not left a trace behind it. Nor did he deserve that it should be otherwise."

"How so? What do you mean?"

"I blame his conduct as a man, my son, and the last, or *Uttara Kánda*, amply supports this condemnation, for it narrates how Sitá was banished by him on suspicion, and abandoned once more to the privations of a forest-life after all she had suffered and borne for him."

"But they were eventually reconciled and reunited?"

"Yes, and translated to heaven, which terminates the story as Válmik has related it."

Monohur heard the account with becoming attention and respect; but it was not in his nature to accept any statement unchallenged.

"Now tell me, Bábájee, do you really believe that Rávana and his subjects were actually Rákshases, or demons, as the poet describes them?"

"There can be no doubt of that when the sacred book says that they were so. Válmik would not have described what was untrue."

"But you have said before that the bears and monkeys described by the poet may possibly have been meant to represent mountaineers and foresters. Could not the Rákshases similarly have been intended to stand for some other savage or ferocious tribes?"

"No, no; fighting bears and monkeys will admit of being interpreted as the productions of a poet's imagination; but Rákshases, or demons, are, or have been, actually in existence, for they are frequently spoken of in all the Shástras, and some are to be seen even now in the Himálayás, and it will never do to ignore them."

"Have we any evidence besides that of Válmik that they were ever the denizens of Lanká?"

"O, yes; the evidences are abundant. All the *itihá́ses* we have of the island describe its inhabitants in the same terms with Válmik."

"Perhaps only because they are all mere repetitions of Válmik? You, as an old traveller, must have heard travellers' stories about the country. What do they say? Has any actual visitor of the place met with a Rákshasa in it?"

"No, for the Rákshases have long ceased to exist."

"How so? How did they come to be extirpated? Ráma did not root them out, for he is expressly said to have left Vibishana in power over the remaining population before he left."

"Yes, and for a long time after Ráma's war Lanká

continued to be inhabited by Rákshases and dragons. But the place was rich, and, Ráma having opened the way to it, merchants resorted to it for trade, for the hope of gain will take men even to the devil's abode."

" Come now, there is a difficulty to solve in that, to commence with. How did the merchants and the demons come to terms with each other? The demons would, it appears to me, be rather ugly customers to deal with."

" Why, at the time of traffic the demons did not come forward at all. They only exposed their commodities for sale with the prices marked on them, just as the English, their descendants, do in their shops at Calcuttá and Bombay. The merchants, if they accepted the prices, paid them down on the spot, and removed the goods."

" Without a word being exchanged?"

" No words were necessary."

" And the demons did not molest the merchants?"

" It was not to their interest to do so."

" Well, after that?"

" These visits becoming frequent, men of various countries came in time to know of the place and its riches, and flocked to it in numbers."

" Unopposed by the demons?"

" Unopposed, because the demons found themselves soon to be much in the minority."

" Then?"

" Two communities came thus to be established in the place, one daily increasing and pushing the other to a corner. The country is said to be delightful. It has no extremes of temperature, neither winter nor summer. The plants and trees in it are always fruitful, and the fields yield luxuriant crops wherever they are tilled, not being subject to the influences of the seasons."

"Well?"

"The peaceful community became more and more populous day by day, and the Rákshases were extirpated."

CHAPTER XL.

THE *DHATOORÁ* POISONER.

THE road forward from the Gográ was not a very cheerful one. It passed through some very thick woods indeed at some places, but the best part of it was too narrow and solitary to be agreeable, and out of the jungle the sights consisted of rocks and ravines merely, neither very imposing in their appearance.

Two individuals of the Dosád caste were going by this road from Lower Bengal to their home in the North-West, some sixty miles beyond Lucknow. They had left Ayodhyá two or three days before, and were approaching a wild defile when they were met by a third person, who said that he also was a Dosád.

"This place has a very solitary and dismal look, and makes one fearful. The road is narrow, and the rocks on both sides lower frowningly."

"You are a lucky fellow then in having found us here," said one of the first two travellers who was named Juggun. "You would not have liked to pass the road alone?"

"No; the very appearance of the pass fills my mind with fear. Who knows but what dark deeds may not have been done here in the past? If these rocks could speak they might tell us very queer stories truly."

"Never mind the past and its stories now," said

Dhooniáh, the second of the first two travellers. "We are three already, and have nothing to fear. But the evening is approaching fast, and we must hasten to find a halting-place."

"The nearest halting-place is Koablásgunj," said the new-comer, who gave his name as Lulloo, "and that is yet three miles distant."

"Then let us mend our pace," said Juggun. "The halting-ground must be reached; it would be no joke to spend the night in such a forbidding spot as this."

The travellers reached Koablásgunj late in the evening, and were soon comfortably accommodated under a large banyan-tree very near the village market.

"Now let us see what eatables we have with us," said Dhooniáh. "Have we enough for three?"

"No," said Juggun, "we have hardly enough for two, and I am so hungry that I think I alone could eat up all we have."

"But we can easily get some flour and vegetables from the market," said Lulloo, "and then we can prepare fresh *chuppátis* and curry for all of us."

"Be quick then," said Dhooniáh; and they each contributed a trifle, with which Lulloo did the necessary marketing for their meal.

The *chuppátis* were made by Juggun and Dhooniáh, while the curry was cooked by Lulloo; and they all eat of the meal heartily. The first two, however, began in a short time to complain of giddiness, and immediately after became perfectly insensible, in which state they were discovered by some of the market-servants.

"Ah, there has been foul play here apparently," observed they to each other. "Who may these people be? And what are we to do for them?"

"Why, friends, what are you consulting about? And what is this gathering for?" inquired a new arrival, who was naturally drawn towards the crowd.

"Come forward and look for yourself, Sunyási. Here be two folks who have been murdered or poisoned by some fellow who has decamped. Will your charms and Mantras enable you to revive them?"

"Give me a chance at least to try my art on them by clearing out the way for me," said the Sunyási. "If it be a dose of *dhatoorá* only you may set your minds easy that I shall be able to plant them on their legs again."

"Ah, I have great faith in Sunyásis," exclaimed the owner of the market who was present. "Make room for him by all means, and let him do his best to help the sufferers."

The Sunyási was now fairly pushed forward by the crowd, and the medicine he forced into the mouths of the sufferers soon succeeded in reviving them, and, by constraining them to bring up what they had eaten, effected a partial recovery.

"How many of you eat together in the evening?" were the first words of the market-owner to the Dosáds.

"We were three."

"Where is the third, do you know?"

"No, we don't. We miss him and our property also."

"Then stay where you are for the present till I find out the fugitive for you. He has had the start of a few hours only, and should not be able to escape us."

The market-man had calculated the chances correctly, and Lulloo was traced and overtaken by his emissaries the very next morning, all the property stolen being also found with him. The mob were for exercising lynch-law on him on the spot, being usually in the habit of

x

taking cognisance of such cases themselves; but the Sunyási interfered and claimed the delinquent as his fee.

"I have cured the people who had suffered from his practice," said he. "Don't you harm him then, if for my sake only."

"Be it so," said the market-owner, "and you may dispose of him in any way you like. But remember that he has been caught with difficulty, and will give you no opportunity to catch him again if you allow him to get off."

"Well, I do wish him to get off notwithstanding," said the Sunyási, "hoping that he may be induced by our very kindness to lead a better life in future. Now, listen to me, Lulloo, or whatever your name may be, and answer my questions truthfully if you can. Did you, or did you not, mix *dhatoorú* with the curry you cooked yesterday for all three of you?"

"I did."

"Did you not eat your share of the curry?"

"No; I took my share, but did not eat it."

"Was this your first essay in the art of drugging?"

"My first essay, Thákoorjee! Surely not. I have promised to make a full confession to you, and am rather proud than otherwise to say that I have lived on the road for the last twenty years."

"Will you promise to mend your ways now that I have been at some pains to get you enlarged?"

"Ah, it is a great sacrifice that you ask of me, father. Will it not suffice if I promise never to be caught again?"

The Sunyási heaved a sigh.

"Get out of the place quickly then, for the good people here will make short work of you if you are found near them after we are gone."

"You advise well, Thákoorjee, and I shall certainly act as you suggest;" and Lulloo was soon out of sight once more.

"Ah, what fearful risks we run, Bábájee," said Monohur, "in these our wanderings! We had, you will remember, a poisoning case before on the Cuttack road, and the peril incurred by the two Dosáds here might have been ours if we had preceded instead of coming after them on the same track. Lulloo would have surely hooked us as his victims as he did them."

"Not very easily, Monohur. I have been travelling far and long, and have come across Thugs, dacoits, and poisoners innumerable. But I am fully awake at all times, and have never come to grief yet."

"I am nevertheless getting somewhat fearful, Bábájee. I could die a hundred times over with the sword or the battle-axe in my hand, but to be drugged and poisoned is really awful to me; and, as our travelling is now objectless, I think we had better return to Bengal as quickly as we may. Whereabouts are we now?"

"About half-way between Ayodhyá and Lucknow," said the Sunyási. "We are very near the Goomti river."

"Let us see the river then, and bathe in it. We can go back thence without exciting suspicions."

"To Boná Ghát?"

"No, not thither, certainly. We shall select our place of residence by-and-by; but I will not re-enter Boná Ghát if I can help it."

They reached the little village of Párroo, which stood about six miles from the Goomti, and took up their abode in the house of a leper, a Bráhman nicknamed Bukshee, who owned the best part of the village as his zemindáry. The man had suffered greatly from his distemper for several years, and had latterly reached that stage when life becomes piteous to the sufferer. For weeks and weeks the days and nights were spent in moaning only; and he had been brought outside of his house and lodged under canvas, having become so faint that death seemed to be fast creeping on him.

"Take me to the Goomti and drown me," was his constant and almost only prayer; but he was loved by his children, and they could answer him merely with tears.

"O, my children, my life is nearly finished. Why do you leave me to suffer so much pain then when you can so easily terminate it?"

"Father, you speak unthinkingly," pleaded the children. "We would not be justified in acting in the manner you desire."

"I tell you what," said the Sunyási, addressing the sufferer in his turn, "Rájáh Parikshit, bit by a serpent, had the patience to listen to the Mahábhárut which was recited to him. Why not apply the same salve to your wound till death relieves you of your miseries?"

A low moan expressed the sufferer's assent to the suggestion made to him, and Monohur was reconciled to his lodgings from his desire to listen to the recital of the Mahábhárut.

CHAPTER XLI.

THE MAHÁBHÁRUT HEARD AND SIFTED.

THE Mahábhárut is a cyclopædia of traditions which the natives of India are never weary of listening to. It is not that Monohur had never heard the story of it before. He had done so frequently, at least in parts. But the tales are unwearying, and are always welcome; and he was not unanxious to hear them retold.

The arrangements made for the recital of the story at Bukshee's house scarcely require to be very particularly described. A pavilion was set up, which was left open on all sides to admit of the easy ingress of auditors from every direction. It was supported on stout timber-posts, festooned and almost covered with foliage and flowers, while the canopy overhead was of sky-coloured canvas, wrought with decorations of leaves, parrots, and roses. The appearance of the tent altogether was indeed not unagreeable, while the accommodation afforded under it was as extensive as the occasion required. The *bedi*, or seat of the Kattak, was in the middle of one side of the square, and Bukshee was conveyed near to it daily on a *dooli* moving on wheels. The Kattak was an old man, who had often to clear his throat in getting on with the recitation; but he discoursed and sang as a nightingale, with a mellow persuasiveness that never failed to carry his hearers with him. The parties assembled were invariably large, and the tone and tears of the speaker were so powerful that his words were often drowned by the sobs they called forth.

"Well, was not the narration delightsome, Monohur?" asked the Sunyási, after the termination of the entire course. "Which parts of the story did you like best?"

"Let us go over the ground a little, Bábájee, that I may be able to distinguish precisely the portions that provoked pleasure or grief from those that taxed my patience rather unduly."

"Taxed your patience unduly! Why, what sort of a compliment is that? I certainly never heard anyone urge such a complaint against the Mahábhárut before."

"Well, if the work of Vyasa be not tiresome at any place, Bábájee, the Kattak's recitation did seem to me to be so at times, that is, whenever he went on rattling pertinaciously with bare facts. I am free to admit, however, that the wearying portions of the narrative were far less, both in number and magnitude, than those which were agreeable or moving."

"Good, so far as the concession extends. But I would still go over the ground as you suggest, if only to understand the causes of your likes and dislikes. My pleasure was so great throughout the narration that I felt as if I was being whirled away through a different and a better sphere, replete with new ideas and new sources of excitement."

"Ah, I understand; for I too felt frequently a thrill passing as through the core of my heart. But there were insipid portions in the discourse notwithstanding, and, if you will go over the *Parvas* consecutively, I shall endeavour to make plain to you what I disliked or objected to, and wherefore."

"Well, the first or the *Adi Parva*, details the history of the two brothers, Dhritaráshtra and Pándu, the birth of their children, and the conduct of the government at Hastinápore. What have you to say against it?"

"Nothing. The preamble of a story, even when didactic, is a necessary account, and always receives the auditor's attention."

"The wives of Pándu were Kunti and Mádree, of whom the first bore three and the second two sons. Yudhisthira, the eldest of the five brothers, was the type of justice and truthfulness; Bheem, the second, of personal strength and courage; Arjun, the third, of great-heartedness and bravery; while the twin sons of Mádree—Nakula and Sahadeva—were both of them at the same time spirited and amiable. Which of the characters did you like best?"

"I was going to ask that question of you, Bábájee. Which did you prize most yourself?"

"Yudhisthira, far above the others," said the Sunyási unhesitatingly; "and you will remember, of course, what the Kattak was so careful to explain at the end of the story, that he alone of all the brothers went straight up to heaven."

"I don't care for that. I would rather be Arjun than Yudhisthira. There was something so endearing in the character given of the former that I could not help liking it better; and Arjun, you know, was Krishna's favourite and friend."

"Ah, yes, the two best characters in the story were undoubtedly those of Yudhisthira and Arjun, and you may make your choice between them. An old man like me will always prize the former better, a young man like you the latter; but I may observe casually that the wise and just is a much rarer character in life than the large-hearted and brave."

"We need not quarrel on that point at present, Bábájee. Let us get on further, and we shall have more light on it by-and-by, I fancy."

"The second, or the *Sabhá Parva*, describes the great assembly of princes at Hastinápore, the play at dice in which Yudhisthira lost his title to the kingdom, and the retreat of the brothers to the woods for twelve years."

"You see here, Bábájee, that it was even your immaculate Yudhisthira that brought himself and his brothers into the difficulties they met with. But for his unjustifiable passion for gambling very much of the troubles suffered by them would not have arisen."

"Perhaps, yes; but the display of rectitude and truthfulness called forth from the hero would, in that case, have also remained unknown, and even your Arjun's valour and generosity would never have been heard of."

"Ah, you are becoming somewhat derisive and scornful, Bábájee. But, to tell you the truth, it was this unusual display of rectitude and resignation that appeared most tiresome to me. The third, or the *Vana Parva*, which narrates the life of the exiled brothers in the forest, was far more interesting, in the recital at least."

"Yes, it is very interesting whether read or recited, and mainly for the episodes in it, which are simply enchanting. There is much of real poetry also in this book."

"It was nevertheless a relief to me when its lengthened sweetness was terminated, and the fourth, or the *Virát Parva*, introduced us to the last year of the brethren's exile and their adventures in the service of King Virát."

THE MAHÁBHÁRUT HEARD AND SIFTED.

" Because of your anxiety to hurry on to the war. Was not that the truth of it, Monohur?"

" Yes; and I was so very anxious on that score that I wished a hundred times and oftener that the Kattak would skip over the *Udyoga Parva* altogether, as the accounts of the preparations made by the contending parties appeared to me to be exceedingly wearisome in their details."

" Wearisome? Why, without them how could you have understood the story aright?"

" O, if I were the poet I would have come at once to the opening engagements as described in the *Bhisma Parva*, leaving the preparations to be inferred. The facts are dry bones merely, which no one cares for in a poetic account."

" But without dry bones of some kind, my son, we can have no correct idea of any form or figure, poetic or otherwise. If the facts had been left out your inferences would have been necessarily inaccurate."

" All that may be very true in the way of criticism, Bábájee; but it was the overcrowding of facts in the *Parva*, nevertheless, that made it so awfully tedious to me. What I decidedly prefer to the enumeration of such details is life-painting, that is, the painting of the age or times, if I may say so, to which the details refer."

" And do you complain that Vyasa is deficient in that? Why, he represents the times he speaks of so graphically that he carries one quite back to them, almost forcibly as it seems."

" Precisely so; but not in the *Udyoga Parva*, which only I was objecting to. The very next book, the *Bhisma Parva*, fully vindicates the poetry of Vyasa, even though it never rises to an equality with the poetry of Válmik, in which the love of nature predominates in yet greater degree."

"But, such as it is, Vyasa's age-painting is certainly not unequal to waft back the imagination to the eras he treats of; and he makes us almost see, as it were, in what respect and to what extent life was different then from what it is now."

"I admit; and in the *Bhisma Parva* in particular the character of Bhisma imparts a singular charm to the book mainly on that account. It is a character almost peculiar to the past, and portrayed, as it seems to me, with a beam of the ideal."

"I am glad to hear you speak of it in such terms, Monohur, for I did like the *Parva* intensely, as being at the same time beautifully calm and intensely exhilarating."

"Then, I felt also a great respect for Bhisma as a warrior, who, old as he was, feared not to encounter the arms of the youthful Arjun. It is a pity that Arjun should have wounded him."

"The achievements and death of Drona, which are described in the seventh *Parva*, are of the same character surely, and ought to have interested you in an equal degree. The Kurus had very brave knights to fight on their side."

"They had; but Bhisma, I think, appears to greater advantage than Drona, as uniting the two characters of warrior and sage. As a warrior simply I would prefer Karna to both, and his achievements and death would not have been unworthy of the best of the Pándavas."

"The war virtually terminates with the *Salya Parva*, which describes the concluding engagements, in all of which the Kurus were defeated. What do you say to the single-fight of Bheem with Duryodhon which it records?"

"I accept the decision of Balarám, that it was most unfairly fought by the Pándava giant. However much I may dislike the character of Duryodhon, that does not vindicate the felon stroke by which he was struck down."

"Ah, fairness and sincerity are not weapons much in use in war, as we ourselves have known in our day, my son. What character would you give then to the night-attack of the Kurus on the Pándava camp?"

"The blackest certainly. It almost makes one doubt if it was an attack made by warriors or by butchers."

"But they say that anything is fair in war, and deceit and stratagem are considered lawful weapons to use. The poet wanted to exhaust and reduce both parties, you know, and a night-attack on them only could have brought down the Pándava faction—then at the height of their triumph—to almost the same state of helplessness as their opponents. How did you like the succeeding, or the *Stri Parva*? Was it not eminently affecting?"

"It was, and here the acting of the Kattak appeared at its best. The lamentations of Gándhári for her numerous progeny were heart-piercing; and all the wives and mothers who bewailed their dead husbands and children were well represented."

"The twelfth, or the *Sánti Parva*, described the coronation of Yudhisthira at Hastinápore, and you must have liked the conference of Yudhisthira with Bhisma, if only for the instructions in the art of government which were communicated by the latter."

"O, Bábájee, I am very unwilling to differ from you, but I tell you the absolute truth when I say that I felt the discourse to be decidedly the most wearisome portion of the whole account; and I cannot conceive what induced the poet to continue the infliction through a second *Parva*, the thirteenth. The lessons are of course all excellent, worthy of Bhisma to impart, and of Yudhisthira to receive; but I would not have been sorry if Bhisma had died at the end of the twelfth *Parva*, which would have curtailed his lectures considerably."

"How ungracious to say that, surely! Did you like the *Aswamedhik Parva* better then, where Yudhisthira performs the horse-sacrifice and ascends the throne?"

"No; but I was greatly affected by the fifteenth *Parva*, which described the retirement of Dhritaráshtra, Gándhári, and Kunti to their hermitage in the woods—the mother of the victors sharing the retreat of the parents of the vanquished and slain appearing, under the circumstances, as a particularly natural and poetic result; and the subsequent self-immolation of the recluses on the forest catching fire was also painfully affecting."

"But you have said nothing of Krishna yet, Monohur, though he acts as the most important figure of all in the story. What did you think of him?"

"What could I think of him, what can anyone think of him, who came as the representative of Vishnu himself, as the incarnation of the Deity in full?"

"I mean, what is your opinion of his life and history; his dances, sports, and adventures, which are mentioned in greater detail in the *Sri Bhágvat*, which your old Surburákár, Nilkant, was never weary of recapitulating?"

"They have delighted generations past and will delight generations yet to come, and I was never weary of listening about them. I have heard the stories repeatedly over and over from my earliest childhood, and they were quite as interesting to me from the lips of the Kattak, to the extent he alluded to them, as I had ever found them before. Some people object at this day to the frolics of the Avatár with the Gopángonás, but is there anything really objectionable in them?"

"No, none whatever. Krishna appeared on the earth as the representative of Vishnu, and Vishnu is pure love solely. It fell to the Avatár, therefore, to teach the world how and what to love, and he taught it personally, since nothing is so impressive as personal instruction."

"But did he teach love only? As Poorna Bruhmu he had other lessons also to impart."

"And these will be found in the *Gitá*, through which he instructed his friend and disciple Arjun, and after him the world, in all that it is worthy of human nature to know and understand."

"Well?"

"His instructions ended, he disappeared as he came, like the lightning's flash, and you have heard the *Mausála Parva* describe the death of the human Krishna and of his brother Balarám, the self-slaughter of their family in a club-fight, and the destruction of their capital Dwárká, by an inundation."

"And the Poorna Bruhmu?"

"Went back whence he had come—to his heavenly seat at Vycant."

"Leaving the heroes of the war to follow him as they might?"

"Well, the Pándavas were overwhelmed with sorrow at the destruction of their relatives and the disappearance of their friend, as the Kattak described it so vividly. They sought for Krishna, but could not find him; they called on him, but he gave them no answer; and the *Maháprasthánika Parva* describes how they renounced the throne they had acquired, and departed seeking for an ascent to heaven."

"And the eighteenth, or the *Swargarohanika Parva*, narrates how heaven was finally attained by them; Yudhisthira having this advantage only over his brothers, that he reached it in the flesh, while the others went through the usual course of nature and had to reach it through purgatory or hell."

"And thereby, as I have said before, was Yudhisthira's superiority over them expressly established. His brothers were of the earth earthy, and one by one fell off from the upward path which they were unable to pursue; while he, as au incarnation of justice, was led on by Indra in person in the shape of a dog, and, adhering to the road, gained the summit, when darkness fell on him, and, instantly after, his soul was wrapped in light!"

CHAPTER XLII.

MIRACLES OVER THE DEAD.

THE life of the leper was extinct just as the recital of the Mahábhárut was terminated, which was held to be a very propitious death, in the same ratio that it would have been accounted unfortunate had he outlived the recital. The widow of the old man was choked with grief, notwithstanding that his end had been so long anticipated, if not wished for; and his children cried bitterly, and felt bewildered and miserable. The neighbours also came and grieved with them; and the servants talked wildly, and had vague and undefined fears, and a feeling of uncertainty as to the future, after the loss of a master who had been so kind to them, and had been by them so respected and beloved.

"We have now to carry the body to the river-side," said the children at last, as being the first to rally; and they asked their guests if they would like to accompany it thither.

"Of course," said the Sunyási, "and we shall remain with you till the funeral rites are concluded."

The body was carried to the banks of the Goomti, and was accompanied, not only by the Sunyási and Monohur, but by many friends and ryots of the deceased; and it was there burnt on a pile of wood, which was set on fire by his eldest son, that being held to be the greatest service that a son can render to his parents.

The pile was composed almost wholly of sandal wood, and an attendant Bráhman recited prayers as the logs were arranged. On the body being laid on the pyre some butter was put into the mouth of the corse, and small grains of gold inserted into the eyes, nose, mouth, and ears, after which the fire was applied by the eldest son walking round the heap and touching the mouth of the dead with lighted straw, while the other sons set fire to the wood at every point, the rest of the party crowding round them to see the cremation get on. The pyre burnt brightly, and melted butter was poured on it in large quantities to intensify the blaze. When the body was wholly consumed water was poured on the pile and a gutter cut to join it with the river below.

The Sunyási assisted at the cremation loyally; but to the unsophisticated Monohur the sight was most painful to behold, and he involuntarily slunk from the spot to where a respectable elderly female was performing *Siva-poojáh* on the river-side. She was seated on the bank, and had made a small image of Mahádeva out of the river-clay; and to this object she was paying solemn homage by pouring water gently at its top with a copper *koosi* or spoon, and by occasionally throwing at it a flower or a *billipatra* smeared with sandal-paste. The Mantras were muttered with folded hands, and the right-hand was occasionally moved round the head, while the fingers and thumb of the left-hand compressed the nostrils, the suppression of the breath being held to increase the efficacy of the prayer.

Monohur had of course witnessed the performance of

the rite a thousand times before, but he had never paid the same attention to the act as now.

"I am twenty-seven years old," said he to himself, "and pass for an orthodox Hindu, yet never have I performed any *poojáh*, the rites at Gayá excepted, with half the faith and devotion of this simple-hearted woman. Is there any reason why it should be so? Or is it that women have a monopoly of faith?"

His further reflections were cut short by the Sunyási calling him away to return to the house of their hosts with them, as the river-side ceremonies were now over.

"Why stay with them further?" asked Monohur. "Can we not proceed on our own business now?"

"It would be unseemly to do so, Monohur, till the *shrád* is over; and I have already told them that we shall be by them to the last. Having remained with them so long, it would scarcely be proper to part with them before they are finally purified."

But a question now arose as to the date on which the *shrád* ought to be performed, the learned being divided on the point because of the distemper of which the deceased had died.

"For a leper the *asoochee*, or period of uncleanness, does not extend beyond three days," held one party; while the other maintained that "the usual mourning of ten days was required to be observed."

The conflict was very distressing to the children of the deceased, and to their mother also.

"Well, how are we to act now?" asked the former in a perplexed tone. "We must come to some decision, and promptly, for there are many arrangements to make."

"Do as your own good sense suggests, without minding the contentions of others," advised the Sunyási.

"Nay, rather leave the decision with Heaven, my children," said the mother, "for sure am I that you will not be left undirected in such a matter long."

And the mother's expectation was realised that very night by the appearance of a remarkable vision to her eldest son—namely, of a golden image ten feet high, resplendent as the moon, and having its head surrounded by a halo as bright as of the sun.

"Who art thou, father?" asked the young man of him in alarm.

"I am the Golden Spirit of the heavens sent to thee by thy father, who is yet waiting by the portals of bliss, and I have to tell thee that he desires that his *shrád* should be celebrated after the usual mourning of ten days, and not on the fourth day."

And the vision vanished as it came.

The supernatural decision was of course final, and was accepted as such by both the contending parties with equal alacrity; and, as Bukshee had died possessed of property, the *shrád* was celebrated with great *eclât*.

"O, my children!" said his broken-hearted widow, "the *Kortá* worked hard, and has left plenty of money for you. All his lands, houses, and effects are yours now. Grudge not then to spend what he has left in silver and gold for the salvation of his soul;" and, while the Bráhmans thundered their "Dhaniya Mái!" "Dhaniya Mái!"[1] on the devoted wife for her charitable heart, her children accepted her order with willing submission.

[1] Praise be to thee, O mother!

The violence of grief had subsided already, the more quickly that the mourners were convinced that the sufferer had ceased at last to suffer; and the household were in a short time actively engaged in completing the preparations for the *shrád*. The old house was decked out, as is usual on such occasions, with dark awnings and canopies, and there was a large gathering in it, and the customary offerings and sacrifices. The feastings were continued for three days, and were prolonged after nightfall daily, and all the guests, including a large gathering of the poor, were sumptuously entertained.

"I suppose this has been the way of the house all along?" asked the Sunyási of an old servant of the family.

"Yes, sir; that is, ever since I have been in the house."

The fact is, old Bukshee had always been fond of feeding the poor, and the poor from miles around had come of themselves to celebrate his funeral.

The ceremony came to an end at last, but in a very strange and remarkable manner. On the last night of it a rat having stolen a burning wick from one of the lamps to suck the oil, it was brought in contact with the skirt of a heavy canopy, and caused a general conflagration, which was not put out without much difficulty. But great was the astonishment of all that nothing in the house, not even the canopy itself which had burnt so long, was damaged, or was even so much as tainted by the fire.

"What does this mean?" exclaimed Monohur, with wondering eyes. "They talk of the impossibility of miracles in these days, but everything that happens here seems to be miraculous. The dream of the shining image and its mission was strange enough; but this harmless conflagration is stranger still, and I do not understand how it is to be explained."

"Ah, Bukshee," said the Sunyási devoutly, "must have been a veritable saint—some god, perhaps, evicted from heaven for a time, and punished with tribulations on the earth. Such miracles appear only in glorification of the pure."

"I have heard of saints, living and dead, Bábájee," said Monohur, "but have never heard of any miracles like these."

"My experience goes the other way," replied the Sunyási. "Miracles I have seen and heard of, but real saints I have never known."

"Have you not seen the Paramhangsa of Sátgáon?"

"Longer than you know of, Monohur. He is a very good and harmless old man, and exceedingly learned, and traditions of holiness and purity do cling about him. But he does not quite come up to my idea of a saint, for all the fine stories I hear of him."

"Then a saint, to your thinking, must be as wonderful a being, I fancy, as the typical things that were churned out of the ocean. I forget what they were, and how many in number."

"They were fourteen in number," answered the Sunyási, with imperturbable gravity, "the first being th Amrita, or the nectar of the gods; the second, Dhanwantari, a learned physician, the doctor of heaven; the third, Lakshmi, the goddess of good-fortune and beauty; the fourth, Surá Devi, the goddess of wine; the fifth, Chandra, or the moon; the sixth, a nymph named Rambhá; the seventh, the nine-mouthed horse named Oochisravá, belonging to Vishnu; the eighth, Kaustabha, a wonderful jewel; the ninth, the Parijáta tree, yielding everything that is desired; the tenth, Surábhi, or the cow of plenty; the eleventh, Airávat, the elephant of Indra; the twelfth, Sankha, a wonderful shell; the thirteenth, Dhanus, an unerring bow; and the last, Holáhol, or poison, which was drunk up by Mahádeva, and dyed his throat blue. But not any of these was quite as wonderful as a saint. They must have sought hard for a being of that character to the bottom of the sea, but there was none there apparently to get at."

"Then how can you say, Bábájee, that Bukshee was one? Did he appear so very exceptional a character to you when alive?"

"We do not see saints in life, my son, or see them in their sufferings only, when we cannot judge of them aright. In the case of Bukshee it is not of my knowledge that I speak, but from the miracles wrought over his death. His sufferings, we know, were intense, and he bore them more meekly than many could have done. The world did not know the man, nor appreciate him while he lived. The miracles come now to proclaim what worth the world has lost."

CHAPTER XLIII.

THE MAID OF ROHILKUND.

Our pilgrims, having left the village of Párroo behind them, were already traversing the well-cultivated valley of the Goomti, when they came up to a large fortress or castle half in ruins, which immediately attracted their attention.

"Pity for the brave edifice!" exclaimed Monohur. "See, Bábájee, how fresh and firm it holds up its battlements and towers through bush and tree, though it has lain apparently so many years in decay. To whom does it belong, and why is it so ill kept?"

"Ah, it has a story of its own, my son, a story of inexpressible sadness, but still one to stir up the spirit of a slave. The building belongs to the Nawáb, but has never been used by him, nor repaired, since one of his ancestors was murdered in it. It was a grand edifice at one time, but has purposely been left to crumble into ruins."

"And the story about it?"

"Rests on mere rumour only, and refers to the circumstances under, and the manner in which the Nawáb's ancestor was slain."

"You make me very curious about the affair, Bábájee. How did it happen? What are the details of it?"

"Well, it is some fifty years now since this castle was

either erected or rehabilitated by the then reigning Nawáb, Soojá-al-Dowláh, for the especial purpose of accommodating a fair Rohillá captive taken by him in war. You must know that this Nawáb and the Rohillás had been fighting with each other ever so long without one being able to subdue the other, till their animosity had risen to the highest pitch. Now the Nawáb dreaded the Rohillás much more than they dreaded him, and so he thought of hiring the assistance of the English to put them down forcibly."

" He must have been a very evil-minded man indeed to bring the foreigners forward in that way against men of his own faith, even though they were his enemies, when they might have more properly combined together to drive out the pale-faces from a country where they had no business to remain."

" O, he was quite a demon in every way, as you will shortly know, and he made his request to the English with the greatest coolness, without even pretending to clothe it in a decent form. 'I want to beat down the Rohillás once for all, and your help to that end. The fighting work will, of course, devolve on you, for the Rohillás are hard-hitters whom I do not care to encounter; but the trouble of plundering, burning, and harrying I shall take upon myself willingly, while you stand by and look on.' And the English, tempted by a large bribe, were only too glad to agree."

" Ah, that has always been their wont in the country, Bábájee, and they have gained ground in it in that way more surely than by any other that I know of."

" Yes, but what they obtained on the present occasion was money, not lands—some forty or fifty lakhs of rupees, which were paid down to them in cash, besides all their expenses being defrayed."

"O, the mercenary wretches! I wish the silver had been poured down their throats in a molten state. Well, what did they do for the amount?"

"Everything that they had bargained for. They led a large army into Rohilkund, which enabled the Nawáb to attack the country with impunity, and, the Rohillás being unable to repel the joint forces of the invaders, died sword in hand, fighting to the last."

"What a glorious death that was, Bábájee! God knows how willingly I would lay down my life in such a cause! Were all the Rohillás so killed?"

"Almost all the great chiefs were, and many of their followers also."

"And then?"

"Why then their villages were harried and burned by the Nawáb, as he had stipulated for, their women violated, and their children butchered."

"Without any overt participation in such acts by the English?"

"No, my son. The two parties had adhered all along to their dirty compact with equal fidelity, and continued to do so now as before. The brutalities were all perpetrated by the Nawáb and his rag-a-muffins, in the presence of an English army, and with the tacit consent of the English Government."

"Well?"

"During this sack and destruction of the country Soojá took many captives—mostly females from the hárems of the chiefs—and among others a daughter of Háfiz Ráhmut Khán, the principal ruler of Rohilkund, who had fallen in the fight. The girl was very handsome;

and her grief for the loss of her father and brethren made her so particularly interesting that even the English Commander took pity on her, and came forward to interpose on her behalf.

"'Why not let her off, Nawáb Sáheb? You have wrought mischief enough on the family already without including her in the sacrifice.'

"'It is too late for that now,' said the Nawáb. 'The witch has made too deep an impression on my heart, and I could not live without her.'

"'Ah, but she will never be yours willingly. She is a Rohillá from the hair-knot to the tip of her toes, and you have wronged the family too much for her ever to forget it.'

"'O, I know how to woo a stubborn maiden,' replied the Nawáb gaily. 'They are more easily broken in than fresh horses, I assure you, and I have several of them already in my hárem. By-and-by you will be pleased to hear, Colonel Sáheb, that she has yielded cheerfully to my wishes.'

"The Colonel shook his head, but he could not interfere; and the girl was carried off forcibly by the Nawáb, after a hurried parting from her mother and her sisters. They were all equally hopeless and miserable now, and had very little to say to each other; and the mother simply kissed her child, and gave her a poisoned clasp-knife as the last token of her affection!"

"A poisoned knife! What for?"

"'Our lot is cast, my child,' said she to her daughter, as they nestled closely within each other's arms. 'The warriors of our house are dead, and there is no one to protect us. But this may help thee in thy need if thou be true to thyself and to thy race, and then let the will of Heaven be done!'"

"Ah, brave, heroic mother! brave even to the last! How did her daughter accept the present?"

"Coldly, for she knew that her movements were watched. But they read each other's thoughts as women only know how to do, and the mother felt certain that her present had been worthily bestowed."

"Say on, Bábájee, say on. How was the knife used?"

"The girl was now removed from the banks of the Káligungá to those of the Goomti, and wept bitterly all the way as she came. But her tears were dried upon this castle being reached, and she was rather pleased to find that it had been exclusively assigned to her use. 'What matters it,' said she to herself, 'where I remain? Happy should I be if I am kept a prisoner here for life without being further molested.' She had grave doubts, however, as to whether such happiness would be permitted to her; and, having no expectations or hopes now —nothing, in fact, but fears—she intuitively kept the knife by her, as the only remaining friend that in all likelihood would not fail her in an emergency. 'Will the opportunity to use it come? Shall I have the courage to use it if it does?' The questions were asked, but were never answered, and the knife was simply kept by.

"Three months were passed in this way, and she was just beginning to get reconciled to the beauty of the scenery here, when her dream of security was broken on finding that the Nawáb had crept up to her side. She saw him, and was startled; but when, after vainly wooing her, he endeavoured to force her innocence, she deliberately drew out the weapon from her hair, within which she had secreted it, and stabbed him, repeating almost the words with which her mother had concluded her address to her—'Let it be then as Heaven has willed it.'"

"Was he killed at once?"

"No. Soojá-al-Dowláh's death is ordinarily attributed to the outbreak of a virulent disease which defied the skill of his chirurgeons; but the general rumour at the time was that he was stabbed, as I have mentioned, and that the wound degenerated into a cancer which no doctor could cure, and which eventually proved fatal."

"And the brave, heroic girl, the glorious avenger of her race! what became of her after the act?"

"According to some accounts she was torn to pieces by the royal guards, while the other women of the castle simply said that she was never afterwards seen or heard of."

"This is the best, the most romantic story that I have ever heard from you, Bábájee. That was indeed a heroine, who by one stroke of her arm avenged her own wrongs, and the wrongs of her family and her country. Let me sit down on the rampart of this castle awhile to grasp a correct idea of her in my brain, where I want to retain the image for ever."

Monohur sat on the rampart of the fortress while the Sunyási went down into the river to bathe. When the latter came out of the stream, after completing his lustration, he found that Monohur had drawn out his writing materials and was scribbling away very intently.

"What is it that you are writing, Monohur?"

"O! I am endeavouring to reproduce your story in my own words, to impress it the more strongly on my mind."

The Sunyási took up the writing, and saw how the muse of Monohur had been running wild with the tale.

"It is incomplete, Bábájee, very incomplete, and you must not be too critical with it. I know well myself that I have not been able to recite the story as you have told it."

The poem may be thus translated and preserved:—

THE MAID OF ROHILKUND.

I.

It was a maid—a noble maid
　Of Háfiz' royal race;
Her heart was crush'd, her sire was dead,
Beside him were her brothers laid,
　With blood begrimed each face.

II.

But they had fought, their dirge was said,
　'Twas not for them she pined;
She mourn'd her country's pride o'erthrown,
For self, for mother old and lone,
　And sisters left behind.

III.

O God! it was a bitter grief,
　Hopeless to hope for aid;
What fears tumultuous rend her heart,
She must from home and country part,
　Her bitterest foe hath said.

IV.

And must thou leave thy natal bower,
　Thy nook of love and rest,
And every little shrub and flower
　Thy guileless heart that blest?
And must thou leave thy mother fond,
　A wretched widow now,
Whose store of earthly joy was gone,
　Whose sweetest prop art thou?

O! must thou leave her side to bear
A life of shame, and woe, and care,
And minister to a base-born slave,
And share a couch thy virtue's grave?

V.

Great God forfend! that thou shouldst e'er
A name disgraced, dishonour'd bear;
For thou art Virtue's purest shrine,
Thy thoughts, thy feelings are divine,
  And should divine remain:
And must it be, alas! thy lot,
Thou, whom the proudest princes sought
  To wed, and sought in vain,
    O, must it be
That coward's arms will 'circle thee?

VI.

The murderers of thy father frown,
  And close to clutch thy hand,
To lead thee to the ignoble doom,
More horrid than the tomb,
  That Soojá hath pronounced;
Low in the dust lies Háfiz' crown,
And none disputes the fate denounced,
  Nor checks the servile band;
O God! shall hands like theirs injure
A maid so fair and pure,
  And Thou the while look on!

VII.

She calls on father, mother, brothers, friends,
  And many a kindred name,
Her haughty spirit loathes to bend,
  Her pure heart shrinks from shame;
But vain her tears, and vain her sighs,
  And vain each outcry wild,
For Ráhmut on the field now lies
  Unconscious of his child;

Her kinsmen all are fled and gone,
    What are the warriors fled?
The British lion still looks on—
And Soojú waves his crimson sword,
Exulting leads his recreant horde,
Beneath the British pennon's shade!

VIII.

Now dares to aid no warrior's hand,
    And thou must hopeless roam
Far from the loved, the blighted strand,
    Thy father's desolate home!
And thou must learn a winning art
To wile Prince Soojá's slavish heart,
Yes, even thou must stoop to be
The minion of his revelry.

IX.

" No, never shall that doom be mine,"
    The shuddering maiden said,
Then shrunk, as shrinks the slender vine,
    And downward droop'd her head;
The words unfinish'd died away
    By shame, by rage, by grief oppress'd,
She sunk as if to eternal rest,
    And on the pavement lay.

X.

Speed, mother, speed! they drag afar
    Thy daughter fair from thee:
" She comes, my angel and my star,
    Off slaves! let me be free,
And, mother, let me cling to thee,
Thou dearest friend in adversity."

XI.

The child and mother fondly twine,
    Commingling sighs with tears,
Each finds the other's heart a shrine

To pour out all her fears.
In vain they look for aid around;
The British flag still braves the gale,
And under it sad shrieks and wail
   Alone rebound.

XII.

"And must I part, for ever part,
   My dearest child, with thee?
O, who will cheer my widow'd heart
   When thou art far from me?
   And yet it must be so,
Behold their haughty pennon streams!
And who shall dare to rescue thee,
   Thou child of misery,
   From sin and woe
Ne'er compass'd in thy dreams?

XIII.

"Alas! these arms shall ne'er again infold
   The fairest flower, the richest gem,
   Of the Rohillá diadem,
The brightest jewel of the bold!
Our star of hope has set in gloom,
   Our warriors press the blood-drench'd sod,
Heaven's canopy their only tomb!
They sleep upon the turf they trod.
Men, at whose names the tyrants quaked,
Men, at whose thought proud Soojá waked
Disturb'd by midnight visions grim,
   Now sleep in everlasting rest,
   Without a single care opprest,
   Without one weary dream!
Their crime was that they would be free,
   The open air for ever breathe;
And Freedom sent her sons afar
To aid Prince Soojá's causeless war;
On Britain's crown the stain will last,
Though years and ages shall have past,
Of butcher'd children, and of ravish'd wives,

Of blazing homes, and slaughter'd lives—
Why of such triumphs wouldst thou make thy wreath,
  Imperial Daughter of the Sea?

XIV.

"Look up, my child, I will not bid
  That faded cheek to smile;
Thy woes I feel, thy pangs I read,
  But cease, O cease! to weep awhile.
What though the splendour of our name has set?
The Lord of Hosts is potent yet!
Though other arms may not now shield thee,
If yet on Him thy faith endure,
He ne'er will leave a shrine so pure,
Nor Soojá's lust, nor Britain's power,
Shall crush the God-protected flower,
  If thou such flower should be."

XV.

She raised her eyes to heaven, and wild
  They rested there,
And, with her kneeling child,
  She falter'd forth her prayer;
And every heart that witness'd them
  Was sad, and every eye was dim,
But still the ruffians stood with terrors crown'd,
And grimly still the British lion frown'd!

XVI.

They clasp'd and kiss'd, and kiss'd again—
  Unwilling they to part,
For each had tasted dregs of pain
  And felt the loneliness of heart;
But of the light of hope no beam
Shed now on them its feeblest gleam,
While uncouth warriors' hastening words
Fill'd up each sighing pause they made;
At last the sobbing maiden said:
  "If such my destiny,
And hope no cheering ray affords,

Allá's great will fulfill'd must be:
Where'er we live, howe'er apart,
O, do thou still remember me,
As I shall fondly think of thee!
And, mother, of thy love bestow
Some token that may solace give
   To thy forlorn and outcast child—
A loved associate for her heart
   Disgraced, dishonour'd, and defiled!"

XVII.

The mother's heart is big with fears,
The mother's eyes are full of tears,
And scarce her tongue her words can tell,
So much her feelings throb and swell:
" What, what have I to give to thee,
   My fairest, weeping flower!
And wherefore shouldst thou harp on me
   In a far and foreign bower?
No gem, no pearl must deck that brow
   Which Soojá would defile,
No jewel rich must grace it now,
   No chain his heart to wile;
But I have one fond token true,
That token fain I'd give to you."

XVIII.

She drew her weeping child apart,
   A jewell'd knife she gave:
" This, this can ease the greatest smart,
   From blight protect, from danger save.
Remember, child, the Rohillá name,
   Remember thou thy father's worth,
Let not his spirit burn with shame;
   Remember thy proud birth.
All, all our sorrows yet avenged may be—
   I speak no more; that start,
That glowing cheek, that sparkling eye,
   Speak of thy feelings well—we part!"

XIX.

They dragg'd the unwilling beauty far away,
Far from the festal regions of the brave—
The loved, the adored of all around!
No more her joyous steps will bound
Beside the Káligungá's wave;
Nor shall her fairy fingers stray
The harp's sweet chords along,
To wake again the rapture-breathing song!
Torn from its stem the virgin flower
Now graced a foreign bower:
But not to smile and not to bloom,
No rest for her but in the tomb;
Her burning eyes for ever wept,
And care within her heart lay deep,
She would not, or she could not sleep,
Or sunk in agony she slept!

XX.

Long, anxious, weary nights have roll'd away,
Thou pinest still from day to day;
How changed since last those eyelids smiled
With gladness pure and mild!
Despair has veil'd her eyes in gloom;
The maiden, shrinking, waits her doom,
Forebodes her ruin'd honour, shatter'd fame,
And bends beneath the pictured load of shame!

XXI.

'Tis night, wild night, on Goomti's shore!
  No star is shining high;
And hideous, vast, and quite obscure
  Frowns the everlasting sky!
Guilt shuns the heavenly blaze of light,
Guilty spirits are abroad to-night;
Háfiz' daughter sits alone
  Beside her glimmering taper's ray,
Blending with the blast her moan,
  And panting for the light of day.

The midnight hour is well-nigh past,
  But hark! a step is at her door;
Perhaps it was the sighing blast,
  O no! it moves again—once more!
She starts in fear; who can it be?
  With caitiff stride who comes?
The veriest caitiff, he!

XXII.

With many a fond, endearing name,
  He woo'd the lovely maid;
She hung her head with burning shame,
  "O do not tempt!" she said;
"And do not add to my distress,
I have tasted much of bitterness:
There are maidens many, sweeter far,
With joy would hail thy prosperous star,
Would stoop with pleasure, sure, to be
Allied by love or lust to thee;
Spare, then, O spare thy weeping slave,
And innocent let her reach the grave."

XXIII.

But ah, fair maid, thou plead'st in vain;
  His heart is proof to prayers,
Albeit like darksome floods of rain
  Thou shedd'st thy scalding tears.
"Thou fairest lily of our vale,"
  Exulting Soojá said,
"Loathing, or fond, thou must be mine;
And I shall swear by Meccá's shrine
To be for ever, ever thine!"
He stretch'd his arms to clasp the maid,
  And press'd her to his heart;
  O, 'twas a grievous smart!
One cry she gave, one shriek of wail;
Her hands her tresses roved among,
Thence drew her mother's parting blade.
Now let the tyrant have his meed,
  Now dagger do thy deed—

The Lord be praised! the deed is done!
Dread spirits of the brave, who throng
The bright Elysian courts above,
If yet one spark of patriot love,
  One gleam of fire,
  Your hearts inspire,
Rejoice, if vengeance can rejoice ye!
Sink, Soojá, sink! thy race is run,
  No art will heal that poison'd wound;
'Tis Heaven has crush'd thy impious pride,
  And dash'd the eagle to the ground!

XXIV.

And she, the flower of purity!
  Her fate, ah! who can tell?
Man knows not if she lived or died;
Her lovely form was never seen again,
  Her voice—so soft, so sweet, so clear—
Was never heard in bower or plain,
  In palace-hall or gay parterre.

"The poem is good enough, I admit," said the Sunyási, wishing to humour the youthful rhymster; "but we are in the Nawáb's country now, and the people here must not know aught about it."

"I do not want to remain in his country longer," replied Monohur. "Let us speed out of it as fast as we may. If the English be bad masters they are surely not so bad as the Mahomedans, for they do not force away people's wives and daughters from them as the others do."

"Ah, step by step you are getting reconciled to the English rule, Monohur."

"Yes, I am really beginning to think that it is the best for us under present circumstances."

CHAPTER XLIV.

HIMÁLAYAN STORIES, AND A NEW ROUTE TO CHINA.

WITH the natives of India generally a return journey is proverbially more expeditious than a forward movement, and Monohur pursued his backward course free-hearted, if not happy, while even the Sunyási seemed to be more at his ease as he marched with sturdier steps than he had done before. Their path had, in fact, become familiar to them, and they were indulging in a feeling of security on it mainly on that account, its grim-looking corners having lost their fears.

"We are fast approaching the English frontier," said Monohur. "Shall we not be able to cross it to-day, Bábájee?"

"We may; but we are still some ten or twelve miles from it, and, if we do cross it, it will be after the daylight has expired."

It was a very close day, and they had just passed the village of Pánágurh, in the Ázimgurh district, where a market had been held for nearly a week, which had now broken up, and the people from it were seen returning to their homes in dozens and scores, in every direction. They were most of them farmers and dealers from the neighbouring villages, and were nearly all of them intent, wholly as they seemed, in recounting their gains.

"There is a lot of men here, Bábájee, whom we do not know. Had we not better keep clear of them?"

"O, they are shopmen and dealers only, not cut-throats or poisoners, Monohur. We have nothing whatever to fear from them."

"We should nevertheless get out of the crowd at least. Our path lies in the direction of the Gorá Nuddee now, I think?"

"Yes, and we have taken to it already, and hope to reach it almost immediately, my son."

There was only one party of market-men on the same track with them—namely, some seven cloth-dealers who lived at a distance of about five or six miles beyond the Nuddee named; and these they overtook to go with.

"We go by the same road with you it seems, if for a short distance only," said the Sunyási to them, "and may jog on together if you do not object."

"With the greatest pleasure on our part, surely," answered the cloth-dealers; and they all went in company, speaking cheerfully and without constraint with each other.

The Nuddee was now reached, a lovely, lazy stream, winding its thin shining course occasionally through sour-looking rocks and defiles, but more frequently through flat, grass-grown swards; and here some of the cloth-dealers proposed that they should halt to refresh themselves, which was, however, not agreed to by the rest. This caused a division among the travellers, and while three stayed behind the other four went on, Monohur and the Sunyási remaining back with the former.

"I would have stayed behind gladly for a while,' said one of the four forward-goers to his companions, after they had crossed the Nuddee, "but for the sinister look of that Sunyási, whose presence with us I did not enjoy."

"For shame!" cried the other three dealers together. "You are surely much too timorous for these marketings. What was there in the old man to be afraid of?"

Before any reply could be made the party was overtaken by a stranger, who asked for a little tobacco, which was given to him.

"You seem to be coming from the market. Did you go to buy or to sell?"

"Both to buy and to sell," replied one of the cloth-dealers with a laugh; "and we are returning home very heavily laden, my friend."

"You had better quicken your pace then, if you have a long way to go. This road is not a safe one at any hour."

"How do you come to know that? Do you belong to the neighbourhood?"

"Yes," answered the stranger, "I live very near the road, I may well say on it, for I live, breathe, and get my subsistence by it; and should I not befriend the passengers on it?"

"You do not describe your calling very intelligibly though. What do you mean by saying that you live by and on the road?"

"Exactly what the words imply, my friend; and it is very hard work, I assure you. But I must be off, for I want rest sadly."

He did not stay for further talk, but left them with a mischievous wink, while the cloth-dealers burst out laughing afresh at the ugly attempt made to frighten them, as they took it; all save the fearful man, who became agitated and nervous again. The path was now getting narrower and narrower at every step, and before they could come into open space they were met by two other strangers, who were particularly anxious to know what they carried.

"Why? How does that concern you?"

"A great deal surely," was the playful reply. "We live by cheap bargains, and to get at them are obliged to be inquisitive."

"Well then, we are not the men you take us for. We have no cheap wares to sell."

There was a little feeling of annoyance now, as was observable from the tone in which the answer was made. But the words were scarcely out of their mouths before the cloth-dealers saw that they were being surrounded by a number of new-comers, who fell upon them, and robbed them of everything they had, even to the clothes they wore, after which all the robbers took to their heels, and were of course unpursued. The other three cloth-dealers and our two pilgrims, who had lagged behind on the banks of the Gorá Nuddee, were now coming up; but they were too late on the scene to go after the miscreants, who were already out of sight; and all they could do was confined to rendering such assistance to the plundered men as they stood in need of, and to conducting them to the nearest thánnáh on the English frontier.

"A pestilent lot of robbers infest the road," exclaimed the thánnádár, "and it is a pity we can do nothing to put them down."

"Why? Can't you pursue them across the border and capture them?" asked the Sunyási.

"No; not at once. We have to apply first to our superior officers for permission to cross over, and the bandits, being protected by the Oude tálookdárs, are always safely housed by the time we are able to start after them. The two jurisdictions cause great trouble and annoyance."

The plea was simply unanswerable, and Monohur took a note of it as he crossed over into English territory with a sigh of relief.

"I had a great love for travelling, Bábájee, but these road-poisonings and robberies have nearly wrung it out of me already. I envy you not the less the enjoyment you have had in that way."

"Enjoyment, Monohur? Well, perhaps you are right. I did enjoy them much in my youthful days—that is, as well as dreary, rugged, and barren routes, such as I have mostly plodded over, can ever be enjoyed."

"But it was not always equally dreary, Bábájee, was it? You must have seen various kinds of places, and the sights must have been of very diversified character."

"My chief pilgrimage, Monohur, was to the Himálayás —to Hurdwár, Kedárnáth, and Budrináth; and the scenes all through were, as I have described them, nothing but rocks before and behind, with dense tangled forests about them, and the *dulká,* or avalanche, descending suddenly down to cover many a poor pilgrim in a grave of snow."

"Ah, I can well fancy the trouble of toiling up and down the eternal hills, and the risk of getting occasionally swamped, or even of being killed by the sliding snow. But the passes cannot be much harassed by poisoners and robbers, I expect?"

"No, for there are no wayfarers there worth poisoning or robbing—none whose rifled rags would fetch two pyce in the market. But tigers and wolves are constantly prowling about the mountains, and there are fire-emitting peaks, such as Nundi Devi, which consume to cinders those who venture too near their summits; so that the Sunyási's path, my son, is not really less dangerous than that of the ordinary traveller roaming through such ill-governed countries as Oude."

"Ah, but the volcanic peaks are well known, and easily avoided."

"They ought to be, but always are not; and pilgrims do get horribly singed by them at times."

"Did you ever go up any of these mountains yourself, Bábájee?"

"Yes; but not when they were emitting fire or lava: and if they had done so suddenly I would surely have got burnt, if not killed."

"Did you go beyond the Himálayás on any occasion?"

"No, my son, I did not. I often formed the wish to do so, from the pilgrim-tales I heard, especially at the *melá* held once in twelve years on the highest accessible point of Nundi Devi, where I met with some strange-looking athletic eremites who gave marvellous accounts of their wanderings. But I was never able to realise my wish. I particularly wanted to visit Cheen, but could never get a companion to go with."

"But is not Cheen approached by the passes through Assam?"

"There were roads to it in the past leading through Assam, but these have long become impracticable. The route ordinarily followed by pilgrims at present lies round the north-west corner of the Himálayan chain, across the east of the Toorki land."

"And what was the character the pilgrims gave of it; I mean those who had actually passed by the route?"

"A great part of the road is naturally the same as that to the Himálayás, except that many more hot-springs are met with in the higher chains of snow."

"Hot-springs in the midst of the snow! Is that not a mere traveller's story, Bábájee? How can such contradictions be accounted for?"

"Why, if the mountains spit fire what wonder is there that the springs issuing from their bowels should be hot and boiling? There is nothing strange at all in that, Monohur."

"And the routes beyond them?"

"Lie through a large sandy desert which has to be crossed, and every account given of it was simply marvellous."

"As how?"

"Why, all the pilgrims said that the desert is full of demons, and that there are also siroc winds there which kill all who encounter them."

"Demons and winds?"

"Yes, the demons riding upon the winds and playing all sorts of pranks with unwary travellers. There are no birds or beasts to be seen anywhere, which makes the sense of solitude there excessively oppressive, while the hazy, hot light refracted from the mountains adds greatly to the discomfort in a different way; and the road is strewed on both sides with the bleached bones of men who have perished in crossing the dreary waste."

"But the pilgrims you spoke with, did they cross the desert and enter Cheen?"

"They did: but for a great distance they found neither dwelling-houses nor people; and the miseries they endured were, they said, simply indescribable. After crossing the desert they had again to pass through a region of mountains very like the Himálayás, covered with snow at all seasons of the year, and here they encountered enormous venomous dragons that spat out poison against them."

"This was a new and peculiar danger to encounter. How did they get over it?"

"Scarcely five out of ten were able to pass through with success; but the dilemma was awkward, and there was no good in turning back from the route. Their watchword therefore was—'Press on, even if it be to perish.'"

"That was a natural determination, and must have given them strength, as, I am sure, it would have given me. 'I will do this' almost means 'It has been achieved.'"

"Yes, submitting to be destroyed they gathered up their strength and pressed forward, but only to meet with fresh difficulties which seemed almost insuperable. The mountains rose like walls of rock before them, and looking over the ice their eyes got confused, while their feet became unsteady, and many losing hold of the rocks fell down and were lost."

"And the survivors?"

"They reached the base of the mountains with the greatest difficulty by granite steps formed by giants or demons for their own descent, and found a rivulet below crossed by a tree thrown over it."

"And then?"

"They crossed several similar streams successively, and eventually reached the land of Cheen, which they found to be as well peopled as India itself, and in every respect quite as flourishing."

CHAPTER XLV.

A TRUE DESCRIPTION OF CHINA, WITH A *SO* AND *DO* WIFE STORY IN THE BARGAIN.

"How is the land of Cheen governed, Bábájee?" asked Monohur of the Sunyási. "Surely with a native ruler over them the people there ought to be much happier than we are?"

"So they are, my son. The whole of Cheen is even like a garden in fairy-land, and yet busy as a mart, the people being both happy and industrious. The Government is paternal, the king is as a father unto his people. The welfare of his subjects is his only concern, and he is so untiring in his efforts to improve and elevate them that they have become absolutely the first of all nations in every respect."

"Indeed! Are they superior to the English then, who brag of their civilisation and greatness so much?"

"I am sure they are, for they excel all the world in the arts and sciences, and in their manner of living also. That some should be richer than others is a necessity of existence everywhere; but nobody is somebody with them because of his wealth. He must know something or do something to be respected or beloved."

"A very good rule that, and very necessary for rousing up every individual member of society to exert himself as a man."

"Yes, and the effect of it has been very salutary in that way. There is no such thing as ignorance or idleness in the country, and no wretchedness or squalidness even among the poor; while the movements of the higher classes are characterised by a refinement, naturalness, and grace seldom to be met with together at any one place."

"How did the pilgrims fare with them then, after all their troubles?"

"O, they spoke rapturously of the hospitality they met with. The men of the higher ranks received them into their houses as old friends, while even the poorest felt grieved if they would not come occasionally to live with them."

"It is really a patriarchal state of society that you are describing, Bábájee—that of a people well-governed, contented, and happy, living as useful and amiable members of society, peacefully among themselves and with all others. They must of course be well attached to their sovereign. O, how faithful I could be to an indigenous king, ruling as a father over his people! But it is our misfortune that we can have none, and this beautiful country, perhaps not less beautiful than Cheen itself, is on that account only what it is at this day."

"You are right, Monohur, for even the people of Cheen speak of India as the richest and the most beneficently-endowed land under the sun. But they do not envy us the possession of it. They commiserate us rather for being the slaves we are, and for what we have to endure."

Monohur was silent for a moment, the words of the Sunyási having very deeply affected him.

"O, tell me more, Bábájee, about the people of Cheen

and their king," said he at last. "Do you think that they are really better off than we are in every respect? Is it possible that the gods should be so much our enemies as to have lowered us below all other human beings in every way?"

"Not in every way, my son; not in every way surely. Our religion is assuredly the best of all religions in the world; the Cheen folks at least have nothing whatever to compare with it, having in fact adopted that residuum of Buddhism which was cast off or thrown into the background by our forefathers: and in letters also we may say that we are yet somewhat ahead of them."

Monohur's face regained its colour on receiving this assurance, and was even slightly touched with pride and joy.

"But they are happier than us, father, and does not happiness make up for every other want? We can entertain no noble feelings, give expression to no honest aspirations, without being regarded as traitors; but they can think and act as they choose without being misunderstood."

"So it is among them indeed. The king is fond of his subjects, and his subjects are as fond of their king, and of his thousand sons, who, the pilgrims assured me, are as good princes as any could wish for."

"His thousand sons? Did I hear you aright, Bábájee?"

"Yes, Monohur; the king has a thousand sons—at least I was told so."

"Has he many wives then?"

"Only two. By the laws of Cheen the king may marry four wives, one *So*, or favourite, and three *Do*, or less favoured; but the present sovereign has only two, of whom the *Do* and *So* have exchanged places by a curious incident."

"Tell me the story, I beg. I am sure it would lighten my mind much of the uneasy thoughts that are oppressing it at this moment."

"Well, the king had two wives, but no children by either of them, and the Board of Rites had many ceremonies performed in all the great temples of the country, and especially in that of the Sun, for the birth of an heir. At last the *Do* wife conceived, and when this became known the *So* was greatly troubled, alike by envy and fear.

"'The odds are mustering strong against me,' said she to herself; 'but I must win in spite of them.' And, on the *Do* being delivered of an unformed fœtus, she represented the event as a misfortune and the harbinger of approaching woes, and prevailed on the king to order the conception to be inclosed in a wooden box and thrown into the Hoang-Ho river.

"She was now as irradiant in her triumph as before, while the *Do*, pressed down by her misery, was forced to abide her time with a sore and despairing heart. In the meantime the box with the fœtus floated up the stream with the spring-tide, which was strong, and was carried far into Kánsu, a country to the north-west of Cheen, the king of which, having opened it personally, was surprised to find in it a thousand very little children, all of one size, and having either exactly the same, or very similar, faces. He brought up these little boys as his own, and they in time became great warriors.

"Several years after there was some great misunderstanding between the two kings, upon which the King of Kánsu sent a large army against his neighbour, headed by his thousand foster-sons. The King of Cheen got terribly alarmed, and his *So* wife also; but said the *Do* to herself—

"'Surely Fortune has veered round in my favour now, and I must be equal to the opportunity to benefit by it.'

"She accordingly sent word to the king that, if he would allow her to march against the invaders at the head of his army, she would certainly be able to avert the danger that threatened them, and that she was prepared to start on the errand at once.

"'How wilt thou do it? How is it possible for thee to do it?' asked the king in reply. 'No, no; the idea is foolish, and I cannot accede to it; nor would my warriors be pleased to have a woman placed at their head.'

"The king had no notion of the facts, nor any inkling of the motives, which had induced the *Do* to come forward with her offer, and, viewing it only as a mad proposal coming from a woman dissatisfied with her position in the palace, he hurried to make his own preparations for meeting the emergency.

"Thought the *So* wife now to herself—

"'Why might not the *Do* be sent out as she has suggested so foolishly? Good would surely come of it if she died; while, if she escaped, there was still the chance of broken bones and other accidents.'

"'O king,' said she, therefore, to her husband, 'let my sister go forth as she has offered, I beseech you. We know not but that she may be cognisant of some charm or incantation to destroy the enemy, and why should we not benefit by her art?'

"'Be it so then since thou wishest it,' replied the king, 'though I fear greatly that no magic will be of much service to us in this affair, while the chances are that the magician may get killed in the fight.'

"Then turning to the *Do* he added—

"'You take too much on yourself in making the request, *Do*, but you may go if you are bent on it.'

"The *Do* became somewhat disturbed now in her turn from indecision, but reasoned herself into compliance by arguing the matter further internally.

"'It is certain that my children are coming, and if I can only see them all together even for a moment I shall not have braved any danger in vain.'

"And the two armies met face to face a short time after, one headed by a thousand youthful warriors with bright beaming eyes, the other by a middle-aged woman still resplendent with beauty.

"The sharp eyes of the *Do* wife counted her children even from a distance, and while one hand was pressed to her heart to repress its beatings, the other was raised to wipe off the moisture from her brow.

"'The breath of life is coming back to me at last,' murmured she to herself, 'but I must not betray any weakness before them yet, lest they should not listen to me.'

"She smoothed her troubled aspect accordingly, and, addressing the young men before her, asked them if they were not her sons, and how they had dared to appear in arms against their own father?'

"'Your sons? Who are you?'

"'Look at my face, and open your mouths;' and while they did so intuitively, she opened her breasts and compressed them, and the milk darted in five hundred jets from each breast, one jet falling into the mouth of each of her sons.

"'You are indeed our mother,' exclaimed the youthful warriors, and instantly laid down their arms at her feet with a shower of joyful tears that poured down their cheeks.

"The king was in raptures on hearing how the expedition had ended; and, as the children came in to him, he folded them one after another within his paternal arms, and pressed them to his heart. The *Do* wife became the *So* wife from that day, the former *So* wife becoming the *Do* now in her turn; and the king, blessed with his numerous progeny, has been exceedingly happy ever since."

"This is scarcely a credible account, Bábájee, as it stands," said Monohur; "but I suppose, like all stories, it has a basis in fact, which I almost fancy I am able to unravel."

"Ah, let us hear your sage construction by all means," answered the Sunyási, rather pettishly. "If the story as I have told it be not to your liking, there is no reason why you should not re-cook it to please yourself."

"But I don't want to re-cook it at all. My object is only to make sense of what sounds like nonsense in its present dress. An unformed foetus in a box would not give birth to a thousand children; no box would contain a thousand children, however small, and float on the river at the same time; no breast squeezed, however dexterously, would give out milk in five hundred jets: and these are all drawbacks to the acceptance of the story as it has been told to you. As I understand the tale it is simply this: The King of Cheen had two wives, a *Do* and a *So* one. He had no children for a long time till the *Do* wife conceived. This made the *So* wife jealous, and being the royal favourite, she had the child that was born (perhaps not fully developed) inclosed in a box and thrown into the river. The box was fished up, probably by some friend of the *Do* wife, and was carried to the King of Kánsu, perhaps one of her relatives. The child thus saved was brought up by the King of Kánsu. He became a great warrior, having the strength of a thousand heroes, just as our Bheem in the Mahábhárut is spoken of as having the strength of a thousand *mast* elephants. On war breaking out between Cheen and Kánsu the youthful prince led his foster-father's army to the walls of the former country, mainly perhaps to avenge his mother's wrongs. The King of Cheen getting terrified now sent for his *Do* wife, and asked her to have the matter settled with her son. She marched thereupon at the head of her husband's army, and, seeking out her son, prevailed on him not to fight against his own father, and possibly also to lay down his arms. Of course the old king was overjoyed, and the *Do* wife became the *So* wife, and *vice versâ*. Does not this appear more intelligible than the story as the pilgrims gave it to you?"

"Perhaps so. But the question is, which of the two versions is the true one? The story as the pilgrims related it was heard by them in Cheen itself, from persons who knew of the facts as they had occurred, while the story as you wish to re-fashion it is nothing more than your individual interpretation of the facts, for which there is no authority."

"With this broad distinction between them, Bábájee, that the one is altogether improbable, and the other not unusual in the least."

"Be it so, my son," said the Sunyási. "There is no need for chewing wormwood over a matter so trivial."

CHAPTER XLVI.

AT PÁTNÁ, AND ABOUT THE MOHURRUM.

THE journey was continued, without any further altercation or difference of opinion between the two companions, but a good part of the road was walked over in silence.

"Whither are we going now, Bábájee?" asked Monohur at last, if only to resume the conversation.

"O, we are approaching the town of Pátná," answered the Sunyási, "but I am averse to enter it."

"Why, what are you afraid of there? Can anyone be lying in wait for us in it, think you?"

"No, not that, Monohur. But the Mohurrum festival is now at its height there, and the people are all in an excited state; and I know of old that very slight causes will on such occasions give rise to a fight amongst them."

"But how does that affect us? Neither you nor I will be for taking any part in such quarrel, I am sure."

"Ah, true indeed—at least as regards myself. But the city is thickly inhabited by Mahomedans, and when the fire burns high among them it seldom flames straight up without crackling and casting forth sparks around, especially in the direction of the Hindus."

"But, O Bábájee, I want to see how the Mohurrum is celebrated in these districts, and, if the risk be not much,

I would certainly wish to enter the city, plucking up a spirit for the occasion."

"To fight out, if necessary, notwithstanding our present position and disadvantages?"

"No, not to fight out, but to learn to be reasonable and on our guard against any provocation that may be offered to us."

"Good," said the Sunyási, "that is rather well said;" and they entered the city the moment they came up to it.

The Mohurrum is the grandest ceremony of the Sheáhs, and is celebrated some time between January and March. It commemorates the martyrdom of Hássan and Hossein, the sons of Áli and grandsons of Mahomet. On Áli being assassinated Hássan retired to Mediná, where he was poisoned, upon which Hossein headed a revolt against Yázid, the ruling vicegerent. Failing in this Hossein was obliged to fly, and for three days took refuge in a dry well near the banks of the Euphrates, where he had nothing at all to eat. His retreat was discovered by a chameleon, upon which he was dragged out by his enemies, and slain, together with all of his family, except Syed, who escaped.

The festival celebrated is throughout a mourning one. It is continued for a period of ten days, during the first portion of which the Mahomedans collect together at each other's houses to hear the story of the martyrdom recited or sung, the *Moolláhs* praying day and night unceasingly for the souls of the dead. The last four days comprise the most important part of the ceremony, when the *tazeáhs* (or mock biers) are carried about and the demonstrations of grief become violent. On the last day the burial of Hossein is celebrated, and the exhibition of sorrow becomes so furious that even women have been known to tear the flesh from off their arms, while all rend their clothes, and beat their breasts till the blood seems to start out of them.

The processions are of course gorgeous, but yet in keeping with the avowed character of the show. The troopers and their horses are all dressed in mourning, and move on with rent banners and muffled drums. The cymbals and kettle-drums are bound round with cloth coloured green; and the mourners are all similarly dressed, not excepting the Hindu servants who take part in the processions as *paiks* and orderlies. The observance of religious rites is of course confined to the Mahomedans; but the Hindu following is by no means inconsiderable, and this is especially the case in Pátná, where the Hindu and Mahomedan celebrants are almost equally divided in number, and where many, if not all, of the former join the processions as to the manner born.

"We are entering what may almost be called an enemy's country, Monohur, and yet you will find almost all the resident Hindus here marshalled on the enemy's side."

"How is that, Bábájee? What may be the cause of it?"

"O, simply the childish love of our countrymen for shows. Naturally we are not much fond of excitement, and would rather keep quiet at home than be going about raving through the streets. But hold up only a flag or two, and beat a drum or sound a cymbal, and the fascination becomes irresistible, and you get throngs of idlers to follow you wherever you may choose to lead them."

"You are referring to the mob only, Bábájee. There must be men of better stamp too, here as in other places?"

"Yes, that of course; and I am now on the look-out for some person of that kind to lodge with, and wish I may find one quickly."

He was looking out very eagerly; but there was a little check to his success by reason of the crowd on the road which did not allow him to see much ahead of him.

"Let us go round the corner there, Bábájee," said Monohur. "The place on the other side is less thronged, and would be more convenient to us, both to pass by and search for."

They did so accordingly, and the result was satisfactory, for they soon met with a very respectable man who was coming in their direction. He was a little bald just above the forehead, and more than a little gray; but his figure was well formed and well filled out, and he had an amiable face and a stately beard.

"I have a great mind to apply to that gentleman there to receive us," said the Sunyási. "I mean him with the long beard and the *Námmálá* in his hand."

"The *Námmálá*? How do you see it? His hand is enveloped in a bag. Is he counting the beads inside of the bag?"

"Yes. He is a Vysnub and has a rosary of the Tulsi wood in his hand, and the bag is the certificate thereof."

"How so? What makes you conclude that he is a Vysnub, and not a Saiva?"

"O, the rosary of a Saiva is made of the berries of the Rudráksha tree, and the beads are necessarily large and rough, such as that small bag would not contain."

"Is the rosary of the Vysnub then smaller than that of the Saiva? My impression was that it was larger, as having many more beads than the other."

"And so it has. The *málá* of the Vysnub usually

counts a hundred and eight beads, while that of the Saiva counts no more than thirty-two or sixty-four; but the former are smooth and small, while the latter are so inconvenient in size that no bag like the one before us would conceal a *málá* formed of them. Besides that, the mere fact of concealment is a sign of Vysnubism."

"In what way?"

"The counting of beads is a work of merit, you know, and jealous demons are always watching to prevent or obstruct its performance. The Vysnub conceals his hand to prevent what he does from being seen; but the Saiva trusts to the imps of Mahádeva, who are always about him, for protection, and considers concealment to be unnecessary."

"Have we good and evil spirits then, always about us, concerning themselves in our affairs?"

"Of course we have. The evil spirits are constantly trying to harm us. Could we have escaped if we had not good spirits to take care of us?"

They stood face to face with the Vysnub now, and he seemed to be a perfect type of what a real Vysnub ought to be.

"A glad greeting to you, friends," said he, coming forward to accost them. "Can I do anything to serve you?"

"A kind greeting to you in return, Mohásoy. If you will be so good as to accommodate us in your house for a few days, or help us in getting suitable accommodation elsewhere, we shall, as strangers and wayfarers, be immensely obliged to you."

"O, don't speak of going elsewhere; I surely will not allow you to do that. My house and everything I have is at your service, and I shall try my best to make you comfortable in it."

"We thank you very much indeed, Mohásoy," said the Sunyási. "My young friend here is anxious to see the Mohurrum procession, and it is on that account only that we have come to this place."

"Ah, then you have come rather late, for the festivities are nearly over, this being the last but one of the procession days. Besides that, a quarrel has sprung up between the Sheáhs and the Sunnis, and there is more likelihood of seeing a grand fight between them than a procession."

"It is all the same to me, Mohásoy," said Monohur. "I would not witness a good fight with less pleasure than a goodly procession."

The Vysnub smiled, and then scanned the form and features of Monohur more particularly as he replied to him.

"You speak foolishly, my son, very foolishly indeed; for a good fight means a good deal of mischief, including heads broken and limbs fractured, and not unoften the loss of lives also. That, surely, is not a pleasant sight to see?"

"Ah, Mohásoy!" said the Sunyási with playful spite, "your picture of a fight is only making it all the more attractive to my young friend. He would not care to get his own head broken if you will only allow him to join a row. Is not that it, Monohur?"

"If it be so, Bábájee, I owe that to your teaching mainly; don't I? Who gave me the name of Kharga Báhádoor, pray?"

"O, never mind those recollections at present, my son. You forget our present character. We are pilgrims now, not soldiers."

Monohur received the rebuke in silence, for he felt that it was deserved, and then, to give a turn to the conversation, asked the Vysnub how the quarrel between the Sheáhs and Sunnis had arisen.

"You shall know all about it, my son, after I have housed you," said the Vysnub. "It is not always safe to talk of these matters in the street;" and he led them away from the main road, which was so full of passengers, to a short blind lane, at the end of which was a small lowly mansion, which he pointed out to them as his home.

CHAPTER XLVII.

A MOHURRUM QUARREL.

THE house of the Vysnub was a very humble building, consisting, on one side, of a rather long, single-storied apartment which was devoted to the reception of wayfarers and strangers, and, on the other, of two or three smaller apartments pertaining exclusively to his womankind, with a capacious cook-shed at one end of the compound, and a well of very sweet water at the other. All the apartments were tile-roofed, and their outside appearance was exceedingly plain. Inside, the walls were painted reddish-brown, and the floor of the reception-room was covered with a thick *durmá* mat, on which the men of the family were accustomed to pass their time, seated or lolling as they chose. For guests and visitors—of whom there were some, more or less, at all times—there were *Morás*, or cane-chairs in reserve in the background, two of which were now brought forward by the Vysnub and placed on the unmatted portion of the floor for the Sunyási and Monohur to sit upon.

"It is very poor accommodation indeed that I can offer you, my friends," said the Vysnub; "but such as it is you are most heartily welcome to it."

"To us," replied the Sunyási, "it is as good as any that a palace could have given, for it is infinitely more comfortable and convenient than what we have long been accustomed to, and your open kindness makes it even more acceptable than it might have been under other circumstances."

The Sunyási's praise of both the place and its owner was equally well-deserved, for the former had a peculiar quietness about it which was not to be easily equalled, and the latter a look of honesty that inspired reliance and respect.

"Ah, I thank you for your words," answered the Vysnub, "and would be sorry indeed if you did not feel quite comfortable with us in all respects. See, there the youngest of my elves is coming with water that you may wash your faces, hands, and feet, and prepare yourselves for such humble repast as they may be able to get ready for you in the house," and sure enough a pretty little girl was approaching them with a well-filled *kulsi* on her head, having set down which in the compound she stood quietly by the visitors, as if awaiting their commands.

"That is a very good girl," said the Sunyási stooping to stroke her head affectionately, while Monohur presented her with a bunch of flowers which he had plucked from the road-side before entering the city, with which she was evidently much gratified.

Having washed themselves the guests were pressed to partake of a homely Vysnub fare, composed mainly of fruits, sweetmeats, and milk, to which Monohur did ample justice, and the Sunyási was by no means indifferent. They then washed their hands and faces again, and, on resuming their seats on the cane-chairs, Monohur hastened to apply for the information which their host had promised him.

"We have restrained our curiosity so long, Mohásoy, that I am sure you will pardon my asking you again to tell us how the Sheáhs and Sunnis have managed to fall out on the present occasion, and in fact all about the matter that you may happen to know."

"Ah, yes," said the Vysnub, "I remember my promise, and will redeem it now with pleasure. The Mohurrum quarrels always originate in trifles, and it was the merest trifle this time also that gave rise to the dispute. The original cause of the quarrel was very different from that now attributed to it. The town, you may perhaps know, is divided into two parties which are contending with each other almost throughout the year. Some months ago one Ábbás Áli, a Sheáh, carried off the widow of one Bakáoolláh, a deceased Sunni, and with her consent married her. There was no crime or offence in this act; but the friends of Bakáoolláh took umbrage at the Sheáhs having had the temerity to take away anyone out of their protection by force, and, collecting together under the lead of one Ketáboodeen, made a raid on their opponents, carrying off three of their women, whom they compelled to perform certain menial duties, such as sweeping their houses, cleaning the family-utensils, and the like. The women were released the next day at the instance of the police; but the Sheáhs were not satisfied therewith, and awaited for revenge.

"'It is not that we are thinking of it now,' said they, 'but we will have our revenge.'

"'Revenge for what?' remonstrated the peacemakers. 'You were the aggressors, and the Sunnis have only repaid your outrage in kind, and certainly not with greater violence. Since you are quits now why not get reconciled with each other from this time?'

"'Ah, but we hate each other, and can never cease to

do so. What is the good of affecting a reconciliation which can never be really effective?'

"Nothing more was said at the time, but when there was a marriage shortly after in one of the principal Sunni families—namely that of Áshghur Áli, the Sheáhs reopened the quarrel by forcing themselves into the house while the bridegroom's party were being feasted, and, creating a disturbance there, spoilt a good portion of the sweetmeats and *pilláos*, and finally set fire to the straw chopper of the barn. The fire was easily extinguished, and apparent concord was again restored by the interference of the police.

"'Now what is the good of quarrelling with each other in this wise,' said some of the Sheáh elders to the Sunnis. 'Let us make up our differences by mutual forgiveness, and be friends with each other for the future.'

"'Agreed,' said the Sunnis, 'though we have had more outrage at your hands than we have inflicted on you. But to be friends it is essential that we should forget and forgive.'

"After this everything went on well between the two parties for about two months till the Mohurrum came, when the Sheáhs invited the Sunnis to witness the celebration of the festival. This is not unusual, though it frequently leads to tumults to end with.

"The Mohurrum songs reflect necessarily on the first three Kaliphs—Ábu Bákr, Omár, and Osmán—whom the Sunnis respect; and on the present occasion the Sunni guests took offence at the *Mooláh*, or priest, reciting the praises of Áli, which happened to include a remark derogatory to Ábu Bákr.

"'Did you invite us to insult our feelings in this way?' asked the Sunnis.

"'No insult is meant to you, friends,' said the Sheáhs. 'The song is recited as it stands; and it has been so sung for centuries—ever since the Mohurrum was established as a festival.'

"'We don't care for that. When you invited us you ought to have expunged from the song what you knew would be offensive to our feelings. We did not come here to listen to what is abusive of those we revere.'

"'You are unreasonable, friends. How can we leave out the praises of Áli from the Mohurrum songs?'

"'Will you apologise to us now for what has been done?'

"'Apologise? What for?'

"'O, for nothing then, if you won't see it. We need not stay here further, friends. Let us be off at once before the insults begin to multiply.'

"The Sunnis went away in a huff to collect their adherents, and it is feared that the result will be a fight, though the police are trying hard to prevent it."

Monohur listened to the account with much interest, and was greatly delighted at the prospect of soon realising the sight of either a grand procession or a goodly row.

"You are tired, and had better take a nap now," said the Vysnub, "till it is time to get out into the streets to see the show;" but Monohur was unable to comply, and the Sunyási did so only to the extent of falling into a fit of mental abstraction which was almost akin to sleep.

"Wake up, Bábájee," exclaimed Monohur at last, giving his companion a rather rough shake on the shoulders when the time to go out arrived; and they were escorted by the Vysnub in person, and did enjoy all the sights that were to be seen.

The *tazeáhs* paraded were richly decorated, that is, as well decorated as ever; and they were followed by a large body of Sheáhs beating their breasts and raving in the usual fashion. The trappings of the horses were of gold and rich green, and the orderlies carried golden staves, on the ends of which were *chámurs* and peacock-feathers. The crowd was immense, and the heat of the day gave a colour and elation to the faces of the mourners. But the gathering was not of the Sheáhs and their admirers only; a large portion of the throng was composed of Sunnis, and a murmur soon went through the common people that these latter were becoming restive. The police were quite on the *qui vive*, passing to and fro from one party to the other with kindly warnings to both; but their words fell unheeded, and there was anxiety and suspense on every face in the crowd.

At this moment some one raised the cries of "*Sere layo*" and "*Már dálo*," and the affray was commenced at once with equal violence by both parties.

It was a hot fight, and the blows fell like hammer-strokes; and, before anything could be done to put down the combatants, one Sheáh was killed, and three Sunnis very severely wounded. Further mischief was prevented by the interference of the police; and Monohur was greatly disappointed at the fight being thus abruptly terminated. The impetuosity with which it had been commenced had raised an intense desire in his mind to see it fairly contested, and he even held it unwise to extinguish it so soon.

"Well, Monohur, are you satisfied with the fight and the show you have witnessed?" asked the Sunyási of him when the row was over.

"With the show—yes; but with the fight—not at all. To insure peace for the future the parties should have been left to carry on the contention a good while longer, for nothing cools the blood so effectually, you know, as a good and full depletion, while the sprinkling of a few drops of blood only keeps the wound green and the debt uncancelled."

"Ah, yes; they would have made a glorious war out of the dispute in the Nawáb of Oude's dominions, but the mode of government is different here, and sadly disappointing. Is it not?"

"You are in a rather bantering mood to-day, Bábájee, and more biting and corrosive than ever. I hate the Nawáb's government, and have commenced to prefer that of the English for many reasons. But I always love to see a fight fairly fought out, and I really do think that the fighters become more peaceful after their eagerness has been allowed to exhaust itself than when it is otherwise."

"You say well, my son," said the Sunyási sadly and regretfully, "and it is time for us to take the entire lesson home to our hearts. We have planned and fought, and fought and planned till we have got completely spent. Had we not better slide down now into privacy and peace?"

CHAPTER XLVIII.

AT ECHÁPORE.

THEY proceeded by hurried marches from Pátná towards Bengal, and in a few days reached the village of Echápore on the banks of the Hooghly, a few miles to the north of the military station of Barrackpore; and Monohur's heart beat high as he saw in azure distance the family-house of the Ghosáls of Echápore, surmounted by three mystic towers for which it was long well known.

"Do you see the castle of my maternal ancestors, Bábájee?" said he, pointing towards the building as he spoke. "It is there that I propose to remain for the rest of my life, since I have not the heart to go back to Boná Ghát."

"Not a bad place to live in, certainly," replied the Sunyási. "But whom are you going to stay with there? Don't you know that the members of your mother's family have all long ceased to live?"

"Yes, I know that; but the building has rooms enough all the same to accommodate me, and the priest of Shámsoondur will perhaps be able to recognise me, and will assuredly befriend me till my affairs are settled."

"Well, I don't know but that that would do excellently well as a temporary arrangement; and, in the meantime, I may pass down to Boná Ghát to regulate your affairs there, and make things ready for you."

"And by the time you finish your work there, Bábájee, I hope to be able to receive possession of the estate here in virtue of my mother's right, after which I shall remain as a fixture here for ever."

"No, no; you must not come to any hasty decision on that point yet. Remain here now by all means, for your presence here is perhaps more needed at this moment than at Boná Ghát. There will be time enough hereafter to determine where you should fix your habitation, and what relations you should bear to the ryots of Echápore and Boná Ghát respectively. The best considered resolutions, my son, have often to be revised after the experience of a few weeks."

Monohur gave no reply. He felt that it was not in his power to return to Boná Ghát. "But there is no occasion to discuss that point further at present," said he to himself, "and it would perhaps sound ungracious to do so with those from whom I expect the greatest aid;" and so the question was dropped by him for the time.

The village of Echápore was at one time a place of considerable importance, and is so even to the present day, being frequently resorted to by holiday-makers from Calcuttá, Serampore, and Hooghly. Apart from the usual cottages to be seen in all places in the Mofussil, it contains a fair sprinkling of *puccá* houses, and fifty years ago the turreted castle of the Zemindárs had a very dignified appearance, particularly the river-face of it, which rose almost from the water's edge, where the ground had been strengthened by piles driven into the bank. The Ghosál family, whose might it represented, was a very well-known one in its day, and at one time very powerful also; but it was much reduced afterwards by the litigious and spendthrift habits of a succession of Zemindárs, and when Monohur's grandfather inherited the estate it was encumbered with a heavy debt.

"We must not mind that; indeed we must not," said the brave man, communing with himself. "If we are only true to ourselves we shall surely be able to make everything square and easy within a few years. I will begin the task at once, and it shall go hard with me if I do not succeed;" and he did succeed by thrift and care, not only to disencumber his patrimonial acres from all their liabilities, but also to raise his cash-balance to a decent and respectable figure, which excited the envy of many a neighbouring squire. What grieved him now was that he had no direct male heir to inherit the estate. His only daughter was married to the Zemindár of Boná Ghát, and was well provided for; but she could not inherit the family-lands so long as there was an heir-male in the way, and this heir-male, his nephew, was such a good-for-nothing spendthrift that it broke the old man's heart to think that what he had redeemed with so much pains must ultimately pass into the hands of such a scapegrace.

"It should not hurt me," would he frequently murmur to himself, "for it really signifies little what becomes of the estate in other hands when I am gone." But he was hurt, very deeply hurt by the thought, for all that; and it was of this grief that he eventually died, being succeeded by the nephew who had been the torment of his life. The debaucheries of the young man were, however, too much for his constitution to bear; he did not live long enough to enjoy, far less to waste, the accumulations his uncle had made; and, while the ryots did not miss their new Zemindár when he died, the estate did not miss much of the savings which had been added to it by his predecessor. Monohur's mother was yet living at this time; but her latter days were so embittered by the disappearance of her son and his erratic life that she never took thought of the Echápore property at all, having hardly the wish to look after Boná Ghát: and it was under these circumstances that the family-*Poorohit*, the priest of Shámsoondur, came to hold the lands in the name of the family-idol committed to his care. The man was of singular habits, perseverance, and discernment, and so simple-hearted and contented withal that he scarcely knew that he had any right to be discontented with anything whatever about him. The estate prospered exceedingly under his care; he watched over it as if it had been his own, but never spent a pice out of it except for its improvement; and it was to him that Monohur went after parting company with the Sunyási, who proceeded eastward to Boná Ghát, which was some forty or forty-five miles further in the interior.

The path that lay between Monohur and the temple of Shámsoondur was well known to him, and he trod boldly over it, though with a sore and heavy heart.

"I have much to do here, and must not break down;" and he did not break down, at least on the way.

It took him quite half-an-hour to reach the temple, which stood on the river-bank, but considerably to the north of the Zemindár's house. It was an old building, perhaps more than a century old, built partly of stone, and having a most queer and inscrutable appearance; but there was plenty of room in it to turn round, and the site it stood upon was a spacious undulating meadow, extremely rustic and secluded, and perfumed by a great variety of flowers.

"You look quite joyless and worn-out, young man," said the priest of Shámsoondur, addressing the stranger who stood before him. "Can I do anything for you? What may be your business here?"

"Do for me, sir? Yes, you can do a great deal for me if you can give me all the information I want. I am told that you know everything about the old Ghosál family of this place, and I have been sent to you to ascertain some particulars in regard to it."

"By whom, and what for?"

"By the priest of Nággesur Mahádeva of Boná Ghát, who thinks you may be able to help Monohur Rái, the young Zemindár of Boná Ghát, in getting possession of his maternal estate."

"Of course I can. Has anything been heard of Monohur?"

"I think so, but am not certain. Did you know the young man personally?"

"Did I know Monohur Rái, the child of my own master's daughter? What a question that to ask of me! Why I have rocked the boy on these knees a hundred thousand times when he could hardly lisp, and I did the same to the mother when she was no bigger than her child."

"You have not heard of Monohur lately, father?"

"No."

"Are there any other claimants to the estate beside him?"

"None."

"The widow of the last Zemindár? Is she not living at Mathoorá or Prayága?"

"She was at Mathoorá for a few years, but has died some seven months ago. She was a very pious woman, who cared nothing for the vanities of life—neither for riches, rank, nor power—and never drew anything from the estate beyond what was absolutely necessary for her subsistence. It was at her earnest desire that I took charge of the estate on behalf of Shámsoondur till the heir to the property was forthcoming."

"Have you any hopes that he will ever turn up?"

"I had none till this moment," said the old man, looking steadfastly at his interrogator, while a single tear-drop was seen to glisten in each eye; "but you surely must have seen him, or know his present whereabouts, or why otherwise should you have been drawing out so much information about him from me?"

"Do you know this token, father?" asked Monohur, showing the priest a green ribbon waistband, curiously embroidered all over with little alternate beads of silver and gold.

The old man held out his hand to receive it, and a flood of recollections came back upon him the moment he had touched it, and he trembled all over with emotion.

"It is the last present I worked up for the boy on the occasion of his *Karnabedha*,"[1] exclaimed he at last in a hoarse broken voice. "Tell me quickly, tell me at once, how you have got possession of the token, where the owner of it now is, and whether he has sent you to me?"

Monohur was too sensitive himself not to appreciate the feelings of the priest, and he hastened at once to relieve him.

"Excuse me, father, for having practised this little deception on you," cried he, throwing himself at his feet.

---

[1] Boring of the ear—a religious observance.

"Your eye is dazed by the glare of the western sky. Look at him again as kindly as in the days of old; it is your own Monohur that has come back to you at last!"

The old man looked steadfastly at the speaker, and recognised him, and his joy was so great that he fainted and fell down on the temple-floor. The exertions of Monohur recalled him to his senses, after which he remained in dreamy silence for some time, looking again and again at the young man's face, till he exclaimed at the end with a sigh—

"Monohur is come back at last, but where is the little mother whom I had also dandled on my knees?"

"Where indeed!" exclaimed Monohur. "It is I that have killed her!" And he stopped abruptly with a hysteric sob, while the priest turned towards him a face glowing with affection and sympathy.

"Hush! Don't speak again as you have spoken, for it is sinful to do so. I feel a deep pity for you, my son, for you have lost such a mother as is not easily found. But it is too bad to regret even for the very best of parents so despairingly. When God smites He smites hard; but we must submit to the stroke with pious resignation. If you accept with submissiveness the lot that Shámsoondur has assigned to you it will surely be made easy for you to bear."

"O, father, I am tired, very tired, just as I used to be in the days of old, when I could hie to my mother's lap for rest, and never fell asleep except in her arms; and how can I help feeling her absence now?"

"Lie down on the temple-floor then as on your mother's lap, my son, and find rest in the arms of Shámsoondur himself, for he will be even as a father and a mother to you! What is past is past; what has happened cannot be recalled. Live now for the future, and may the gods grant a blessed future to you to make amends for the past!"

Monohur stretched himself out on the temple-floor as the priest directed him, and a deep sleep fell on him after a few more piteous cries of—"Mother! O, my mother!"

CHAPTER XLIX.

THE AGGRIEVED VYSNUBI.

It was on the outskirts of the village of Poorá that a woman was sitting alone in the evening at the foot of a mango-tree. Her face was youthful and interesting, but sodden with care, her age was not more than five-and-twenty years, and she wore the dress of a widow.

"He vowed eternal constancy to me," said she to herself. "It is less than two years now that he did so, and I am already forgotten and neglected. But I will watch his movements night and day till I find out who this new beauty is that has supplanted me in his affections, and when I have both of them in my toils I shall know how to avenge myself."

Thus spake Koosum, a female of the Kybarta caste, who since the death of her husband had become a Vysnubi, and had been living under the protection of one Nakool Ádock, a young man of about thirty years, who had also accepted the Vysnub faith, though he was much better known as a reckless libertine. Koosum was greatly attached to him, and Nakool had promised to devote his life to her; but it was not in his nature to be constant, and the girl had not the art to retain his love. If she had no art in her, however, she had a large share of determination and boldness, and it was evident from her very appearance that her love for Nakool was fast giving place, for the time at least, to an anxious desire to get avenged.

"Who art thou, daughter, sitting here alone by yourself, and what are you musing upon?" asked a Sunyási who had approached her unawares.

"O, father, I am a friendless, unfortunate woman, who was enticed away into error and victimised, for which I am now repenting leisurely."

"If your repentance be sincere it is all the amends humanity can offer for its shortcomings. But you were complaining even now of the fickleness of your lover, and were planning vengeance on him and his new mistress, if I understood your murmurings aright. That is not a fit mood for repentance."

"I am not in a mind, father, to listen to your homily now, and you should not have overheard my self-repinings. Pass on your way, Mohásoy. We have no concern with each other that I know of."

"Ah, the afflicted should not be so impatient. I want your service, daughter, and may be of use to you also in return."

"What service can you seek of me? I cannot even conceive how I can be of any use to you."

"Do you know the Gossáin of your village—Nundarám Thákoor?"

"I do; he is the master of the Vysnub I was speaking of to myself. If you know the Gossáin intimately you can indeed, sir, be of help to me with Nakool."

"I be of help to you with your lover? Why, girl, you mistake my character when you expect me to act in that way for you. Go, however, to the Gossáin, and tell him that the Sunyási and his *Cheláh* have returned from their pilgrimage, and that if he will proceed at once to the shrine of Nággesur Mahádeva at Boná Ghát he will meet with the former there, and be able to complete the calculations that were left unreconciled when we parted."

"Your message is a mysterious one, father, and sounds very like a riddle to me. Why should I carry it? What is to be my advantage if I do?"

"The Gossáin shall know how Nakool has deceived you, and will no doubt punish him as he deserves."

"Ah, then you need not say a word about the matter, either to him or to anyone else. There is no call for your interference in our affairs, and I entertain no personal feelings against Nakool certainly. A Vysnub takes or discards his Vysnubi as he pleases, and Nakool has only acted as many others do daily. What I want is to discover the new Vysnubi he has taken, and you can only help me by asking the Gossáin, when you see him, to send Nakool on some errand which would take him out of the village for a time."

"Ah, that I shall do surely, and shall probably employ Nakool myself, if he be a bold man and true."

"He is both; yes, both bold and true—true in all matters except love. But I waste time, father. I shall go immediately to the Gossáin and communicate your message to him;" and off the girl went to the Gossáin's house in a state of mind which we shall not attempt to describe.

"This Vysnub and Vysnubi system of living together as man and wife without accepting the responsibilities of the alliance, is a great religious scandal," muttered the Sunyási to himself, "and I must really speak sharply about it to the Gossáin. It would be much better if the parties thus connected were married outright notwithstanding any differences existing between them in caste and position, and brought up children like other folks."

He had no time, however, to spend on such thoughts. His message to the Gossáin sent, he hurried forward on his way to Boná Ghát, which he reached rather late in the night. In the meantime Koosum had hastened to the Gossáin's house, and, after being mischievously kept at the door for some time by Nakool, had begun to strike at it lustily, which led to its being opened to her in haste.

"What do you mean by knocking so hard at our door in this fashion, Koosum?" said Nakool to her in a rather sharp tone. "What is your business here?"

"Nothing with you now. My business is with the master of the house."

"With the master of the house! Think you he will speak with such a baggage as you are, and at this hour?"

"He must. I have an urgent and important message for him."

"Indeed! Tell me what it is then, and I shall carry it to him directly."

"No, my message has to be personally delivered. It does not pass through go-betweens."

"Then I will close the door upon you again. You don't see the master to-night, surely."

But the master had heard the irritative altercation between the once ardent lovers from his own apartment, and, hurrying out, was at the door in a trice, which compelled Nakool to slink off from the spot.

"Well, girl, what is your business with me that you are so importunate and clamorous for an interview?"

"Ah, sir, I met with a Sunyási just half-an-hour ago, and he told me to tell you that the Sunyási and his *Cheláh* have come back from their pilgrimage, and that you could meet the former at Boná Ghát, at the temple of Nággesur Mahádeva, if you repaired thither to-night, to complete some calculations which were left unreconciled before."

"Returned! Both of them! Nakool, I must go to Bouá Ghát at once, and you must accompany me."

"This night, sir?"

"Immediately; this moment, man. Don't you understand me?"

"And must I go with you too? Who will keep watch and ward over the house here in our absence?"

"You need not trouble yourself about that in the least. There are other servants in the house quite as able-bodied and vigilant as you are, and I shall give the necessary directions to them myself. You get ready at once for the start, for I am prepared for it already."

Nakool pouted as a spoilt servant; but his master was unusually resolute, and they started for Boná Ghát within half-an-hour.

"Shall I not now find out the *inamoratá* who will be looking out for Nakool throughout the night? I don't feel sleepy in the least yet, and it won't tire me at all to go about from house to house till I discover this additional saint of our holy calendar."

If anyone had stood by Koosum at this moment he would have heard her quickened breathing and the fierce beating of her wicked heart. She had toiled and schemed, and the scheme had unexpectedly ripened for being carried into effect; and she felt so eager for the completion of her triumph that she could brook no further delay. She burst forth into the street with a half-suppressed scream; and her feet once set agoing moved on and on with untiring assiduity. Her research was at last crowned with the fullest success. The house-door of Románáth

Koloo remained open the whole of that unending night, and, as the watchful spy passed and repassed it, she was careful to observe that the widow-daughter of the oilman was in fidgets, and always on the look-out, as if anxiously expecting somebody to come in.

CHAPTER L.

THE NIGHT CONFERENCE, AND RECONCILIATION OF ACCOUNTS.

They sat up the whole of that night in the temple of Nággesur Mahádeva—namely, the priest, the Sunyási, and the Gossáin, and talked of many things, but especially of Monohur and his affairs. The night was cloudy and starless, and the east-wind had a biting breath; but they sat up all the same, reviewing in detail the subjects that were discussed.

"It makes me feel twenty years younger to see you here again, Bissonáth," said the priest, opening the conference, "and to know that you have brought back with you the scion of an ancient house, whose return has been so anxiously, I may almost say, so hopelessly awaited for by his friends."

"Ah, yes, we have turned up once more, my brother, after having wandered almost from one end of Bengal to the other, with various divergences in different directions; and I have much to report to you about the journey. But your countenance tells me that you would prefer to give us an account of your ministry before listening to the stories of our travels and escapings."

"Nággesur Mahádeva be praised that you have returned, and especially that Monohur has come back. I shall take it for granted that you have gone through great privations and hardships, and perhaps perils also;

and I shall always hear the stories you have to relate with interest and sympathy. But you are right in yielding precedence to business, and I had better explain to you at once, as briefly as I can, how the Zemindár's affairs now stand."

Do not speak to us of such dreadful things, exclaims the impatient reader; and we won't, for there is no occasion for us to do so. The account given was, of course, very important; but the gist of it was in a bundle of papers which the priest threw down before the Sunyási, who, after having turned them hurriedly over, put them into his wallet.

"They are the records of what I have done," said the priest, "and have to be carefully studied."

"And so they will be," replied the Sunyási, "when we have light and time to do so. Now let us have the main features of your service in words, Dada Mohásoy."

The priest explained thereupon the state of affairs verbally, and the account given was extremely satisfactory, both as regards the condition of the zemindáry and the feelings of the people towards its owner; and the Sunyási was glad to learn that the latter had never wavered from their attachment to their master, notwithstanding the prolonged absence of Monohur and the varying character of the reports they had received of him.

"O, brother, I am so happy, so very happy to hear of the steadfast affection of the ryots for him that I have hardly anything now to pray for even from Nággesur Mahádeva himself."

"Ah, yes, they are all almost passionately fond of him, and it was the intensity of this feeling only that buoyed me up in conducting the affairs of the estate, which gave me a good deal of trouble at the outset, but were afterwards made easy by the active co-operation I received from everyone. Bring him here, and they will welcome him with delirious ecstasy."

The Sunyási shook his head doubtingly.

"I fear, brother, that he will be in no haste to come here, for the remembrance of his mother is a sore grief to him, and the house of his fathers he believes to be haunted by the phantoms of the dead. You know, of course, that he visited it once in concealment, but was obliged to depart as quickly as he came?"

"Yes; and he came here too, but so suddenly that I was almost staggered by the sight of him. That, however, was years ago. He has had plenty of time since then to brace up his mind."

"Yet on the subject of his mother's death he is as sensitive still as ever; and even the possession of ease and security, and all the benefits which go hand in hand with the occupation of one's own paternal estate will not, I think, reconcile him to a residence at Boná Ghát very quickly."

"I am not surprised to hear that," said the Gossáin; "but he must come here notwithstanding, for the attachment of his ryots is not a thing which a good Zemindár can afford to forfeit."

"We must take care that he does not forfeit it," replied the Sunyási. "The people, after having missed him and searched for him so long, should be well pleased to hear that he has turned up at last, and is now in their neighbourhood; and, when a decent interval has elapsed, it may not be impossible perhaps to persuade him to spend at least half of every year at this place."

"And his prospects at Echápore, are they quite as hopeful as his prospects here?" asked the priest.

"He seems to think so himself, and, as the priest of Shámsoondur is a faithful man and true, I have no doubt that everything will go on smoothly with him there."

The priest of Nággesur Mahádeva drew a breath of relief, and his face was even flushed with a bright and happy look.

"I am glad, very glad, to receive this report, Bissonáth," said he; "for with the savings of the two estates Monohur ought to be able to set himself up at once with dignity and ease. His maternal estate is particularly productive, and the accumulations there should be very considerable."

"The paternal assets, however, always take precedence of the maternal in accounts," observed the Sunyási, with a smile. "With how much hard cash will you be able to assist him to start with?"

"The savings immediately available to him here amount to about five lakhs of rupees, and there will be some forty thousand more in his hands within four or five months after."

"And this after Government revenue fully paid?"

"Yes; the Government revenue has, of course, always been very punctually paid to prevent the estate from getting into even greater difficulties than were created by the absence of the Zemindár. It was in this that I was most cordially assisted by the ryots."

"You have done everything then, brother, that could have been done, either for Monohur or the estate; and have, in fact, left nothing for us to do."

"Thou art in error there, Bissonáth," said the priest with laughing eyes. "One important thing remains yet to be done, and that is to give Monohur a wife."

"Yes, brother, yes; and I requested the Gossáin

Mohásoy to come over hither that we might discuss the subject of marrying Mádhavi with Monohur, for he loves her to distraction still."

The reader will understand at once that Mádhavi was the daughter of the Gossáin, and the niece of both the Sunyási and the priest of Nággesur Mahádeva, whom Monohur had seen and prized in the Ferázee camp at Nárkelberiáh when she was no more than ten or eleven years old. The girl was the pride and joy of the family—handsome, noble-hearted, and worthy of the love they bestowed on her; but her life up to this moment had been rather unpleasant, if not unhappy.

"O Mádhavi, it is time to give thee a fitting husband and see thee settled in life," would her parents often say to her. "Why wilt thou further resist our wishes on this point? Monohur is fickle and inconstant, and will never return."

But the pleadings of her parents made not the least impression on her. Poor Mádhavi had treasured her first childish love within the deep recesses of her heart, and would not give it up for all that they could urge against it.

"I have sworn to be faithful to him for ever, mother. How, then, can I be faithless to him by agreeing to any other match?"

"But had he loved you, Mádhavi, as ardently as you love him, would he have stayed away so long from you? He has broken the troth already, and it is madness for you to regard it as still binding on yourself."

"He has not broken his troth, mother; he is incapable of doing so. We know not where he is now, or how he is detained. But surely, he will come back at last to claim the fulfilment of our vows."

And her eyes would fill with tears even when she thus forcibly buoyed up her heart with hopes which she dared not believe in herself.

All the endeavours made to get her married were thus strenuously resisted by her. She would not allow herself to be talked over, and necessarily grew up a *Thoobri*, or big unmarried girl, in her father's house. This is not unusual in Bráhman, as in other Hindu families. The caste rules for the Bráhmans are so strict that many girls get no fit husbands till almost towards the decline of their life. This was not Mádhavi's case; the offers of marriage to her were many. But she voluntarily chose the unmarried state for herself, and there seemed no likelihood of its being changed till now.

"But are you sure, brother, that Monohur still desires to have her?" asked the Gossáin again of the Sunyási, almost trembling from very joy.

"Would I have dared to speak to you on the subject otherwise? I have watched him at all times, and under all temptations, and he has always appeared to me to be perfectly indifferent to every other woman, while the slightest allusion to Mádhavi invariably brings either a flush of eagerness on his face or tears into his eyes."

This clenched the matter, and virtually settled the account which had been left unadjusted when the Sunyási and Monohur were obliged to run away from their homes. Monohur was an excellent match personally, and an alliance with the Sándyals was in all other respects also a very desirable one for the Gossáins; and if the Gossáin had sought for other matches intermediately it was only under the conviction that Monohur would not, or could not, return.

"I am not sorry now," said he laughingly, "that

Mádhavi proves to be wiser than her parents. She deserves to be happily married, if only for having refused the other matches which we attempted to force on her."

"Yes, she must have felt much troubled by your worryings, brother," said the Sunyási; "but all's well that ends well, and you had better make your arrangements now for the bridal as fast as you can."

"Have you any further directions for me, Bissonáth?" asked the priest. "I hope not, for I have got sick of stooping over *nuthees* and figures, and am very anxious to sink the man of business again in the priest."

"But you have managed the zemindáry so well in our absence—so very much better, in fact, than any professional manager could have done it—that I greatly fear that Monohur may still wish to have you for his Surburákár. What shall I say to him if he proposes it?"

"Say that it is impossible that I should undertake such duties for good even for his sake. During the Zemindár's absence from home I did all that I felt bound to do for him by my obligations to the house. But he has returned, and I must be permitted to revert wholly to my spiritual duties now, for Nággesur Mahádeva will not allow me to have two masters for ever."

"Then the whole responsibility devolves on me, and I breaking down so fast, and so illiterate withal!"

"Why should you fear that, Bissonáth? Is not Monohur young and intelligent?"

"Yes, Monohur is very intelligent, and gives good promise for the future; but he has no idea of zemindáry work at present, and will require much training yet to be able to do justice to it."

"Ah, in that I shall take my part cheerfully with you.

But the best course of tuition, you know, is to throw all the onus on the principal. Let him learn everything by practical experience, and then he is sure to do credit to himself and his ancestry, and be of benefit to his country."

CHAPTER LI.

A CHANGE OF MASTERS.

THERE was an uproar in the little village of Poorá, created by Koosum's proclaiming with stentorian lungs the connection that existed between the daughter of Románáth Koloo and Nakool, which the accused girl had not the hardihood to deny. Old Románáth was of course greatly incensed at it, and gave full swing to his wrath by abusing his daughter immoderately; but he was not of a savage disposition naturally, and gradually became less violent as he perceived the inutility of his ravings.

"Bidhoo, you know not what you would have had to endure if you had a less kinder parent than me to deal with. Your conduct has been grossly wicked. A crime so disgraceful I should never have suspected in one so seemingly pure as you are, and no other father would have pardoned his daughter for it easily. But I am willing to forgive you if you will promise never more to communicate in any way with Nakool."

At first no answer came from the girl, who lay on the clay floor of her apartment, and placing her hands before her eyes, was indulging in a paroxysm of tears.

"I had the most implicit faith in your conduct," continued the Koloo, "and the very fact of your having been able to deceive me shows what a father I have been to you. I gave you credit also for greater sense than you have shown. But I will not allow you to deceive me, or to be befooled yourself again, and I insist on your abandoning your lover for good, and will be obeyed."

"You shall be obeyed, father," murmured the girl through her tears, rolling towards his feet. The day was unusually hot, but the external heat was as nothing to the fever that was raging in her heart. Her pulses were beating rapidly, and a life-time of repentance was in each beat.

"Give me a direct answer, Bidhoo, that you will never again communicate with Nakool in any way whatever, nor have any evil-dealings with anyone else."

"Never again, not with anyone," was the sobful reply.

"Then go, my child, to your usual work. I forgive you as freely as I hope to be forgiven, though the bad name which Koosum is circulating of us may well force one to go mad."

Peace was thus re-established in the Koloo's house, or rather the unpleasantness that had arisen in it was allowed to die out. But it was a long time before Bidhoo could resume her accustomed avocations with ease; nor, it must be confessed, was Románáth sooner able to regard her with his usual tenderness.

Still less was the Koloo able to forgive or forget the crime of Nakool against him.

"I never had occasion to feel ashamed of my life before till this injury was done to me, and must I sit down tamely under it because I am spiritless and old?"

It was very hard indeed to do so, but his heart failed him when he considered how unequally matched he would be in a personal quarrel with a dare-devil fellow like Nakool if he attempted to punish him, and he could only think of appealing against him to those who had him in their power.

"I shall go over to Echápore," said he, "to the priest of Shámsoondur, who is the landlord of Nakool, and can assist me against him if he will, and it certainly does befit his calling to help me in such an affair as this."

He was disappointed, however, to find that the priest either would not, or could not, espouse his cause as heartily as he wished. He was received by him, indeed, with great kindness and urbanity; but the grievance he complained of was viewed by the priest only as a personal affair, which he was unable to back up at once owing to his being then very busy with more important concerns.

"I fully sympathise with you, Románáth," said he, "but have really no time now to help you. Besides that, Nakool is neither at Echápore nor at Poorá at this moment, but with his master Nundarám at Boná Ghát, and nothing can be done till they return."

"He has done me a great injury, sir," urged Románáth, "though Heaven knows I had always thought kindly of him. If I wish to see him punished now, I do so more in the interests of our village, than from any personal feelings merely."

"I understand that fully," said the priest, "and I do think that it would be very proper to punish him. But there is a time for everything, and my hands are too full of other business at present for me to attend to yours immediately."

Románáth could not press the matter further after this reply, and, deriving little consolation from it, sped back to his village dissatisfied and aggrieved. The case, however, was, at about the same time, taken up and more thoroughly gone into elsewhere, though the final result there even was not altogether disadvantageous to the delinquent.

The Sunyási having spoken of Koosum's revelations to the Gossáin, the latter, who kept a strict discipline over his household, peremptorily demanded an explanation of the matter from his servant, upon which Nakool, taken unawares, endeavoured at first to brazen it out.

"It is true, indeed, Mohásoy," said he, "that there has been some flirtations between the girl and me, but really nothing more, I assure you. I was obliged to visit her father's place frequently in your own service, and the hussy, being fond of gossiping, always made it a point to detain me, which necessarily led to a little flutter or flapping of wings on both sides, if I may so describe our entanglement, but never to anything beyond that certainly."

"You had better drop your metaphors, Nakool," said the Gossáin sternly, "when you are speaking to me. You do not escape this time with your impudence as easily as you have done on other occasions. The woman's disclosures have given the lie direct to your account already, and I have greater confidence in her words than in yours."

"Well, sir," replied the servant, with increasing audacity, "if the woman has confessed her guilt, I suppose I may admit as frankly that I was indeed duped by her. But I have not been the less a good servant to you for all that."

"I do not deny that you have, on the whole, been a good servant to me, Nakool. You suited me so well, in fact, that I cannot help regretting that I am obliged to dispense with your services now. The offence you have committed is not so venial as you seem to think. It is too rank, at any rate, for me to tolerate; and I cannot permit you to disgrace my livery after having been found guilty of it."

"But I have a request to beg of you, brother," put in the Sunyási at this stage, not wishing that Nakool should be thrown out of employment altogether on a complaint preferred by himself. "I want the man on the Zemindár's affairs—that is, if you will not give him another trial at your place. He has acted against our True Church surely, but only as several others do; and we need not lop him off altogether for that if we can induce him to recant and be a true Vysnub for the rest of his life."

"Well, brother, you may make what you can of him. I sincerely wish that he may recant and reform, but such as he is at present I have no place for him at home. He is a good serving-man I admit, and, if you take him into the Zemindár's service, he will, I doubt not, work faithfully for him in all respects; though whether he will cast off his wickedness, or walk in it with bolder and firmer footsteps, may well be questioned."

"O, I shall keep a sharp eye on him, brother," said the Sunyási, "and if he does not mend I shall know how to deal with him."

And so Nakool changed masters with a threat, but less to his disadvantage than he could have hoped for.

CHAPTER LII.

ESTABLISHED AT ECHÁPORE.

The servants of the Echápore household and the ryots on the estate gave themselves up to uncontrolled rejoicings when they knew that the handsome gentleman whom the priest of Shámsoondur had brought in amongst them was no other than the young truant of Boná Ghát, the true and legitimate heir of the Echápore estate. Their gratification would perhaps not have been quite so great if he had been uncouth in either face or figure; but there is always an unaccountable prejudice in favour of manly beauty and an intelligent appearance, and their possessor in the present instance had the further advantage of having returned with renovated health, life, and energy. This drew forth the villagers of all classes around him almost from the first day that he was introduced to them, and their attachment became stronger and deeper the more they remained with him, so that in a few days he came to be completely hemmed in by them at all times, every movement of his limbs being watched as if to anticipate his wishes.

"What strange things come to pass!" exclaimed the men. "Who would have thought that the wild madcap of Boná Ghát would have turned out such an excellent bargain for us within a few years!"

"See with what grace and dignity he assumes the

state he was born to," observed the women, particularly captivated by his frank and open countenance and engaging manners. "Since he has come hither we must not allow such a sousy face as that to depart from us."

"Surely not," responded a stout farmer, who stood next to him in the crowd, "at least, not till he has taken a wife from amongst us, as his father did before him. A little love-making would do him a world of good now, and you women should set him to it."

"O, that his good mother had lived to see this day!" exclaimed a village wife, who was as closely stationed as the other speaker; and the words rang in Monohur's ears as if the whole air were laden with their burden, bringing tears into his eyes as he lifted them upwards in search of the parent who had become so dear to him.

This at once drew on him the earnest sympathy of every person present.

"Ah, never mind it a jot," said the men, as tenderly as their rough natures would allow. "Such losses come even to the best, and should not be so distressfully regretted for."

"Don't think that you stand alone in the world because your parents are not living," cried the women. "There is not a house in Echápore in which you will not find a mother or a sister to love you."

The welcome thus given to him was unto Monohur as the murmur of a running brook in the ears of a wanderer in the desert. He was refreshed and comforted by it, and within a short time felt as much at home in the place as he possibly could have been at Boná Ghat. The memory of his mother was of course coming over him at all times, recalled almost by every slight thing that was said or done. But it ceased now to disquiet him, nay, gave him satisfaction instead of pain, and he already felt as if the shade he had seen at Boná Ghát was always hovering about him, brightening the welcome offered to him from all sides.

"O mother! dear mother! be always with me, and I will not be unworthy of your love," cried he from his heart of hearts. "If I deserted you in life I shall never give up your memory, which shall both brace me up to exertions and support me under tribulations."

"Let it be as thou hast said!" murmured a voice to him in reply, though he saw nothing before him but an autumn cloud passing over the meadows, fringed in its outline by the dying brightness of the evening sun.

The undying love which filled his heart displayed its magic virtues quickly by giving a charming development to the man, for it made him modest and unpretending, and at the same time discerning, critical, and keen-sighted; and the oldest servitors of the zemindáry were quite surprised to find how well the giddy-pated youth, who had been wandering up and down, hither and thither, all over the country so long, understood that work which had cost them the application of a life-time to master, and was able even to direct them when they were either nonplussed or at a fix.

"You had better assume personal charge of the zemindáry now, Monohur," suggested the priest of Shámsoondur to him, and he did not shrink from accepting the responsibility, though still seeking the support of those around him.

"Indeed, sir, I have no wish in the matter apart from yours and that of my ryots. I should not have ventured to propose such a step myself so early; but, if you consider it necessary that I should take it, I shall do so at once, not doubting that you will all continue to help me as heretofore."

"We shall of course do that," was the common reply of everyone around him, and, while a few of the small-brained and evil-hearted felt aggrieved in getting a master over them at last, the higher and better-disposed servants crowded around him, manifesting the greatest eagerness to serve, direct, and obey.

The Zemindár showed great intelligence, quite as much intelligence as the old dependents of the family had expected of him. He showed great perseverance also, which is always a rarer qualification among those born in the higher grades of life. The daily round of a common task is often to many of these the hardest to perform; but Monohur, once set a-going, would go over every detail of the business in his hand with untiring precision, and this was hailed as a very favourable indication of the man by all.

"That is a formidable *nuthee* that you are bringing up, Peshkár. What is it about?"

"A dispute between Tárá Moni Dabya on one side and Chunder Kánto Surmá on the other, for the possession of a *Hát* at Sumboogunj, which is claimed by both; and neither of the parties has, on the pretext of the quarrel, paid the rent due to the zemindáry for the *Hát*."

Monohur received cheerfully the bundle that was handed to him, and was soon absorbed in reading through it, while the Peshkár exhibited his zeal by giving his own version of the case, and suggesting how it might be decided.

"Tárá Moni has the reputation of being a very quarrelsome woman, and it does seem that the Surmá, though perhaps of no better character than his opponent generally, has the right side in the present quarrel between them, for—"

Here he stopped abruptly, for he saw the sharp eyes of the Zemindár fixed on a document which he was examining with particular scrutiny, and that he was not attending at all to the hints that were being thrown out for his guidance.

"I side with the lady," exclaimed Monohur, "for I see that the Surmá has, among other papers, submitted an ante-dated document in support of his claim, the stamp sale-date borne by it being later than the date affixed to the writing. His claim must be false since he has stooped to this deceit. I would back the lady with the ryots, and realise pending dues from her."

Insignificant as the order was, it made a great impression on the people, who had been awaiting for the Zemindár's fiat with breathless attention.

"He has eyes of his own to see with, and judgment apart from that of his officers. This is a new rule, and a change very much for the better for us," whispered the ryots to each other.

A yet bigger bundle was the next to come up, and this also was handed to the Zemindár.

"What may this be about again?"

"A contest for the possession of the Kátimghurrá lands between two applicants, named Moorali and Básdeb, the former of whom claims it under a Mokruree title granted to him by the latter, while the latter has filed a *fowteenámáh* which gives a later date to his father's death than that borne by the Mokruree grant, and necessarily vitiates the grant, since, if he was not the owner of the property at the time it was made, he could have had no right to give away the title claimed."

There was not much information to be extracted from the papers submitted, though they were examined with the Zemindár's usual care; but he understood their drift well enough to come to a correct conclusion notwithstanding this disadvantage.

"There is a bad smell about this matter," said he, "for I suspect that the knave Básdeb has been purposely falsifying the date of his father's death to deceive the party who had dealt with him in good faith. But here the Zemindár need not interfere. Refer both parties to the Civil Court. We can defer realising the rents due to us till after a court of justice has decided between them."

Many other cases were similarly gone through day by day, and always determined with equal promptness and intelligence, which made the Zemindár a great favourite with the villagers. But what added yet more to his good name with them was that, on the cutchery labours being terminated, he made it a point to fly out into the open air to wipe off the tedium of work with rural amusements.

"This is not worthy of you," would some too-forward official often whisper in his ear. "It does not look well for the Zemindár to amuse himself with and alongside of his subjects."

"Ah, my good friend, this is the background of the stage on which I have to act through life, and I would get broken-hearted indeed if such little enjoyments were denied to me. I am a Zemindár it is true, but still a member of the great human family to which my ryots belong. Why should I not mix with them then? Were I to stick to the common round of working for an allotted time, and then dawdling about my house ever after, would I eat with relish, or get good sleep at night? No, no; let me play the peasant, as well as the Zemindár, unblamed, if only to relieve the loftiness of a position which would otherwise be too tiresome to endure, and to earn for myself the peasant's hunger and his sleep."

"He is too honest and open-minded," observed the priest of Shámsoondur, "to understand the meaningless distinctions the world makes about what is 'proper' and 'improper,' and that is perhaps the best feature of his character. So long as he preserves his own self-respect, what matters it that he mixes with the humbler classes in their play? He takes a pride in owning fellowship with them, and need one find fault with him on that account when, without sinking him to their level, it gives him the firmest hold on their affections?"

The dictum of the priest was incontrovertible, and was accepted by all, and, while Monohur was relieved by being left uninterfered with, the ryots were greatly delighted.

CHAPTER LIII.

AT BONÁ GHÁT, AND ABOUT AN INDIGO DISPUTE.

WHILE things were getting on at Echápore in the way described in the preceding chapter, the course of true love was running quite as smoothly also at Boná Ghát. The priest of Nággesur Mahádeva had a complete hold on the hearts of the people within his spiritual jurisdiction, and even those over whom his influence did not extend were not behindhand in expressing their gratification on hearing of the return of their long-lost master, whose radiant face, so exquisite in its fresh beauty when last seen by them, had left a deep impression on their hearts. The sensational element in their attachment was, however, apt to run short in the absence of the object round which it was expected to chafe and foam: and this forced the Sunyási back to Echápore, to press upon Monohur the importance of repairing at once to his native village.

"You must come among your ryots, my son, if only to thank them for cherishing their old partiality for you so continuously and long. You cannot hope to retain your hold on their affection if you do not show that you reciprocate it."

"I shall certainly do as you suggest, Bábájee," returned Monohur, "if only to thank your brother personally for the great love and kindness he has evinced for me. But I shall not put up at the old family-house on any account, nor remain in the village longer than may be absolutely necessary, for really it is not in my power to do either."

These conditions were readily agreed to by the Sunyási, and within a short time after the young Zemindár and his Mentor were journeying towards Boná Ghát, not as solitary travellers or pilgrims, as had been their wont so long, but in the style of a landlord, accompanied by a train of attendants and well-wishers.

"I am glad you have come," exclaimed the priest of Nággesur Mahádeva the moment he saw Monohur approaching the temple to prostrate himself before the deity. "The blessings of Eklinga be on you and your house for ever! Your people have asked for nothing but your presence here since they have heard of your return, and this surely is your proper place to live in."

"O, father, next to Nággesur Mahádeva himself, I am beholden to you and your brother for everything that belongs to me here, and it will always be a pleasure to me to remain under your guidance in all respects. But I have already explained to Bábájee why my stay at this place must be exceedingly brief, and, as my sorrow must be as sacred to you as it is to me, I am sure you will not ask me to prolong my presence here further than may be absolutely needed."

"So be it then, my son, for the present," replied the priest; "but the final issue does not rest either with you or me. See how tumultuously the people are coming to welcome you, and remember that you owe a duty to them as to yourself."

There was indeed a mighty bustle round the temple already, and the ryots were seen pouring in crowds from all sides with shouts of joy.

"Ah, there he is at last; he whom we have been so anxiously waiting for, who fled away from us, almost in his boyhood, as if on wings. Is it not a happiness to look at him after such a long, long delay?"

"Let us go up nearer to him and scan him more attentively, for have we not kept ourselves alive to this day only to see him back again amongst us?"

Monohur thanked very kindly all who pressed so eagerly about him; but their name was legion, and their questions and exclamations were too turbulently rapid either to be noted or answered.

"Yes, this is indeed our long-lost heir, though he has reached a man's stature now whom we knew but as a boy, a smooth-chinned boy, when he left us!"

"Whence come you to us so unexpectedly after an absence of so many years?"

"Where have you been? What did you go for? What are the sights you have witnessed?"

"Why did you never send us tidings of yourself while we were in suspense and fear?"

Many similar questions were rapidly launched forth, to which no answers were expected, or could be given; and the people themselves put a stop to Monohur's replies when he attempted any.

"No matter, no matter. It is enough that we have you again with us. We are fully satisfied now, and have no more complaints."

And they seemed to forget all their own concerns, and did almost nothing the whole day but flock around him, to feast their eyes on him and listen to such words as he was able to utter.

This went on for days; but Monohur was not disheartened thereby, and while the men were charmed by his manners and conversation, the women felt astounded by the genius they discovered in him, verily believing that no cleverer young man had ever before been known on the earth. This gave to their warmth and admiration a rather oppressive character, which made the Zemindár wish ardently at times for the hour of retirement that he might slip into his bed. But he always reappeared punctually at daybreak to begin the exhibition afresh, and never completely broke down but once, on finding that an old blear-eyed woman was raving for him and addressing him as her "own poor child."

"Ah, my own poor child," cried she, "are you come back to me at last?"

Monohur was taken unawares by the words, and turned suddenly round, almost expecting that his mother had made herself visible again. But he averted his face as quickly on seeing by whom he had been accosted in such terms, and instantly after burst into tears.

"Mother! O mother!" he cried out with a voice choking with emotion, "what is all this welcome and rejoicing to me where I find you not?" and he beseeched both the Sunyási and the priest of Nággesur Mahádeva to send him back to Echápore and comparative quietness again.

"Ah, my darling!" exclaimed the old woman in confusion, "I did not surely mean to grieve you. We doat on you with the fondest love. Are you not even as a child to all of us?"

"He is," replied the Sunyási, speaking for Monohur; "and he will always try his best to retain that position in your hearts. But do not address him again as 'your own poor son,' good mother, for the name recalls many associations which cannot be remembered without tears."

The crowd at Boná Ghát was getting greater and greater every day, for not only the residents of the village proper, but visitors from many adjoining places were constantly on the move in it to have a sight of the returned Zemindár.

"He is getting tired and breaking down under this now," said the priest of Nággesur Mahádeva at last, addressing the Sunyási, "and may well retire for a time to Echápore, as he proposes."

"Without getting through the Indigo case when he is on the spot?"

"What case do you allude to, Bábájee?" asked Monohur, who had heard his companion's query with a quick ear. "I would remain here of course if there be any business to perform."

As at Echápore so here also, Monohur was keenly alive to his duty, and eager to do justice to it; and he now offered of his own accord to prolong his stay on hearing that an Indigo quarrel within his zemindáry had terminated fatally, and had to be inquired into.

"In a show so busy as ours this was not reported to you till now; but I knew that being here, and having the clue of discovery almost wholly in your hands, you would not wish to depart hence without digging out the case."

"I am bound to do so, Bábájee," was his brief reply; and he went to work with such promptitude and earnestness that he was able in a very short time to have the entire circumstantial history of the murder fully cleared up.

This history was as follows:

The quarrel was between two planters, namely, of the Rájcote and Neemdangá factories respectively, which were situated, one immediately to the north and the other immediately to the south of Boná Ghát. The Rájcote factory belonged to a Mr. Tomlins, the owner of several other factories in the district, and it was managed by a person named Jemmy, *alias* James Archer. The Neemdangá factory was the property of one Mr. Beaton, and was worked under the superintendence of a person named Broom. Between the planter-principals the disputes about the lands cultivated were constant, and the quarrels between their respective managers were nearly as frequent. On the last of these occasions there were high words between Jemmy and Broom, after which they came to blows; but the conflict not being satisfactorily terminated even in that way, Broom went out after nightfall, at between seven and eight o'clock, to the house of Jemmy, taking with him eighty or a hundred *láttiáls*, who broke through the fence of the house and rushed into the compound.

"What is the meaning of all this?" cried out Jemmy in surprise, as he came forward to meet them.

"You shall see it soon enough," said Broom, ordering his people at the same time to seize hold of him.

A mistress of Jemmy, named Goro Ándee, who was living with him on the premises, now came out crying—"*Dohye, Company Báhádoor ke Dohye;*" and Broom being enraged at this struck her with a spear on the forehead, while Jemmy, who had been seized, was carried off in the direction of the Neemdangá factory, a *gámchá*, or bathing-towel, being tied round his mouth to prevent him from screaming. He had twice asked for water before his mouth was tied up, but it was not certain if any cries were afterwards heard from him. It was a moonlight night, and the witnesses saw everything that was done to him. The Neemdangá factory-building was under repairs, but Broom lived in a tent pitched close to it, and thither Jemmy was conveyed, the men who carried him crying out—"Shib Shunkur! Hari, Hari, Bole!"[1] He was thrown down before the tent and the *gámchá* removed from his mouth, and some said that he cried out faintly—"I am dying!" while others said that he did not speak at all, and the breath had then left the body. Several of the factory people then struck the body, some with whips and sticks, others with shoes, and Broom was seen to kick at it several times. Again it was asserted by some that they heard a sound from Jemmy's mouth, while others said that they observed only a slight trembling motion all over the body without hearing any sound. Broom then ordered the *Márká* to be heated, and said that he would brand Jemmy's posteriors with it; but his chuprássis, who had put their hands to Jemmy's face, said—

"There is no use of marking him; he does not breathe."

"If that be the case," said Broom, "drive away all the crowd, and we shall see what is to be done with him."

The people were accordingly driven away, but they could still see from a distance what was done with the body. A hole was dug in the ground, and it was thrown therein, and was afterwards covered up with cow-dung.

All the above-mentioned facts were brought to light by the personal exertions of Monohur, which helped him also to get over the sickness of an overkind reception, at the same time that they drove out from his mind the wish to return quickly to Echápore.

[1] Outcries usually uttered when the dead are carried out for being burnt on the pyre.

"After having taken so much pains to unravel the case, how do you intend to dispose of it, my son?"

"I? O Bábájee, I have neither the power nor the wisdom to deal with an affair of this nature myself. The Zemindár has become wiser now than he was when he decided the school-affray case some ten years ago, and knows that he has only to send intimation of what has occurred to the police, and hand over the witnesses to them; and I shall do both without the least delay."

The case was tried by the proper authorities in due course; but the result of the trial was somewhat surprising. Broom, as a European, was tried by the then existing Chief Court at Calcuttá, and acquitted, while his subordinates, as natives, were tried by the Chief Court for the Mofussil, and were convicted and punished! The people were aghast at the dissimilar character of the two decisions on one and the same case. The uncertainty of the law is nowhere more glaringly illustrated than in India.

CHAPTER LIV.

THE ENGLISH *VERSUS* THE MAHOMEDANS.

"WELL, what do you think of these Englishmen, Monohur? You have latterly been rather partially inclined towards them. Does this Indigo case exhibit them in any favourable light?"

"No, I suppose not, Bábájee. But we must not judge ill of an entire people, you know, from one particular case of this kind, the chief actors in which, moreover, can hardly be regarded as patterns of their race."

"If they do not represent their race fairly they represent well enough all the Indigo-planters and their managers we have in the country. High and low, rich and poor, they appear to be men of the same stamp throughout, all equally mean, cruel, and heartless, regardless of every interest but their own."

"It does not become me to dispute your assertions, Bábájee; but it occurs to me that there have been such events before as those we are commenting upon, alike among the natives and the Europeans, among the Indigo-planters and other people; and it does seem unfair to me to make any general deductions from them while their character is apparently so exceptional."

"Ah, a man who lives long," replied the Sunyási, "sees very many things in a different light from those who have not had equal opportunities with him to observe and discriminate. My knowledge of the English has been a rather diversified one, and, though I have of course seen a great variety of shape, colour, and behaviour among them, I have no reason to think that the character I have given of the planters is not generally applicable to the entire race, laid on with a lighter hand on some, and with a heavier hand on others."

"Ah, brother," remarked the priest of Nággesur Mahádeva, "your loves and antipathies have always been strong, and I think I see a glimpse of their nature here. I, too, have had a varied experience of the world and of the English race; but I do not think so ill of the latter now as I did before, and as you do to this day; though of course I abominate them as a godless people quite as much as you can. Mean, cruel, and heartless they certainly are not; that is, not more so than other races generally."

"I should like very much to hear your general opinion of them, Mohásoy," said Monohur. "To say the truth, I bitterly hated the English to begin with; and I thought that both of you did so as well, since you induced me to join the Nárkelberiáh revolt."

"You need not refer to that or to any other similar affair now, Monohur. We need not remember them at all, since it may not be to our advantage to do so. It is true that I did wish for the subversion of the English power at the time you speak of; but only because I regarded the English as being indifferent to their religion, contemptuous towards the world generally, and spiteful towards their equals. I wanted their self-conceit and presumption to be punished; but I have since got much reconciled to their rule, which seems to me to be in every respect better suited to our present condition than the Mahomedan Government ever was, and to have already bettered that condition to a greater extent than the Mahomedan Government ever attempted to accomplish."

" How so, brother? In what way?"

" Why, in diverse ways, as I shall try to explain to you. During the Mahomedan period no day-labourer ever earned more than thirty to thirty-six rupees in a year, nor lived on anything better than rice, pulses, and pot-herbs, with occasional fish chiefly of his own catching, while by way of clothing he had two or three *dhotis* only annually, and, may be, two *gámchás* also. His wife had perhaps a larger supply of clothing; but she was much worse fed, and her ornaments were made simply of beads, glass, or shell. Now a labourer earns from fifty to sixty rupees a year, is able to afford a daily purchase of fish (or fowl, if he be a Mahomedan); and his clothing has the addition of a *chádur* in the place of the *gámchá*, while he can, in some cases at least, boast of a pair of shoes also. The women, likewise, are better fed than before, more decently clad, and wear brass bracelets and necklets, and silver ear-rings; while the household utensils, which formerly consisted of mud vessels only, now frequently include brass *lotáhs* and *thállas*, and occasionally a few *báttees* besides."

" You have observed well, Dádá Mohásoy, and are not far wrong in the facts you have stated. But is the advance you describe attributable to the exertions of the English Government, or of the labourer himself? The labourer works harder now than before, and the Zemindár has become more civilised and less rapacious; and is it not to these circumstances that the changes you allude to are owing?"

" Yes, most certainly so. But reflect, and it will be

clear to you that the labourer works harder than before only on account of the more settled character of the Government he lives under, and the Zemindár is less exacting than before, merely because the laws are now more equitably administered and enforced. Justice, brother, you must admit, is now better dealt out than it used to be in the past."

"Justice better administered, Dádá Mohásoy? Notwithstanding that Broom passes unpunished?"

"Yes, notwithstanding the occasional vagaries of particular courts, which are not dishonest if they be whimsical and absurd. Education also is now better promoted—"

"What education? An education the only object of which is to sap the foundation of true religion, that the whole country might be Christianised. Has not the Englishman an especial design in furthering it?"

"To be sure he has. He has conquered the country, and his chief aim is to spread his own belief, or disbelief, broadcast over it, to further his own interests. But the result includes an improvement in the condition of the people also. The religion he wants to propagate has made no advance to speak of, for falsehood is falsehood, and will remain so to the end. But the education that has been imparted has given birth to a higher feeling among the mass; and so far the result has been extremely satisfactory."

"Now, Bábájee, what are your arguments on the other side? What have you to say against the recommendations advanced?"

"Simply that they are no recommendations at all. My charges against the English are very heavy, and nothing that my brother has yet stated has shaken my convictions in the least. Throughout the land the Englishman is criminally truant in all his acts, heedless of the lives he destroys. The world is instinct with life, but he carries death with him in every place. He shoots at birds and animals which never dreamt of molesting or annoying him, merely to derive a transient pleasure. He shoots even at men, almost as heedlessly, and the courts which administer justice so equitably, as Dádá Mohásoy maintains, never punish him when the victim is a native, nor even when he is an unbefriended Englishman, as in the case of Jemmy against Broom. 'Live and let live,' says the Vysnub; there is no such doctrine in the Christian's creed."

"Of course not, my brother," replied the priest; "there we do not differ in opinion in the least. The Englishman has no religion, as I have said already; but in that respect the Mahomedan was no better, and the utter disregard of life to which you refer characterised the latter even more than it does the former. Did it not?"

"Then," continued the Sunyási, without heeding either the interruption or the inquiry, "the English Government is constantly interfering with our habits, customs, and usages, notwithstanding our protests and their own denials."

"How so? To what do you refer? The English Government does not force conversion as the Mahomedan Government did."

"It has abolished Suttee, which the Mahomedan Government never dreamt of doing. Are there no widows now, think you, who would prefer to be burnt alive with their deceased husbands if the law allowed them? The spirit of Suttee still survives; but it is smothered down so ruthlessly that it cannot exhibit itself."

"But surely," said Monohur, "that redounds more to the credit than to the discredit of the English name. Think, Bábájee of the pain and cruelty which the Suttee rite involved?"

"Pain? What pain? See you not the Urdhoobáhoos holding up their arms above their heads for years and years, clenching their fists firmly till the finger-nails pass through their hands? Do they fear pain? Did the Suttee fear pain when she dressed herself with garlands, and perfumed herself with *Chandan*, before ascending the pyre?"

"This is taking a very extreme view of the case, surely," said the priest of Nággesur Mahádeva. "I of course approve of the Suttee, and would be glad to see it re-established. But, if it was their sense of humanity only that made the English abolish the rite, how can we blame the motive that suggested the interference?"

"Ah, the motive! Every one vindicates his motives when he is not able to vindicate his acts. Well, even the motives of the English, Dádá Mohásoy, are, I fear, not always as disinterested as you have understood them to be. They affect, for instance, that the conquest of the country was dictated by the most benevolent motives, that they hold us in subjection simply for our own good only. Don't they?"

"But we certainly do derive considerable benefit from the subjection," observed Monohur parenthetically; "I mean as compared with what we derived from our subjection under the Mahomedans."

"Possibly so," said the Sunyási, "but the greater advantages remain still, and wholly, with our conquerors; there is no disinterestedness, no indubitable purity of motives, in the case, as they are so eager to assert. First of all, they derive all the benefits of an unlimited commerce with our country by the conquest. Had India belonged to any other nation it would not have been English products that would have inundated all our markets."

"Ah, but look at the comfort which that brings to us; is that not greater than ever it was under the Mahomedans? What does it matter whether the products in the market are English or Mahomedan?"

"A great deal, surely. What the Mahomedans produced were produced in the country—by denizens of the soil. The English products are imported from some distant island with which this country has no concern. Then again, they enjoy the immense advantage of finding lucrative employments for the mass of their countrymen here, who, but for the Indian field, would have been all but beggars in their native land. Have you any idea, Monohur, of what shoals of Government officials come out to this country, year by year, to suck it dry? What shoals of military officers, lawyers, doctors, clergymen, merchants, and tradesmen also? Could these have earned anything like the princely fortunes they go home with in any other part of the world?"

"These facts, Bábájee, are patent to all," said Monohur, "and I, as a native Zemindár, will never admit that we are better off under the English rule than we could, or might be, under princes of our own race and creed. What I maintain is that the English rule, with all its drawbacks, is still better than what the Mahomedan rule was; and this, as I understand it, is also what the Poorohit

Mohásoy contends for. Have we not ourselves seen this position verified in our travels, Bábájee?"

"No, Monohur; you won't extract a single word from me in favour of the English *Ráj*. What was verified in the course of our travels was this only, that Oude is worse governed than Bengal; that the Nawáb is a greater rascal than the Company Báhádoor. But the Mahomedan Government, as a rule, was not so bad as that of the Nawáb; and I won't concede that the English Government is better than the Mahomedan Government was, though you, as a Zemindár under the English Government, need not accept my views on that point."

CHAPTER LV.

THE HOGS.

THE days were passed pleasantly at Boná Ghát, but the rejoicings came at last to an end on Monohur renewing his wish to return to Echápore. This caused much regret and repining among his ryots; and the women went so far even as to object to his departure clamorously. But the priest of Nággesur Mahádeva and the Sunyási were in accord in supporting the Zemindár's request, and the people were finally obliged to acquiesce in it.

"I owe you a great deal, my friends," said Monohur, addressing the latter, "and knew beforehand how warm your reception of me would be; and it has really been as a holiday to me here. I would have given anything to remain with you for good. But you all know by this time why I cannot do so, and should gladly make allowances for my feelings which are so easily affected. Believe me, I pray you, that, wherever I may be, I shall at all times cherish the most ardent attachment for you, and always endeavour to do as much good to you as I can."

The people applauded him much as he spoke, and felt that the power of objecting to his wishes had been, as it were, extracted out of their hearts. They followed him a long way as he proceeded towards Echápore, but were eventually prevailed upon to fall back and return to their homes, which they did with rueful faces and wet eyes;

and it was not without much persuasion that even the priest of Nággesur Mahádeva was induced to revert to the service of his god, the Sunyási only following the Zemindár as his lifelong friend.

"I feel that I am growing foolish," said the priest of Nággesur Mahádeva to Monohur in a gruff voice, in taking leave of him, "for it ails me to part with you here. But you remain in very safe hands so long as you have my brother with you, and you will always find him to be as sure as a rock to depend upon. Walk ever according to his counsels and you will be both prosperous and happy, for he is a man of strong common sense, notwithstanding any particular prejudices that he may entertain on particular points. Your first duty, my son, is to your country; and never, never be you unmindful of your people, whose care Providence has committed to your charge, and who have vindicated their claim on you by the strong affection they have shown for you."

"O, Mohásoy, I shall certainly always act as you direct. I can have no wish in my heart apart from the good of my people, and I shall endeavour at all times to give effect to that wish in the manner you and your brother may point out."

The Zemindár and the Sunyási then went forward together, as they had done such a long portion of their lives, and were only followed by their suite; while the people of Boná Ghát dispersed to their homes.

"Thus far, Monohur," said the Sunyási, "everything has gone well with us. But you have made no inquiries yet about the bright eyes you met with at Nárkelberiáh, which made so much impression on you at the time. Has my niece passed out of your memory since?"

"No, Búbájee; that dream has been the stay of my

life, and can never be forgotten by me. I have never seen her since that time; but I have dreamt of her as my playmate, and embraced her, and kissed her, and wept with her in my dreams. If I had not thought of her life would have been unbearable to me. Has she thought of me, father? Does she know that I am alive, and live only in the hope of making her my own?"

"Ah, my son, it is not usual with us, as with the English and other uncivilised races, for the female to disclose her love; but how well she loves you you may understand from the simple fact of her remaining unmarried to this day, notwithstanding the many tempting offers that were made to her, and the pressure of father and mother that she should close with one or other of them, and get settled in life."

"Then where are her parents? Why will you not carry me to them, that I may claim her as my own, and be at once united to her?"

"Ah, we have been settling all that for you, my son— I and my brother—in anticipation of your consent. Have I your authority to conclude the final arrangements now?"

"Most certainly you have. Have you not my authority to do everything for me? Do not you and your brother stand in *loco parentis* to me, and is it not usual with us for our parents or guardians to tie the nuptial knot on behalf of their children?"

The Sunyási was pleased with the reply, and then changed the subject of conversation adroitly, by directing attention to less important topics.

"There is another matter, my son, which has to be immediately determined. The sugar-plantations at Káchigrám are deteriorating day by day, and require to be carefully superintended. Have you any idea on the subject? What would you wish to do with the property?"

"Who, I?" exclaimed Monohur, his mind still dreaming of the beautiful image which had been recalled to it, and quite unable to grasp any other question simultaneously, "I—I have no recollection of the matter at all."

"Ah, but it presses for a decision, my son, and you must make up your mind quickly about it; and, notwithstanding my known antipathy against the English, you must not be surprised if I recommend to you the appointment of an Englishman to take charge of the estate."

"An Englishman! O, why an Englishman, Bábájec, in preference to any other person? Are there none among our old zemindáry servants who could fill the post as efficiently?"

"No, none, Monohur, or I would not have thought of an Englishman at all. The fact is, these sugar-plantations are much infested by wild-hogs, and no Hindu, or Mahomedan either, will have anything to do with those dirty creatures. The priest of Shámsoondur has been maintaining an army of *Kaorás* to destroy them; but they are lazy drunkards, and do nothing. Now an English Superintendent would naturally take an interest in hunting the hogs, for the English are very filthy eaters, and the plantations would thus be soon rid of a most pestiferous nuisance. You can also make the Englishman otherwise useful, that is, in any way you like."

Monohur could not suppress a smile to hear the Sunyási press for the destruction of the hogs so strenuously after having deliberately condemned the English practice of desultory shooting.

"Well, Bábájee, I have no objection to your proposition. But the Englishman will be destroying the hogs in our interest, and will not that make us participators in the crime?"

"No, it won't. We will benefit by the crime it is true, but the guilt will be the perpetrator's alone, our obligation in the matter being compounded by the money-payment we shall have to make to him. There is no *Pátak* except for the actual perpetrator of a crime, you know."

"That is scarcely fair to all the parties concerned. But I will not discuss the point further with you, Bábájee, for I now recollect that I intended the very same arrangement that you suggest. I do want to employ a European manager on the plantations, particularly as that would give me an opportunity to learn the manlier accomplishments from him, Englishmen being generally held to be very proficient in them. There is none better qualified than an Englishman, I am told, to teach one to ride and hunt."

"Ah, but you must not learn to shoot in sport, my son, as these English fellows do. Shooting at birds and beasts without any object at all is unnecessary cruelty, and has no justification whatever, as you have heard me urge before."

"I agree with you there, Bábájee; but still are manly accomplishments desirable for men in my position in life. Kharga Báhádoor has learnt the use of the sword pretty well, and mainly from you."

"Yes, but only to take advantage of the expertness

whenever there may be any noble object to attain; not to kill merely for the killing's sake."

"Just so; and he may also learn the use of firearms and other similar accomplishments with precisely the same object, that he might be of use to himself and to his country should a proper occasion for the exercise of such acquirements arise."

The Sunyási was still unwilling that Monohur should personally betake to such exercises at all. But the Zemindár's proposition was only a corollary to that suggested by himself, and he was obliged to acquiesce in it silently, without expressly committing himself to any extent. The result was that a man named Emanuel was appointed superintendent of the Káchigrám sugar-plantations, which adjoined to Echápore, immediately after the Zemindár's return to the latter place; and he was most commonly employed, day by day, in instructing his young master how to ride and shoot, which made the latter very expert in both attainments, in a very short time.

CHAPTER LVI.

THE DEVIL NOT SO BLACK AS HE IS PAINTED.

EMANUEL was appointed at the suggestion of the Sunyási. Judge then of the consternation of the good man on finding that the superintendent was not only a crack shot, who destroyed both the wild-hogs and birds on the plantations in large numbers, but that he was also a free-thinker in religion, and laughed alike at Christianity, Mahomedanism, and Hinduism.

"What a man we have got indeed! and he riding side by side with Monohur, morning and evening, and doubtless dropping all sorts of poison into his ears."

Thus soliloquised the Sunyási in his fears, as he stood on the road by which he expected that the equestrians would be passing out to their sport. He was immediately after joined there by Monohur, not on horseback as he had expected him, but on foot like himself, and quite unarmed.

"You are not for any sport this morning, Monohur, I see. Is anything the matter with you?"

"O, nothing whatever. I have done enough of butchery in the shooting line during the past few days, and have preferred a quiet walk this morning by way of a change."

"But your hunting-master? He, I suppose, will be out at work as usual notwithstanding the want of his pupil's company, and will be destroying large game and small game alike, as he is accustomed to? Nothing comes amiss to him under any circumstances."

"Of course not, Bábájee. We want work from him, and must allow him to keep his hands in exercise in his own way. He is a very good fellow on the whole, I assure you; and I am glad of having taken him into our service, for he suits me well in every respect."

The Sunyási shook his head disapprovingly as he pondered over the words Monohur had spoken.

"You say that you like Emanuel, Monohur. What sort of conversation does he usually indulge in?"

"Conversation! O, I have very little of that with him. He is a capital hand at the gun, has a firm seat on the saddle, and also a submissive and agreeable manner; but he does not speak much, and I like him the more for that."

"I am glad to learn that he has not a long tongue; but you need not like him particularly for anything whatever, my son. You know, I suppose that he is a freethinker; one that believes in nothing—neither in God, nor in the fiend, and sees nothing but the clouds in the blank, blank sky."

"I don't think he *fears* anything," replied Monohur, with something like a sigh; "but I never talk with him on such subjects, Bábájee. It is always best to keep men of his rank at a distance, you know."

"You are right there, my son," returned the Sunyási in a pleased voice, for he felt that even if the disbeliever had been sowing foul seeds into Monohur's mind they had not sprouted yet. "Never speak of religion with people who have none. Those only are freethinkers who care not to think at all."

"I doubt if I understand you aright, Bábájee. I

thought you Kartá-Bhajás based your religion on faith, not on thought. Is it not the Buddhists and the Vedantists only who base their religion on thought, comtemplation, or knowledge, or whatever other word they may use to express the idea?"

"All religions are based on thought, my son," said the Sunyási. "Faith does not necessarily imply the absolute negation of thought, but only the negation of continuous thinking, which is so apt to unsettle the common mind. Worship is of two kinds, the worship of the heart and of the judgment; but that of the heart is not necessarily thoughtless, for in that case it would be aimless also."

"Ah, Bábájee, it would be foolish in me to carry on a discussion with you on such an abstruse thesis as this. I do think that Emanuel has no religion; but I am told that the educated classes in all countries are similarly circumstanced."

"A doctrine which you must have received from Emanuel himself, I suppose? It may be true; it is certainly true to this extent that the educated men in this country—as our agent Rám Mohun Rái, for one instance—have very distinct notions of religion from those entertained by the masses around them. But they have philosophy, literature, and the sciences to form their minds, and may well be trusted with their aid to keep themselves safe in the ways of truth and rectitude. Emanuel is not a man of that stamp; he is not an educated man any more than I am. He has no knowledge of philosophy or letters generally; and for such persons there is no religion better than that of faith based on contemplation in its simplicity, such as the Kartá-Bhajá creed, which I value mainly on that account."

"Why not try to convert him then to the same belief with yourself, Bábájee? They are every now and then converting Hindus into Christians. It is surely worth trying to convert a Christian into a Hindu."

"Yes, but not such a Christian as Emanuel."

"Well, even such a man as he is. Would you not try to save him if you can?"

"If I can! But the *can* in the case is a straining of possibility which it will hardly stand. It is more likely that you may be able to convert Emanuel than I; for he may be converted to any creed by gold."

Just at this moment the person spoken of was seen galloping by on horseback at a very rapid pace, bent on araiding on some owls' nests in the village; and there was a large number of urchins running after him. He saw the Zemindár, and made an obeisance to him; but he affected not to see the Sunyási, evidently to spare himself the trouble of a nod.

"Take care, Superintendentjee," cried out the Sunyási. "The birds are harmless, and you should not destroy them; and you are holding your gun too carelessly considering the number of children at your heels."

"Tut!" cried Emanuel, casting a sharp look towards the speaker as his only reply; and almost immediately after there was a sound of firing, followed by the shrill cry of a child in pain.

Both Monohur and the Sunyási came up promptly to the spot, and were equally aghast at seeing what had happened. The gun had been fired at a big old owl, but the bullet, instead of striking the owl, had refracted from a tree and mortally wounded a ragged urchin about ten years old.

Emanuel had alighted from his horse at once, and

taken up the child on his knees; but he was too much agitated himself to be of any use to him. The bullet had entered the temple of the boy, and there was no hope of extracting it. Nor was the pain of the sufferer long protracted, for he died in Emanuel's lap just as the Zemindár and the Sunyási came up to the spot.

"He is gone!" exclaimed the unhappy huntsman, with a look of horror and grief, "and only because I would not mind the warnings of the Sunyási."

Both the Zemindár and the Sunyási joined in comforting him, and pointed out that it was but an accident, though so very lamentable in its result; and the cry of fury which arose from the villagers was soon silenced by the liberal money-payments made by Monohur to the parents of the child, and a sincere expression of his sympathy for their loss.

"What shall we do? How can we receive money as a price for the life of our child?" urged the parents at first in their grief.

"O, good people, you must not view the matter in that light. The Superintendent had no wish to injure you, and could not possibly have borne malice to your boy. This is a lamentable loss to you surely, and a loss also to me. But it is God's doing more than Emanuel's, for you know that he never fires amiss."

"Must not the matter be reported to the police?"

"Of course it must," said Monohur; and fifty men ran off at once to inform the police of what had happened.

But the view taken of the occurrence by the police was precisely the same as that which had been arrived at by the Zemindár, and the hubbub in the village was necessarily immediately after allayed.

"O, Sunyási!" exclaimed Emanuel, still in despair, "why does this accident make me so uneasy, when I have killed beasts and birds continuously for years without feeling any grief or remorse? Does a human being make so much real difference then in the reckoning?"

"He has the right stuff in him after all, I see," muttered the Sunyási to himself, without giving the querist any direct reply. "The devil is not so black as he is painted."

CHAPTER LVII.

THE QUESTION MOOTED.

The Gossáin returned to Poorá three days after he had left it. The sun had nearly set, and the villagers were enjoying the evening breeze under the friendly shade of their *burr* and *bokool* trees. The Gossáin was an important man amongst them, almost as important as their Zemindár; and the talk was mostly about his hurried and mysterious departure for Boná Ghát.

"Why has he gone there at all?" "What can be his business there?" "Why did he start so hurriedly at night?" These were some of the questions that were eagerly put forth.

"He must have gone on some religious errand, I fancy," said one in reply. "Or on the summons of the priest of Nággesur Mahádeva, who is related to him," said another. "Or perhaps to settle a match for his daughter, Mádhavi," said a third. "It would be a burning shame indeed to us all if she remained a *Thoobri* here for life, and she so pretty and sweet-hearted withal." "Or it may be that the young Zemindár of Boná Ghát is expected back from his travels soon," said a fourth, "in which case the Gossáin would, of course, be wanted to set matters right for him among his numerous *Jajmáns*, or disciples, both at Boná Ghát and Echápore."

The Gossáin passed by the speakers as a whirlwind,

but could not help overhearing what was being said amongst them; and it troubled him much that his movements should have given rise to so much frivolous discourse.

"I do not see why people should be talking about us in this way," murmured he to himself, "though I don't mind in the least what they choose to tell of us."

His house was before him already, wearing its accustomed aspect of utter peacefulness, and he bounced into it eagerly, without further heeding the idle nonsense that was being ventilated outside of it; and, as the whole establishment was astir the moment he appeared among them, the disagreeable feeling that had arisen in his mind was quickly chased away.

"Well, Mádhavi, here I am back again. Your father has always been an odd man, and you must not be surprised to see him turning up in this way at odd times."

The young lady heard the well-known voice with a radiant face, and darted out of her apartment to welcome back her returned parent; and the reader may as well take the opportunity to renew her acquaintance after the long interval that he has been separated from her.

Mádhavi was now a fine girl of above twenty years, or rather a handsome young woman, as she was well entitled to be called in a tropical country, even though her habits were yet girlish, more so than is usual for maidens of her age in the East. Her face was singularly sweet, and beautiful, far sweeter, in fact, than when Monohur had seen it at Nárkelberiáh; her figure extremely graceful; and her eyes, broad, large, and dark, and much resembling in lustrous mildness those of the ringdove and the gazelle. The dress worn by her was similar in fashion to that of other girls of her age, and consisted of the voluminous garment called *Sáree*, which was very modestly wrapped round the whole body, leaving only the face, arms, and feet bare. The neck and arms were loaded with ornaments of gold and precious stones; but, what was more beautiful to look at, was the ingenuous and amiable expression of her countenance, which conveyed an idea of truthfulness so marked that it appeared almost impossible for her either to hide her thoughts or to prevaricate.

"Ah, how could you keep away from us for three whole days, father?" cried the maiden, as she sprang forward to greet him. "What was the business that detained you so long, which made us so unhappy here in your absence?"

"O, it was a matter of great importance, my child, and you will know everything about it, but not till I have discussed it with your mother. Tell her to come to me presently. I have some particular tidings for her."

The mother was bustling about the house, intent on domestic work, but came up the moment she knew that she was wanted, confronting her husband however with a rather startled look.

"Has anything gone amiss? What is the news that you have to tell me?"

"O, some wonderful things have happened, and I want to have a long talk with you about them. You must give me a patient hearing for at least half-an-hour."

"So be it," said she, resignedly, "but tell me briefly the character of your news to begin with, for you have alarmed me somewhat by your suddenness."

"Pooh! How excitable you are, wife! When did I bring any but good news to you? And what I have to say now is about the very best that I have ever had to unfold."

"Tell me all about it then without keeping me further in suspense. We are alone now, and I am ready to listen to you."

"Briefly, it is this then: the Zemindár of Boná Ghát has returned."

"Returned! You astound me. Returned at last? Praise be to Brahmamoi (Káli) then that it is so! I am very glad indeed to hear of it—for his mother, you know, was my childhood's dearest friend."

The woman was overborne by her feelings, and stopped short for some moments before she could launch forth the questions that stuck in her throat; but they were asked with great volubility immediately after.

"When did he come? Where is he now? Have you seen him yourself? In what plight has he come back? How have his ryots received him?" were what she wanted to know of her husband, all in the same breath.

"Ah, if you come out so thick with your queries, wife, I shall never be able to answer you. Confine yourself to one inquiry at a time, and I shall endeavour to satisfy you in the best way I can. He arrived at Echápore just two days before I left for Boná Ghát. I have not seen him myself, for he still remains in the halls of his maternal ancestors, and will not come to Boná Ghát because of the unpleasant associations it might bring up to his remembrance. He has passed through great privations and hardships of course, as was indeed to have been expected, but has returned hale and vigorous; and the people of Echápore, I have just heard, have received him with open arms."

In her inmost heart the Gossáin's lady doated on Monohur, for he was the only son of her earliest and best-prized playmate. He had come back from his erratic wanderings at last, after having been taken for lost for so many years, and was already a general favourite with the ryots of one at least of his ancestral estates. These were very cheering tidings to her. But there was an episode to the story which was full of fears to the mother's heart. Her only daughter had led very like a widow's life for the truant merely from a childish penchant they had felt for each other some ten years ago. Was he true to her yet? If not, how would his return affect the tenor of Mádhavi's life?

"Have you no further questions to ask of me, wife?"

"Ah, I would like to hear of my brother, the Sunyási, now. Has he come back with Monohur?"

"Yes."

"And what is he about then?"

"Why, scheming as ever. He has schemes enough in his mind to occupy him for twenty years to come. But they are now of a pacific character only, and refer mainly to the well-being of Monohur."

"Ah, that is just what I wanted to know, and I accept the information with great relief. Monohur stands alone in the world now, and needs staunch friends by him, and never can he get better friends than my two brothers are sure to be to him."

"And do you know, wife, these precious brothers of yours have, between themselves, made up their minds to give a wife to Monohur at once. What do you say to that?"

The lady's eyes became dim of a sudden, and her cheeks were blanched with fear.

"What do you mean? What can I have to say about it?"

"What can you have to say to it when they propose to marry Monohur to your own daughter, Mádhavi? Why, the marriage can never take place till you agree."

The calm self-possession of the mother returned the moment her fears were dispersed. Monohur had come back, and it was proposed that he should marry the little bride he had selected for himself at the Ferázee camp. But proposed by whom? How was the mother to be certain that the Zemindár wished for the union yet? The entanglement at Nárkelberiáh was altogether a childish affair. In Mádhavi it had matured into a heartfelt passion. But what were Monohur's feelings for her all the while? Then, again, Monohur had been passing the best part of his life abroad. How had it been spent? Was he worthy of her love yet?

"What, quiet still?" exclaimed the Gossáin. "Shall I report to your brothers then that you say 'Nay' to the union?"

"No, not that, surely," said the mother. "Mádhavi's heart is fixed on Monohur, as we both of us know so well. Must we not assure ourselves now that Monohur has not become indifferent of her since? I want proofs that he loves her still, loves her as well as in the days of old; and, also, that he continues to be worthy of her. Is it not right that we should be very certain on these points?"

"Of course it is; and I was not unmindful of them in making my inquiries of Bissonáth. He has assured me in return, several times over, that Monohur thinks of none but Mádhavi, and has never done otherwise; and there was nothing in the story he gave me of his life to diminish our old estimate of his worth. What better assurance can you have than that of your own brother on such points, and he Monohur's constant companion so long?"

"But why this haste to conclude the union after such long delay? Can't we wait a bit to ascertain facts for ourselves?"

"How can we? Monohur stands alone in the world now, as you have just observed, and this life of solitariness has to be immediately remedied. The family of the Ráis has long been without a mistress, and that void has to be filled up. Matters have, in fact, come to that pass that the Zemindár has to be wived at once. We know that the young folks love each other. Why should we create an obstacle then where none really exists?"

"But must not Mádhavi herself be consulted?" asked the mother at last, in the expectation of gaining some little time in that way if possible.

"Assuredly, yes," answered the Gossáin, "and I wish you to broach the matter to her without the least delay."

Almost as if she had heard the last words of her parents the daughter was seen that moment running up to her mother.

"O, Mádhavi! Your father has asked me to reopen the old subject again, for another very likely suitor has come forward to ask for your hand."

"I have given my answer before, mother dear, and the new suitor must be satisfied with the reply the old ones have received—namely, that Mádhavi desires not to leave the protection of her parents."

"But it must not ever be so, my child. The matter is daily getting more and more serious than before, for your father and I are both waxing old. Who will protect you after we are dead and gone?"

"O, mother, are you so anxious to get rid of me that you try to frighten me into marriage? God, the common protector of us all, will not desert me, even if I should be so unfortunate as to survive both my parents."

"I have no doubt that God will protect you, Mádhavi, at all times, for you fully deserve His love; but it is His ordinance, girl, that all men and women should marry, and perpetuate the universe He has made."

Mádhavi heaved a little sigh.

"Yes, mother, you are right there as in every other doctrine you lay down. But I have a heart to satisfy, and I have not yet seen or heard of any man whom it would accept as its companion for life."

"Why, what manner of man does thy heart seek for, if not of the same stamp as other girls are contented with? Why not take the best of the many that have offered, as others do?"

"Ah, mother! Not the best of those who have offered, but the very best of men for me, or none. And where is the very best to be found?"

"Suppose he has turned up at last, girl," said the Gossáin, coming at once to the fore. "Will you have him then?"

Mádhavi's face was suffused with blushes, but in a moment after she was deadly pale.

"O, father, you cannot be trifling with me. Speak plainly what you mean, for I do not comprehend you."

"This only, child, that Monohur Rái of Boná Ghát has returned, and both I and your mother, and your two uncles also, wish anxiously that you should marry him."

Poor Mádhavi was unable to reply; her whole frame was agitated, and shook violently, and she sank crying into her mother's arms.

"I am afraid the girl does not know her own heart well enough at all times, and may perhaps not wish to have Monohur now after having waited for him so long," said the mother, unable to understand the intensity of her feelings aright.

"No, no, it is not that," said the father. "The fire that lay deep hid among the ashes is glimmering up again, and the long cherished love will soon be ablaze."

CHAPTER LVIII.

THE KNOT TIED HARD.

The nuptials were to be celebrated with becoming pomp and splendour, and the Gossáin was loyally aided by the Sunyási and the priest of Nággesur Mahádeva in completing the arrangements. They invited widely on both sides, and the elite of all Datteáh came crowding to assist at the ceremony.

"The wedding must take place at Poorá, the residence of the bride?" observed the priest of Shámsoondur inquiringly. "Had we not better remove to its neighbourhood in time that the bridegroom might go out thence in state, as usual, without discomfort or confusion?"

"Yes," said the Sunyási, "and there is a handsome *bágh*, or villa, within about two miles of the Gossáin's house, which would not be a bad place to stay in for the time, and start from."

"Ah, I remember; but to whom have we to apply for the use of it?"

"To the Zemindár of Poorá, I believe. It is his hunting-lodge, or country-seat, or whatever else he chooses to call it."

The Zemindár of Poorá was, of course, only too glad to oblige his neighbour of Boná Ghát when the proposal to occupy the lodge was put forward in his name; and Monohur, in repairing to the place, felt that he had alighted on a small Arcadia, from the agreeable scents and sounds that came to his heart. The *bágh* was, in fact, one continued wilderness of roses and jasmines, overshadowed by a confusion of citron and other fragrant fruit-trees, and it was so full of birds and their little gushes of melody that the general effect on a new-comer could not but be revivifying in the highest degree.

But Monohur's time for thought here was of the briefest, and he was too impatient at heart now to enjoy its quiet beauty even during that short period without demur.

"This is indeed a happy and secluded spot," said he to himself, "and as full of rural loveliness as any one could wish for! Why does it not satisfy my heart, then, as completely as it ought? Why is it that I am almost getting tired of it already?"

Ah, impatient lover, you are burning to clasp the fay of Nárkelberiáh in your arms! Wait a bit only. They are even now forging the shackles in which you are to be fettered for life, never, never to be loosened again!

The preparations in the Gossáin's house were indeed being very actively proceeded with. The house was a large one-storied one, the outside of which would be called extremely plain at the present day, but which had, nevertheless, much beauty within, especially when viewed from the *Oothán*, or square compound in its centre, which was surrounded on three sides by a colonnade of well-proportioned pillars, while the fourth side was bounded by a spacious *Chandimandab*, devoted to the worship of the gods and the performance of other religious ceremonies of every kind. The general aspect of the building was at the same time cleanly and neat, which may be taken as the chief distinguishing mark of respectability; and it had, moreover, been thoroughly whitewashed and repaired, and the walls painted in several places with brilliant colours.

The house had been wholly refurnished, and, on the marriage-day, the floors were all covered with luxurious carpets, including the floor of the *Oothán*, where the bridal party were to be seated, while, in the midst of the cushions and pillows scattered for the guests, were left rich nosegays and fans gaily bedecked with flowers, the entire floor of the passage leading to the compound being at the same time strewed with rose-leaves. Against the walls were hung numerous lanterns and lustres of various designs, with decorations of red and gold in particular places to heighten the beauty of the show; and when the lanterns were lighted towards the evening, in expectation of the bridegroom's arrival, the effect was simply magnificent.

The bridegroom's party started from the *bágh* immediately after sunset, the procession being preceded by caparisoned horses and elephants, rich flags of gold carried by little urchins dressed in tinsel, and a whole band of musicians playing on all sorts of instruments, which produced a discordant and bewildering sound, obeying none of the laws of harmony, and yet without being altogether destitute of an undercurrent of melody.

Immediately after the musicians came the bridegroom, seated on a *Tuktrámá*, or open throne, carried by gaily-dressed porters. He wore on his head a rich turban of gold brocade, wrought over with pearls and surmounted by heron-plumes and diamond-drops, while, brighter even than the diamonds and pearls, flashed the light of his dark eyes, with an intensity of life and animation that bordered almost on sauciness. His noble features were further adorned by the manly down of youth which graced them, while on his neck was a brilliant string of pearls that were not to be easily matched in size or price. The upper garment which covered and set off his lithe and muscular figure was a tunic of gold brocade reaching below the knees, fastened round the waist by a sash of blue and gold, and the lower garments were of equally rich materials, the dress being completed by a pair of gold slippers on his feet.

Following the bridegroom came on foot his own personal friends, and such respectable neighbours as had been invited to join the procession; while the tail of it was brought up by a crowd of men, women, and children, all shouting with delight, or trampling on each other's toes and cursing and screaming dreadfully in their eagerness to get nearer to the bridegroom's throne.

The procession came to a stand at the gate of the Gossáin's house, when the musicians attached to the bride's party advanced to welcome the bridegroom and his friends, raising a shrill and piercing blast of triumph that drowned all ordinary exclamations of joy. They then arranged themselves sidewise to allow of the father of the bride, accompanied by his most intimate friends, to do the honours of reception; and the manner in which the Gossáin went through the task was so urbane and charming that all his guests were mightily well-pleased.

The company were then conducted to and seated in the square compound prepared for their reception, the bride and bridegroom being both placed in their midst, the former deeply veiled and resplendent with gems and gold, her red satin *sáree* being literally covered all over with gold sprays and spangles.

The marriage followed immediately after. It was

what the Shástras describe as a *Gandharva Bibáha*, the essence of which is that the bride and bridegroom select each other.

"We have had no marriages of this kind for ages amongst us," observed the Gossáin in an objecting tone.

"It does not matter. It is valid according to the Shástras," was the Sunyási's reply; and the priests of Shámsoondur and Nággesur Mahádeva bowed to the assertion in acquiescence.

The bride was now presented with a new silk-cloth and shell-bracelets by the bridegroom, on her selection of him being made known, and she retired to put these on, the bridegroom also retiring to exchange his rich procession-dress for a silk *jore*, or *dhoti* and *chádur*. On returning to their places there was an exchange of garlands between the pair, and, the bridegroom being permitted to raise the bride's veil and look her full in the face, the ceremony was held to be fully and completely concluded.

"Is that all?" asked the Gossáin, in the same objecting tone as before. "Should there be no religious rites to complete the union?"

"None are required by the texts of the Shástras," said the Sunyási.

The Gossáin was uneasy; the marriage without a rite seemed as no marriage at all to him. But he did not know what objection to urge to it, when word was brought from the inner apartments that the mother of the bride was not satisfied with the formula observed, and insisted on the usual forms for ordinary marriages being also gone through.

"Does the bride herself wish it?" asked the priest of Shámsoondur.

Mádhavi bowed her head in acquiescence, upon which the services of regular marriage Poorohits were at once brought into requisition to celebrate the union in common fashion. The place selected for this fresh ceremony was the *Chandimandab*, to the north of the *Oothán*, where the priests were accommodated on *kusásans*, or small mats of the *kusá* grass; and the bride and bridegroom were conducted thither to the presence of Náráyana, as represented by a small round stone called the Shálgarám, after which the officiating Poorohits began their intonations. The rites were commenced by the worship of Ganesa, the obviator of all difficulties. The bride was given away by her father, aided by the Sunyási,. the marriage formula observed, apart from a long string of meaningless ceremonies, being nearly as follows :

"Water is Náráyana, or God, and His emblem is present before us. Is that your belief?" asked the priest of the bridegroom.

"It is," responded he, in a deep reverential voice; upon which a *kusá* knot was tied to a finger of each of his hands after having been wetted with water.

"Worship him with flowers and *Chandan*, and offer burnt-oblations to him."

The bridegroom did so.

"Now let the bride be led three times round the sacred fire."

She was led round the fire in the manner pointed out.

"Pass the marriage-knot now lightly round the shoulders of both bride and bridegroom, and tie their garments together."

They did this with great address and celerity.

The chief priest then addressed the bridegroom once more.

"In the presence of Náráyana, as represented by his emblem and by water, do you accept this maiden as your wife?"

"I do."

"To love her and to cherish her all the days of your life?"

"Yes."

"Then is the selection of the bride confirmed."

This was followed by a brief pause, as if all the parties present were trying to realise the sense of the few weighty words which had been spoken, after which the priests resumed intoning their Mantras and prayers, till the ceremony was finally concluded by the solemn dictum that "those whom Náráyana had united were never more on any account to be dissevered."

"Are you fully satisfied, brother, with the ceremony now? Is it complete and to your liking in all respects?" asked the Sunyási of the Gossáin a little derisively.

"Yes, brother, it is. Now let us bless the youthful pair, the Poorohits who have tied the knot so firmly leading the way."

This was done accordingly and the ceremony terminated, the benedictions of the Gossáin, the Sunyási, and the priests of Shámsoondur and Nággesur Mahádeva being of course by far the most fervent.

"Stable and abiding be your happiness, O, my children!" exclaimed the Sunyási in the fulness of his heart, "even as the centre of the earth is fixed and immovable. Be ye ever the dearest to each other, and undear to no one."

CHAPTER LIX.

THE RETURN TO BONÁ GHÁT.

THE wedding-feast at the Gossáin's house was kept up till a late hour of the night, and not less than eight hundred or a thousand persons sat down to it. The victuals placed before the guests were sumptuous to a degree and consisted of several courses, and every individual was delighted with the attention and honour paid to him.

"Just one *metoy*[1] more, sir; only one?" and some three or four were poured down the moment the assent to the addition of one was obtained.

"O, thank you; but don't heap my plate like that, though I think I never did taste such a dainty sweetmeat before."

"Another *kuchouri*,[2] sir, if you will permit? just one only? Made at home, I assure you."

"And very well made indeed," responded the gratified guest. "So nice and pleasing that it melts in the mouth as of itself."

And these civilities were of course extended to all.

There was feasting on as liberal a scale for the servants of the guests and for the village poor in the outhouses and compounds; and, when hunger was appeased, both

---

[1] Name of an Indian sweetmeat.
[2] Indian *Patty*, made of wheat and pulse.

the masters and their servants had *pán* and tobacco served out to them *ad libitum*, the natives of all classes being equally fond of them.

It was next the turn of those to be attended to who had not eaten at all, such as the Poorohits and the Adhyapaks,[3] the common practice with whom is to take their shares of the victuals home with them; and the good things were put up for them quickly and on a munificent scale, which was of course eminently satisfactory to each recipient.

"And now we must be going," said the guests after all their requirements had been gratified; and the company broke up, though not without an effort, as being loath to depart: nor did they eventually separate till they had repeated their wishes for the happiness of the bride and bridegroom a hundred times over. There were also affectionate *kollákoolis*, or respectful embracings, before parting, between all the elder guests and their host, while the younger gentlemen whom he had entertained made their *pronáms* to him deferentially as each took his leave.

The guests then divided themselves into parties, all who went in the same direction starting together. The night was splendid, there never had been a clearer night; and all the stars were sparkling brilliantly in the sky.

"Do you happen to know the way across that hedge there?" asked the retiring people one of another. "If not, we had better go straight through the lawn till we reach the main road;" and so they went, across lawns, and through hedges, and over flower-beds, all extolling with noisy tongues both the uncommon beauty of the

---

[3] Eminent Bráhmen scholars, or Principals of *Toles*.

bride and the untiring civility of her father, till the sound of their voices died away in the distance.

Monohur had sat down to the banquet with the other guests as is usual on such occasions; but he had hardly eaten anything. His heart was too full to allow him to do so; he felt so intensely happy that the sense of his felicity was almost overpowering him. A whole array of recollections had come back to his mind, hot and cold, sad and pleasant, but all lit up now with the sunshine of Mádhavi's smile, and even the remembrance of his mother was no longer distressing to him.

" My dream of dreams is realised at last! " exclaimed he in ecstasy on being finally left alone with his wife. " O, dearest! how lovely and good you are indeed! and now mine for ever! "

Mádhavi could not answer. She laid her head on his breast and wept.

" I thought I never could be happy in this life again, my love," said Monohur, " but am happier at this moment than I ever was; and I feel that I shall now be able to pass rejoicingly through the world, notwithstanding all that I have suffered, till the time comes for me to rejoin my mother."

" O, my husband, if we love and bear with each other, if we endeavour to do good to others to the best of our power, is there not happiness for every one of us in life, even for all the blights and misfortunes that so frequently overtake us?"

" That was not my creed, my dearest, a few short months before; but I have now secured the one bright vision of my youth, and can scarcely think of any circumstance under which I could be miserable with thee."

" Well, I certainly ought to be entirely happy," responded the wife, "and surely I am; but I do not know what is pressing on my mind since I had a most singular dream the night before last."

"A dream?"

"Yes, and I am somewhat troubled about it, for I can make nothing of it, though it was unusually distinct, and I am quite certain was meant to be understood."

"Let me know all about it then, my sweetest, and we shall put our two heads together to interpret it."

"It is soon told. On account of the agitation and anxiety of the past few days I did not sleep well during the first part of the night I am speaking of, but fell into a heavy slumber later—from midnight till morning. I do not know how long the dream lasted; it seemed as if it was continued throughout the time I slept. I thought I was sitting beside the pool of water that lies to the east of our house. The water appeared to be unusually clear, so that I could see the fishes chasing each other at some depth below. I looked intently at the fishes, and methought there was a big otter now in the water swallowing up the fishes with great celerity. I was much distressed at the sight, but I could not, for all the strenuous efforts I made, drive away the animal from its prey. I heaved a deep sigh, and immediately after saw a black man in the water hastening to the rescue of the fishes. On seeing him the otter fled out of sight through deep water, and my delight was extreme. But great was my surprise and terror when I saw the black man the next moment seated at my side.

"'Who and whence are you?' I asked.

"'I come from the East,' said he, 'from a place your bridegroom-elect knows well, and I was your bridegroom's greatest friend, but he has deserted me.'

"'But what are you?'

"'Look at me steadily,' said he, 'and see if you cannot discover it.'

"I could not look at him steadily; I found it impossible to do so: but the only glance I was able to cast towards him was sufficient to show that the colour of the being had sharply changed from black into white—a dazzling silvery white. My terror was intensified, and I could speak to him no longer, for my tongue clove to the roof of my mouth; but he continued to speak to me as before.

"'Fear not,' said he, 'for I am still the Zemindár's friend, though he has deserted me. Bring him back to me after you are married to him, and I shall be a friend to both of you for evermore.'

"'In what way can you befriend us?' I stammered out at last, breaking through my fears, 'and in what matter would we require your aid?'

"'In every way, and in everything,' said he. 'When you are in the greatest distress I can help you; from your most involved difficulties I shall extricate you.'

"I felt that it was a spirit that was speaking to me, for the whiteness of his colour had now become blinding bright.

"'Father!' said I, 'whither then must we go to find you?'

"'The Zemindár must go back to the home of his fathers to find me, and his wife must go with him,' and saying this he vanished into air, and I awoke."

"O, my wife! my blessed wife! You are surely blessed, for the apparition you have seen, the black being and the white, can be none other than Nággesur Mahádeva himself, the god of my fathers, who has taken offence at my abandonment of Boná Ghát. He will not allow me to live at any distance from him, and his will must be obeyed."

The parting from her parents was very painful to Mádhavi, and to the lady-Gossáin also, who protested that she would never be able to get over it. But it was effected all the same, with sobs and tears, till nothing could be heard between them beyond snatches of those usual heart-piercing refrains—

"My dearest mother!"

"My darling child!"

"I must depart from this place also," said Monohur, after returning to Echápore, "though I had once made up my mind to settle here for good. Is not the seat charming, my love, and is it not a pity that we should have to leave it?"

"Yes, the site on the river-bank is indeed very sweet and ecstatic," said Mádhavi, "and there is also considerably less of heat and dust here, I think, than at Poorá. But we must leave both of course now to go home to Boná Ghát."

How sweet the word "home" sounded in the ears of Monohur when pronounced by the lips of Mádhavi, and applied to his own native village! and he lost no time in repairing to the temple of Shámsoondur to take leave of the priest.

"O father, I feel quite ashamed to tell you that I have come hither to solicit your permission to go back to Boná Ghát, though it was only a few short days ago that I said I should never be able to do so again."

"Ah, my son, I shall certainly never object to your returning to your own paternal home, and I may even say that I am pleased to hear that you wish to do so now. But how has this new wish arisen?"

"It is not I, father, that wish it at present any more than I have hitherto done. But the god of my fathers has appeared in a dream to my wife, and has demanded my immediate return;" and he related to him all the particulars of Mádhavi's dream.

"Haste back then, my son, and haste at once where the deity desires to have you. His wish must be as a law to all of us, and I have no power to direct you otherwise, for Shámsoondur and Nággesur Mahádeva are not two distinct deities, but one and the same."

Very great was the rejoicing of the Sunyási, of the priest of Nággesur Mahádeva, and of all the people of Boná Ghát, on the re-occupation of that village by the Zemindár. The old family-house there, which recalled so many disagreeable associations to his mind, was now pulled down and a superb new one erected on the site; and, when he and his wife took up their residence in this edifice, a great festival was held in honour of Nággesur Mahádeva, and his protection and blessing formally invoked. The priest replied in the name of the deity, and was fully equal to the occasion.

"This was the dwelling-place of your fathers, Monohur," said he, "and blessed is the judgment which has brought you back to it with your wife! The god blesses you through me, and will protect and befriend you, as he did your forefathers from the days of Kooláye Chánd Rái. You will have brave sons and fair daughters, who will by their own deeds long keep the virtues of their parents alive in the recollections of their descendants. Be happy then; and sinless likewise, that you may be happy evermore!"

THE END.

www.ingramcontent.com/pod-product-compliance
Lightning Source LLC
Chambersburg PA
CBHW022133300426
44115CB00006B/172